Train Up a Child

YOUNG CENTER BOOKS IN ANABAPTIST & PIETIST STUDIES

Donald B. Kraybill, *Series Editor*

Train Up a Child

Old Order Amish & Mennonite Schools

Karen M. Johnson-Weiner

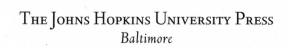

THE JOHNS HOPKINS UNIVERSITY PRESS

Baltimore

© 2007 The Johns Hopkins University Press
All rights reserved. Published 2007
Printed in the United States of America on acid-free paper
2 4 6 8 9 7 5 3 1

The Johns Hopkins University Press
2715 North Charles Street
Baltimore, Maryland 21218-4363
www.press.jhu.edu

Library of Congress Cataloging-in-Publication Data

Johnson-Weiner, Karen M.
Train up a child : Old Order Amish and Mennonite schools / Karen M. Johnson-Weiner.
    p.   cm. — (Young Center books in Anabaptist and Pietist studies)
Includes bibliographical references and index.
ISBN 0-8018-8495-0 (hardcover : alk. paper)
1. Amish children—Education. 2. Mennonite children—Education. 3. Amish—
Social life and customs. 4. Old Order Mennonites—Social life and customs.
I. Title. II. Series.
LC586.A45J64 2007
371.071'97—dc22   2006007079

A catalog record for this book is available from the British Library.

Contents

Preface

The average North American sees little difference between one Old Order Amish person and another, or between an Old Order Amish person and an Old Order Mennonite. In their plain, archaic-looking clothes and horse-drawn buggies, they all seem firmly anchored in the nineteenth century, as ignorant of mainstream culture as any pioneer from a forgotten past.

The different Old Order church-communities[1] are not lost in time, however, nor are their members naïve Luddites. United by history, these groups trace their roots to the radical Anabaptist movement of the sixteenth-century Swiss Reformation. Each remains a voluntary church of believers, marked by adherence to the principles of nonresistance, pacifism, and nonconformity to the dominant society. They reject mainstream American values of individualism, personal success, and civic responsibility.

Yet Old Order church-communities vary considerably in how they realize this rejection and how they position themselves vis-à-vis one another and non—Old Order society. They all belong to the broad category of "Old Order" because their members chose in the nineteenth century to remain faithful to the *Alte Ordnung* (old order) of their forebears rather than succumb to pressure to change and assimilate. However, within the category of Old Order there are groups such as the Swartzentruber Amish, who have been among the most adamant in their rejection of technological change; the Groffdale Conference of Mennonites, also known as Wenger Mennonites, who have permitted electricity and telephones in their homes while rejecting the automobile; and the Stauffer Mennonites, who continue to reject electricity. Some Old Order Amish church-communities permit gas refrigerators, bicycles, and telephones in shops. Other Old Order Amish groups, in company with the Swartzentruber Amish, reject all of these innovations.

In short, all Old Order groups stand apart from the world but not all in the same way. The boundaries of an Old Order church-community are established by the practices of its members. Each church-community defines itself in opposition to other Old Order groups and to the world by its choices of dress, lifestyle, and technology use.

As Hostetler (1989, 130) has noted, "Amish elementary schools support the values taught in the family. The school helps the child to become a part of his or her community and to remain within it." Thus, in their difference and similarities, Old Order schools offer a window to the diversity of Old Order life. Founded by church-communities to resist unacceptable developments in public education, Old Order schools have become agents of change as well as agents of resistance to change. In his study of language shift in the Papua New Guinean village of Gapun, Don Kulick notes that "villagers' ideas about literacy, the millennium, and Christianity form a framework into which all aspects of the modern world are fitted. One domain in which all these themes coalesce is in the villagers' understanding of schooling" (1992, 175). Similarly, in Old Order communities, private schools are defined by particular beliefs about the place and practices of church members within the church-community and within the larger society. Each group's understanding of what it means to be Old Order shapes its educational philosophy, strategies, and tools; and these, in turn, reinforce distinctive community values.

Asking how Old Order education reflects and shapes Old Order values and reinforces social and linguistic norms, this book explores the way Old Order schools function within the larger symbolic framework that structures everyday Old Order life. It is based on archival research, interviews, and fieldwork conducted in eight areas of Old Order settlement: the Elkhart-LaGrange Counties, Indiana; Centreville, Michigan; Perry County, Ohio; Fredericktown, Ohio; Ashland, Ohio; Holmes and Wayne Counties, Ohio; St. Lawrence County, New York; and Lancaster County, Pennsylvania. The Old Order communities in these regions vary in size, proximity to other communities, and interaction with the non–Old Order world; thus, they represent the diversity of the Old Order world.

In this ethnographic study, I describe Old Order schools in the context of Old Order culture. In her study of bilingual education among Quechua speakers in Southern Peru, Nancy Hornberger (1988, 4) refers to the ethnographer as a "marginal native" who should "participate with the community without judging it, and . . . without forgetting to observe it."[2] This I have tried to do.

Conducting field research in Old Order communities is challenging. In my experience, members of Old Order communities favor personal interaction, tending to be suspicious of questionnaires and surveys and generally declining to take part. Most Old Order groups will not permit photography or sound or video taping in their homes or in schools while school is in session, believing that these violate the commandment against the making of "graven images" (Exodus 20:4). As Enninger (1987) notes, "In this culture, the choice the field worker has is to work on the basis of the obtainable data or to gain no insights at all" (149–50).

In researching schools, I drew on personal connections established over a number of years of participant observation in the Amish communities of upstate New York and in Old Order Mennonite communities in Lancaster County, Pennsylvania. These connections enabled me to stay with Old Order friends in the different communities, to eat with them, play with their children, and accompany them to church services. I visited schools; talked with students, parents, teachers, and school board members; attended teachers' meetings and teachers' suppers; helped children with spelling; and graded workbooks. I interviewed parents at home while helping to prepare meals or wash dishes, and I interviewed teachers while we stood together on the playground to supervise children or eat lunch. I had a very interesting conversation with a teacher while we waited our turn to bat in a game of "rounders." Perhaps the most formal interview I conducted took place in Indiana, when we gathered around the kitchen table after a meal to drink coffee and to talk about schools.

These interactions led to a valuable correspondence with members of the different communities. In personal letters, Old Order teachers and others responded to my observations about what I had seen in their schools and to my questions about testing, discipline, textbooks, and teaching religion. I often asked in letters many of the same questions I had asked in person, finding that my correspondents gave far more elaborate answers in writing. The insights of this lively correspondence have richly informed this project.

In addition to participant observation, interviews, and correspondence, I found the collections at the Heritage Historical Library in Aylmer, Ontario, and the Muddy Creek Farm Library in Lancaster County, Pennsylvania, to be particularly useful in researching the texts used in Old Order schools, the development of Old Order textbook publishing, and the history of Old Order private schools. I also interviewed a number of Old Order publishers who, as a result of their ongoing efforts to ensure that Old Order schools are provided with appropriate reading material, provided a unique insight into Old Order education.

The first chapter outlines the scope of the study and discusses in greater detail the communities whose schools are the focus of this work. Chapter 2 contrasts the popular view of Old Order schools with the reality of twenty-first-century Old Order education. It explores broadly how, in response to organizational changes in the school systems of the dominant culture, the Old Orders have developed private schools that meet the standards imposed by the state but realize the educational goals of the particular church community rather than the goals of the dominant society.

Chapters 3 through 7 describe schools in nine Old Order communities, looking first at the community's relationship to other Old Order settlements and to the dominant society and then suggesting how this has influenced such aspects of Old Order education as pedagogy, student-teacher interaction, discipline, selection of classroom materials, the physical structure and location of the school in the community, the extent to which students are drawn from one church community or several, the teaching of religion, and parental participation at school events. Focusing in particular on the Swartzentruber communities in upstate New York, chapter 3 discusses the ultra-conservative Swartzentruber Amish schools. Chapter 4 treats the schools in the smaller, relatively isolated and homogeneous settlements in Somerset, Ashland, and Fredericktown, Ohio, and Norfolk, New York. Turning to the largest area of Amish settlement in the world, chapter 5 looks at the schools in the diverse Amish settlement in the Holmes County, Ohio area. Chapter 6 explores the schools in the large, wealthy, progressive, and homogeneous Amish settlement in Elkhart and LaGrange Counties, Indiana, and those in its neighboring settlement in Centreville, Michigan. Focusing on the Old Order schools of Lancaster County, Pennsylvania, chapter 7 explores schools in which Old Order Amish and Old Order Mennonite children study together, often under the guidance of a teacher who is not from their own church.

Chapter 8 explores the textbooks used in the different schools and the publishers of these texts. Old Order publishing has evolved hand in hand with the Old Order private schools, and this chapter investigates the links between publishing, education, and the maintenance of Old Order cultures and lifestyles.

I argue that, in every way, Old Order schools demonstrate the values of the Old Order church-community. The study of these different schools highlights the diversity of Old Order life and the myriad ways in which Old Order schools reinforce community boundaries and Old Order values.

Ochs and Schieffelin (2001, 269) point out that the ethnographer "faces the problem of communicating world views or sets of values that may be unfamiliar and strange to the reader." While I have spent much time in Old Order communities researching and writing this book, I am neither Amish nor Mennonite and thus speak as an outsider, a point asserted by an Old Order Mennonite educator who, after reading a draft of the text, noted, "As far as I can discern, your facts are correct and also your in depth reasoning of where we (the plain communities) come from and why we do as we do. That's not saying you didn't miss certain aspects of the spiritual understanding as we understand it although that kind of knowledge is too abstract (intangible) to fully convey it on paper. 'Faith' can only be learned and realized through experience as given by the Holy Spirit."

Old Order parochial schools are expressions of faith, realizations within the church-communities of biblical teachings on separatism, nonconformity to the world, and the parents' duty to "train up the child." I hope in letting Old Order teachers, parents, and other church-members speak for themselves that I have made this clear.

§ ❦

THIS BOOK COULD NOT HAVE BEEN WRITTEN without the help and support of Old Order teachers and friends who willingly talked with me; welcomed me into their homes, schools, and church services; wrote long letters to me; and kindly gave me comments and advice on earlier drafts of this work. In addition to those who wish to remain nameless, I want to express my gratitude and indebtedness to David Luthy and his wife, Mary, for welcoming me to work in the Heritage Historical Library; to Joseph Stoll, for his willingness to read and comment on my work and to talk with me for long hours; to my dear friend Sue Ann Wickey, who first welcomed me into an Old Order classroom; to Amos Hoover and his wife, Nora, for their encouragement as I worked at the Muddy Creek Farm Library. I am also grateful to Alta Hoover and her husband, David, who welcomed me to stay with them while I asked endless questions on publishing, and to Mary and Ivan Shirk and their family for the opportunity they presented me to just be "at home" with them.

In the non–Old Order world, I owe a special debt to Donald B. Kraybill for his mentoring, encouragement, and advice; to Bruce Weiner for reading and commenting on numerous versions of this work; to Werner Enninger for his encouragement; to the Anabaptoids—M. J. Heisey, Bethany Usher, and Stephen Foulke—for their willingness to listen and to read lots of drafts; to Kathy Tyler for proofreading help; and to Janet Schulenberg for her help with graphics. I am also grateful to the anonymous readers who have offered comments on this manuscript. The comments of many of the above on drafts of this work improved it greatly. I accept full responsibility for the faults that remain.

This work could not have been completed without financial support from the National Endowment for the Humanities (Ref: FB-37315-01), the Spencer Foundation (no. 200200164), and the Research and Creative Endeavors Program at SUNY Potsdam.

Finally, to Bruce, Seth, and Miriam, thank you, for I couldn't have done it without you.

Train Up a Child

CHAPTER 1

Private Schools and Old Order Life

Train up a child in the way he should go: and when he is old,
he will not depart from it.
—Proverbs 22:6

In 1937, writing to "our Men of Authority" in the Pennsylvania state government, a group of Old Order church members from Lancaster County, Pennsylvania, argued against a new law that would extend the school year from eight months to nine and raise the age at which children could leave school from 14 to 15 years old. "We do not wish to withdraw from the Common Public Schools," they noted, "but at the same time we cannot hand our children over to where they will be led away from us" (Shirk 1939, 86). Following years of legal battles in several states and finally in the U.S. Supreme Court, the Old Order Amish and the Old Order Mennonites have established their own schools, and in the last fifty years the number of Old Order private schools has mushroomed. As Meyers (1993) notes, today maintaining private schools has become essential for the preservation of Old Order culture.

Within the larger symbolic framework that structures everyday Old Order life, Old Order schools function to define and perpetuate a system of social relationships and community norms that helps to maintain Old Order religious beliefs, values, and patterns of language use. In their schools, in the choices they make about pedagogy, curriculum, textbooks, assessment, parent-teacher-student interaction, and even school design,

Old Order church-communities[1] realize and reinforce religious beliefs and preserve the social, cultural, and linguistic markers of Old Order identity.

The Amish and the Mennonites

Today's Amish and Mennonite church-communities have their roots in the suffering and martyrdom of the Radical Reformation of the sixteenth century. Frustrated by the slow pace of church reform, several students of Ulrich Zwingli, leader of the Swiss Protestant Church, defied their teacher and the Zurich City Council by meeting secretly in January 1525 and illegally rebaptizing each other. In so doing, these early Anabaptists— the term, a pejorative one in the sixteenth century, means "rebaptizer"— set out to establish a church of believers "according to evangelical truth and the word of God." Their goal was a church separate from the state, in which membership was voluntary and marked by adherence to the principles of nonresistance, pacifism, and non-conformity.[2]

The Anabaptists came to be called Mennonites after Menno Simons, a Dutch priest turned Anabaptist preacher whose teachings helped shape Anabaptist views of baptism, nonconformity in attire, pacifism, and the shunning of excommunicated members. In 1693 an Alsatian preacher, Jacob Amman, argued that the Mennonites were becoming too "worldly," that they were interacting with and even marrying non-Mennonites.[3] The majority of Mennonite preachers and congregations rejected Amman's call for greater separation from the world, so Amman excommunicated them. The conservative minority became known as Amish Mennonites or simply Amish.

Since arriving in North America, Amish and Mennonite churches have experienced additional schisms. Today the most conservative of modern-day Anabaptists, the Old Order Amish and the Old Order Mennonites, remain distinct from the dominant society in their dress, their mode of transportation, their use of technology, and their patterns of language use.

The Old Orders

The early Anabaptists saw clearly that the church of true believers must be opposed to the outside world and would be persecuted by it just as the early Christian martyrs had been. Their Old Order descendants continue to maintain a lifestyle informed by "religiously based conflict with the secular environment" (Redekop 1989). The church is the one pervasive force in Old Order life. Not just a building or a ritual service, the church is a redemptive community of those dedicated to putting the teachings of Jesus Christ into practice (Cronk 1981; Hostetler 1993). The Old Orders call it *Gmay* in Pennsylvania German, from the standard German *Gemeinde*, which means community.

One joins the *Gmay* by being baptized. Like the first Anabaptists, the Old Order Amish and the Old Order Mennonites believe that baptism is literally a covenant with God. Only adults can appreciate the importance of this commitment, and they are urged to think carefully before taking such a step. The Old Orders do not believe that baptism brings salvation. It is instead a public symbol of one's repentance and vow to serve God and God's church. In joining in fellowship with others in the community and being guided by its wisdom, the members of Old Order churches gain the strength to lead lives they hope will be worthy of salvation.

Choosing to be baptized means vowing to maintain the discipline or *Ordnung* of the church-community. The *Ordnung* is a "code of conduct" that reflects the beliefs of the community and controls most aspects of Old Order life, from dress to the use of technology (Kraybill 2001, 112). It separates the church-community from the world, serving as a *Zaun*, a fence enclosing the individual within the larger community and protecting the community from the outside (cf. Keim 1975, 10). A church member who violates the rules of the *Ordnung* risks excommunication (*Bann*) and shunning (*Meidung*).

The Old Orders are obedient to the laws of the secular state, provided that these laws do not conflict with church doctrine. Yet they remain staunch in their view that worldly authority is separate from the kingdom of Christ to which they commit themselves in baptism. Like their Anabaptist ancestors, the Old Orders believe that the Christian way will not be chosen by the majority of society, and thus members of Old Order church-communities attempt to remain "a peculiar people" (Titus 2:14), separate from the world and prepared to suffer at its hands. For members of Old Order church-communities, rejecting the dress and lifestyle of the dominant society and choosing to obey the *Ordnung* signals willingness to be a committed disciple of Christ, to take up the cross and suffer inevitable persecution.

In short, Old Order religious ideology defines the church-community as "God's realm" and demands its separation from the world. All aspects of Old Order culture, from dress to home decoration to economic activity, are circumscribed by community beliefs about proper Christian behavior. Fearing assimilation or "worldliness," each Old Order community weighs potential change carefully, for changes in one domain of Old Order life affect norms and activities in all other domains. Believing that individuals are inherently weak and susceptible to temptation, the Old Orders find strength in community behavioral standards. Changes in the norms of social interaction between members of a church-community or between the church-community and the outside world generally indicate changes in the religious beliefs that constitute the community's sense of itself.

Keim (1975) suggests that it is significant that the Old Orders were defining themselves as a distinct ethnic group at the same time as the states were developing comprehensive school systems: "By the time most states had legislated compulsory attendance statutes, the Amish *Ordnung* had been defined and the Amish community was consciously at variance with the urbanizing secularizing tendencies of the larger society" (1975, 12). Thus, early on, schools became contested territory, a space in which children raised in the *Ordnung* confronted the world.

Old Order Schools

Although a relatively recent phenomenon, Old Order parochial schools[4] are an important institution in Old Order life. Conducted in English, the school is the locus of the Old Order child's introduction to the non–Old Order world, and thus it plays a key role in perpetuating religious ideology and reinforcing community norms, including the maintenance of Pennsylvania German and patterns of German and English usage. Enninger (1999) sees in Old Order schools "a means of tightening the boundaries between the church-community and the dominant society," a view echoed by many in Old Order groups who argue that the private school is as important as the home in preparing children for Old Order life and in maintaining Pennsylvania German and other aspects of Old Order identity. More recently, as economic forces make it increasingly difficult for Old Order young people to earn a living from farming in the traditional way, Old Order schools appear to have become a site of resistance, preparing children to engage in the economic interaction that is necessary for the survival of the community, and at the same time, reinforcing values, beliefs, and patterns of language use that will keep the church-community separate from the world.

Given the importance of the private school to the continued existence of Old Order society, it is ironic that it was not an Old Order innovation, but rather a reaction to organizational changes in the school systems of the majority culture (Enninger 1999). Until only a few decades ago, nearly all Old Order children attended local one-room schools with non–Old Order (English) neighbors. Although public, these little schools allowed Old Order parents a measure of control over the classroom. They were usually within walking distance, and Old Order children were schooled with the same friends with whom they played, did chores, and socialized outside of school. Old Order parents knew all of their children's classmates, and even children who were not from Old Order families were likely farming and doing chores like their Old Order counterparts. In some communities, Old Order parents even sat on school boards (Lapp 1991).

In the mid-twentieth century, however, the public school system was changing. Many rural one-room schools were being consolidated, the length of the school year and number of years of mandatory schooling were increasing, and new subjects were being added to the curriculum. Old Order Amish and Old Order Mennonites became increasingly uneasy about the direction in which public education appeared to be headed. Noting that "necessity is the mother of invention," Old Order Amish educator Uria R. Byler asserted:

> Half a century ago there was less need for parochial schools. The countryside was still studded with one-room schools in which the three R's [sic] were emphasized minus the modern embellishments of TV and radio. The progressive educational theories of John Dewey were still in their infancy [. . .] all this was changed. The country schools were closed one by one. Consolidation, under the label of more "efficient" instruction methods, became the rule. Local districts almost fell over each other to join forces. [. . .] This consolidation trend brought other problems in its wake: long bus trips to and from school, gym classes, and more homework. Many Amish parents were finding it increasingly hard to go along with these developments. Here, then, was being created the necessity for

a change. [...] Plainly, the need for our own schools was there for anyone to see. (Byler 1969, 8)

Kraybill (2001, 175) suggests that the Old Orders "intuitively grasped that modern schools would immerse their youth in mainstream culture" and "separate children from their parents, their traditions, and their values." Similarly, Nancy Nichols Jackson (1969, 39) has asserted that, "in essence, the Amish object to public schools which are no longer homogeneous and within their control because they recognize that the public school is a prime Americanization agent, equipping children for a way of life opposed in many respects to Amish expectations of their children." As school consolidation and centralization in rural areas threatened to remove Old Order children from the watchful eyes of their parents and the church-community, the private school became a way to maintain community boundaries, a way to keep the Old Order world separate from the dominant English one and to protect children from a world of unknown people and different lifestyles (Enninger 1999, 222).

While non–Old Order society changed the way it educated its children, the Old Orders maintained the status quo, taking over abandoned one-room schoolhouses and maintaining a curriculum that emphasized the "3 Rs." Insisting that eight years of formal education were sufficient and that schools remain under the control of parents and church leaders, the Old Order Amish and the Old Order Mennonites began to establish one- and two-room schools that would, like the old public one-room schools, keep children close to home with little opportunity for unsupervised interaction with non–Old Order peers. In this way, Old Order communities began to limit the children's introduction to "worldly fashions" in dress, literature, and technology in a way that they could not when their children attended public schools. As they had when church members served on the boards of education of one-room public schools, church-communities regulated the content of education, limiting the curriculum to subjects and topics that the community deemed appropriate. Schooling had always been about providing children with particular language and arithmetic skills that they could not learn at home. In fact, thanks to a century of public school instruction in English, English had become the primary medium of written communication within Old Order communities (Johnson-Weiner 1997). When they began to establish their own private

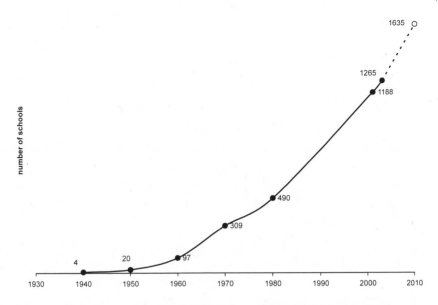

Overall Growth in the Number of Old Order Amish Schools (*The Blackboard Bulletin*; Huntington, 1994: 86)

schools, English remained the primary language of instruction. However, the context of instruction became strictly Old Order.

The first Old Order private school, the Apple Grove Mennonite Private School in Dover, Delaware (later called the Apple Grove Amish Parochial School), was founded in 1925. A directory of schools published in 1957 listed 59 Old Order Amish schools in ten states and the province of Ontario; in 1982, the same directory listed 130 Amish private schools in Ohio alone (see Newcomb 1986, 60). Similarly, Lapp (1991) reports that before 1950 there were four Old Order Amish private schools in Pennsylvania; by 1960 there were 29, and by 1990 there were 245 (cf. Hostetler and Huntington 1992; Kraybill 2001).

Demographic Differences in the Communities Studied

This work explores schools in nine Old Order settlements in five states, including schools in the oldest settlement (Lancaster County, Pennsylvania), the largest settlement (Holmes and Wayne Counties, Ohio), and several of the smallest settlements (the Norfolk community in St. Law-

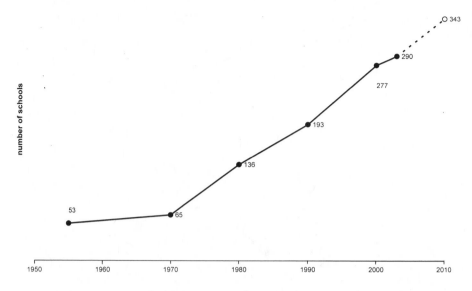

Overall Growth in the Number of Old Order Mennonite Schools (*The Blackboard Bulletin*)

rence County, New York, with seven families, and the Somerset community in Perry County, Ohio, with eleven).[5] It also looks at schools in the
very conservative Swartzentruber communities in St. Lawrence County,
New York, and Holmes and Wayne Counties, Ohio; in the much more
progressive settlement in Elkhart and LaGrange Counties, Indiana; and in
the long-established settlements in Fredericktown, Ohio; Ashland, Ohio;
and Centreville, Michigan. These communities are similar in a number
of important ways. Each has imposed limits on the use of technology, has
standardized dress and transportation, has maintained a dialect of German
for oral intra-group interaction, and has limited formal education. Differing in size, age, and economic base, and in the nature of their interaction
with other Old Order communities and with the dominant non–Old Order society, these communities demonstrate the range of variation in the
Old Order world. More importantly, these communities also demonstrate
varying degrees of "worldliness" (Hostetler 1993, 93) and together present a range of *Ordnungs*, from "low" to "high."

Hostetler (1993, 93) defines low churches as "the most simple and
humble," with a strict *Ordnung* that encourages separation from the world.
A high church, on the other hand, has a more relaxed *Ordnung*. The Old

Orders draw the distinction between "high" and "low" on the basis of a variety of factors, including dress (e.g., the length of a woman's skirts and how much of the hair is covered by her cap), the degree to which a group uses technology (e.g., the presence or absence of indoor plumbing, the use of chain saws or iceboxes), and the construction of a group's buggies (e.g., whether there are windshields or tops on the carriages). The Swartzentruber churches, which have severely limited the adoption of technology, are among the lowest of all Amish affiliations or fellowshipping groups, while the settlement in the Elkhart-LaGrange area is among the highest. Communities such as those in Somerset, Fredericktown, Norfolk, and Ashland, fall in between. Similarly, the Wenger Mennonites, members of the Groffdale Conference of Mennonites, are lower than the Horning Mennonites but not as low as the Stauffer or Reidenbach Mennonites.[6]

The differences between these communities demonstrate the impact of population growth, urbanization, economic change, and religious schism—the variables that have shaped Old Order life across North America. For example, whereas the community in Elkhart and LaGrange Counties is relatively homogeneous, in Holmes and Wayne counties, the largest region of Old Order Amish settlement in the world, members of many different Amish church-communities live intermingled lives as neighbors and co-workers, and their children study together in the private schools. Like the Amish in the Elkhart-LaGrange area, the Lancaster County Old Order Amish community is large and homogeneous, but its members mingle daily with Old Order Mennonites from different conferences. In Lancaster County, some private schools are run by the Old Order Amish, and others are under the supervision of the Old Order Mennonites. Children simply attend the school closest to their homes, resulting in classrooms in which Old Order Amish children study with Old Order Mennonites from a variety of backgrounds.

Patterns of Interaction with Others

These church-communities also interact in different ways with the non–Old Order world that surrounds them. Holmes and Wayne Counties in Ohio, for example, are popular tourist centers. Buggies share the narrow roads with tourist buses, and farmers compete with developers for valuable, high-priced land. Similarly, Lancaster County, also a popular tourist destination, is only an hour from Philadelphia, and farmers struggle with the influx of tourists, developers, and commuters. In contrast, the Somerset settlement in Perry County, Ohio, is a small, homogeneous farming community relatively isolated from other Amish communities in the state. Although living only three hours south of the heart of Amish settlement in Holmes and Wayne counties, Somerset families seldom travel to more populated areas of diverse Amish settlement and have limited interaction with their non-Amish neighbors.

Like Perry County in central Ohio, St. Lawrence County in upstate New York is relatively isolated from the large urban regions of the state. It is the largest county in New York State and the least populated. The Old Order Amish first came to Norfolk in St. Lawrence County in 1974, lured by cheap land and relative isolation from urban influence. Forty miles away from its nearest Amish neighbors, the much larger Swartzentruber settlement in the Heuvelton-DePuyster area, the Old Order church-community in Norfolk is relatively homogeneous, like those in the Elkhart-LaGrange region from which many of the Norfolk residents originate.[7] However, while the Elkhart-LaGrange settlement is wealthy, and many of its members earn their living as hourly workers in local factories, the Norfolk Amish live in poor farming country and are dependent on the dairy industry. There is little in the way of heavy manufacturing, and the Norfolk Old Order Amish often supplement farming with work in town as carpenters or housecleaners.

In contrast, the Swartzentruber Amish, who moved to St. Lawrence County from Holmes and Wayne Counties in Ohio in 1974, are forbidden by their *Ordnung* to work "in town" or as permanent wage employees for non-Swartzentruber employers, so factory employment is out of the question.[8] The same prohibitions limit the work available to Swartzentruber Amish in the Holmes and Wayne Counties settlement. Their Amish neighbors in Holmes and Wayne Counties, and Amish in other Old Order settlements in Ohio, Pennsylvania, Michigan, and Indiana, find work in town in local retail establishments and factories, and on carpentry teams working for non–Old Order employers.

Despite these differences, the communities explored in this study illustrate the broad network of family, religious, and commercial relationships that binds diverse Old Order settlements to each other in important ways. For example, although the Old Order Amish in the Somerset settlement in Perry County, Ohio, which began in 1990, do not fellowship formally with the Amish in the Fredericktown and Ashland, Ohio, settlements, they share ties of family and friendship. As one Somerset woman put it, the church-communities do not share ministers, and, although the young folk continue to socialize with each other and attend church back and forth, they do not intermarry.[9]

The Fredericktown and Ashland Old Order Amish settlements do fellowship formally with each other—that is, their *Ordnungs* are very similar, and ministers from one community preach at church services in the other and sanction intermarriage between the groups. Moreover, family connections tie them to the small settlement of Old Order Amish founded in Norfolk in St. Lawrence County, New York, in 1974, and there is much visiting back and forth. In addition, each of these smaller groups in Ohio and New York has ties to the Old Order Amish settlements in Elkhart and LaGrange Counties, Indiana, and in nearby Centreville, Michigan. Indeed, Centreville was the birthplace of a number of the original Old Order Amish settlers in Norfolk, New York. The Elkhart-LaGrange and Centreville settlements, and thus the settlements in Fredericktown, Ashland, Somerset, and Norfolk, are also linked by family, and to some extent by church discipline, to the Old Order Amish churches in Holmes and Wayne Counties, Ohio. Traveling long distances, members of any of these settlements can find a welcome in homes in all of the others.

The large Swartzentruber Amish settlement in St. Lawrence County has no religious ties to the Old Order Amish settlement in nearby Norfolk, although they engage each other in economic interaction. Established in 1974 by families who moved up from Holmes and Wayne Counties in Ohio to find cheaper land and isolation, the St. Lawrence County Swartzentruber churches continue to maintain close ties to family, both Swartzentruber and Old Order, and to their sister churches in a number of states, including Indiana, Kentucky, Michigan, Minnesota, Tennessee, and Pennsylvania, and in the province of Ontario, Canada.[10]

The Old Order Amish in Lancaster County, Pennsylvania, perhaps the most well-known region of Old Order Amish settlement, have fewer ties to the other areas studied. The Lancaster Old Order Mennonites, however, are linked to churches across Pennsylvania, New York, Ohio, and beyond. In Lancaster County, Old Order Mennonites and Old Order Amish mingle socially at farm sales and auctions, in school, and at work.

Separation, Diversity, and Old Order Identity

Not a random sample but representative of the range of lifestyles and Ordnungs found in groups otherwise united by family and religion, the nine
communities that are the focus of this study demonstrate what it means to
be "Old Order." Sociologist John A. Hostetler has noted that "a sectarian
movement must establish an ideology different from that of the parent
group in order to break off relations with it. Emergent beliefs tend to be
selected on the basis of their difference from the parent group" (1993, 48).
In living according to biblical precepts, the first Anabaptists consciously
attempted to create a new society in which each member of the church
would not be "conformed to the world" (Romans 12:2).[11] By separating
the church from the world and distinguishing the true believer from the
outsider, the early Anabaptists attempted to establish new patterns of behavior that would, in contrast to worldly actions, reflect biblical teachings.[12]

In North America, the need to be separate from the world has continued to shape the social practices of Old Order communities. Committed
to the Alte Ordnung, or "Old Order" of their ancestors, today's Old Order
Amish and Old Order Mennonite church-communities control the use of
technology and preserve distinct styles of clothing, architecture, worship,
education, transportation, and patterns of language use in their attempt to
function "in the world but not of it" (1 Peter 2:11).

Yet, since the Old Order Amish churches are congregationally based,
with no strong, organizing body uniting them and standardizing behavior, each church-community makes its own decisions as it negotiates its
place in the world. Different communities may be in fellowship with
each other, but decisions made by one church-community are not bind-
ing on another. As a result, although books, articles, and TV specials refer
to the Old Order Amish as one group, they are, in fact, plural; for no two
Old Order Amish groups are alike. This does not mean that one group
is "more Amish" than another, but rather that the "Amish" are variously
constituted. For example, in their use of technology and interaction with
the dominant society, the Swartzentruber Amish of upstate New York are
different than the Old Order Amish of LaGrange, Indiana.

Old Order Mennonites differ obviously from Old Order Amish in
their use of meetinghouses for church services. Moreover, although indi-

vidual Mennonite congregations have considerable input through counsel meetings into church decision making, individual congregations within a conference are bound by decisions taken by their ministers and bishops. These meet together prior to the twice-yearly communion services to resolve differences and ensure that the church communities "stand in peace, love, and unity with each other" (Horst 2000, 35).[13] When differences cannot be reconciled, a schism may occur. In this way, the variation between Old Order Mennonite conferences is similar to the variation between fellowshipping and non-fellowshipping church districts in Old Order Amish communities.

Like the Old Order Amish, the Old Order Mennonites evolved in opposition to innovations taking place in the broader Mennonite world, including Sunday schools, revival meetings, the use of English for church services, and higher education (Johnson-Weiner 1998; Kraybill and Bowman 2001, chap. 3, esp. p. 61). Like the Old Order Amish, the Old Order Mennonites continue to limit formal education to the eight primary grades: "For Old Orders the sources of spiritual renewal were found in new affirmations of older ways, not in innovative practices from the outside. More than mere reactionaries, they sought to renew the church by reclaiming and revitalizing the precious patterns of the past" (Kraybill and Bowman 2001, 61).

Unlike any of the Old Order Amish communities I am considering, many of the Old Order Mennonites use electricity and have installed telephones in their homes. In the 1920s, some Old Order Mennonites adopted the automobile. This study focuses on "Old Order Team Mennonites" (Kraybill and Bowman 2001, 65–66), who continue to rely on horse and buggy for transportation.

The groups that call themselves plain—Old Order Amish, Swartzentruber Amish, and Old Order Team Mennonites, including Wenger, Reidenbach, and Stauffer Mennonites—are linked generally by history and common Anabaptist beliefs, and more particularly by the use of horse and buggy for family transportation, plain dress, and a desire to remain separate from the world. Yet within these parameters they vary widely in size, geographic location, and, more fundamentally, in their pattern of social and economic interaction with other Old Order groups and with the dominant society.

Old Order Schools and Old Order Diversity

Strikingly similar and yet different, the Old Order communities that I visited for this study reflect the reality of Old Order life across North America. Similarly, the schools presented here, although only a small percentage of all Old Order schools in North America, are representative of Old
Order private education. Even church-communities separated by great
distances may be "in fellowship" with each other and thus share a common
understanding of the goals and standards of education. Thus, a school in one
church-community represents the reality of education in many others.

Yet, while each individual school in this study is representative of educational practices common in many communities, as a group they demonstrate the diversity of Old Order private education. Popular wisdom has
it that Old Order education ends with eighth grade, which is generally
true but not for all; that Old Order teachers "have no teacher training before they take their job" (Klimuska c. 1989, 3), which, again, is generally
true but not for all. Nor are *all* Old Order schools simple one-room buildings, *all* Old Order children in a class "peas of the same Swiss-German
Anabaptist pod . . . sharing homogeneous values," *all* Old Order curricula
"the unsweetened 3 Rs" (Klimuska, c. 1989, 3). Indeed, one cannot even
make these claims for all Old Order schools in Lancaster County or Holmes County.[14]

Simply put, Old Order schools are not all the same because Old Order
communities are not all the same, and the multiple forms of "Old Order"
are revealed daily in the operation of Old Order schools. Most of the research on Old Order private schools has focused on the Old Order Amish.
Certainly, the Old Order Amish appear to have been most prominent in
resisting school consolidation and other changes in public education. But
Old Order Mennonites have followed closely behind. Particularly in
Lancaster County, Pennsylvania, the Old Order private school movement
has involved Old Order Amish and Old Order Mennonites working together,[15] although, as historian Amos B. Hoover has noted, the Old Order
Amish, guided by Preacher Stephen F. Stoltzfus, took the lead.[16]

In 1966 Aaron E. Beiler, presiding over a meeting of the Amish School
Committee at which a number of Mennonite school directors were also
in attendance, warned that the proliferation of private schools was "getting too big," and so "there was a danger of things being geared toward

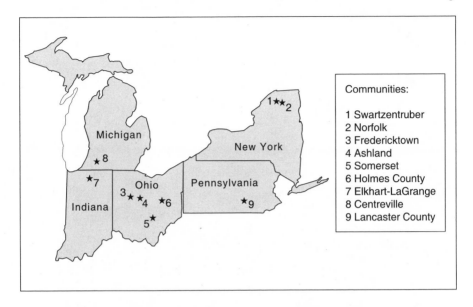

The communities visited during this study are spread across five states.

higher standards, and that there was a danger of things running out of control" (*Background*, 13). The first meeting of the committee for the Mennonite Parochial Schools of Pennsylvania was held in March 1968. From the beginning, however, Old Order Mennonite children attended Old Order Amish schools and vice versa. Still today, Old Order children in Lancaster County attend the neighborhood private school, whether it is Amish or Mennonite (Kraybill and Bowman 2001, 83–84). Given this practice, and given that Old Order Mennonites have expressed the same fears about public schools and have similar goals for private schools as their Amish counterparts, it is useful to include both in this study.

Studied together, Old Order schools reveal how community size, economic base, and pattern of interaction with other Old Order communities and the surrounding society reflect and shape community values and the community's sense of itself and its place in the larger society (Dauenhauer and Dauenhauer 1998).

Table 1. Characteristics of Old Order Schools and Communities Discussed in this Study

Schools (Location)	School (A) and Community (B) Characteristics
Swartzentruber Schools (Upstate New York [Heuvelton]; Holmes and Wayne Counties, Ohio)	**(A)** One-room schools serving only a few families; primitive construction with no electricity or indoor plumbing and stove in classroom; no playground equipment; teachers employed for only a year or two and receive no training; archaic textbooks; minimum number of subjects taught (English, arithmetic, German); only German singing; no prayer in schools; minimal parental involvement in school functions.
	(B) Very conservative communities; no electricity or indoor plumbing in homes and strict limits on technology; "working in town" or as permanent wage labor for non-Swartzentruber employers is not permitted; limited interaction with non–Swartzentruber Amish groups.
Small Amish Schools (Somerset, Ohio; Fredericktown, Ohio; Ashland, Ohio; Norfolk, New York)	**(A)** One-room schools with no electricity or indoor plumbing; teachers may receive some training and may have teachers' meetings; mix of archaic and more current texts, often public school castoffs; most offer history and geography in addition to basic subjects; German and English singing; morning devotions and prayer before noon meal; parents involved with Christmas and end-of-year parties and may visit schools.
	(B) Small, homogeneous, rural communities; primarily agrarian; communities interact though they may not fellowship; very conservative in dress and use of technology, but communities vary (e.g., some have indoor plumbing, but others do not).

Mainstream Amish Schools (Holmes and Wayne Counties, Ohio)	**(A)** Larger schools, many with two classrooms; teachers may belong to a different church than their students; up-to-date texts from Amish or Mennonite publishers; singing in English and German and morning devotions; wide range of subjects, including history, geography, and art; teachers often employed for several years and some make teaching a career; regular teachers' meetings; parents actively involved in schools. **(B)** Largest Amish settlement in the world; quite diverse, with a number of different Amish groups and a range of lifestyles; much economic and social interaction with the non–Old Order world, but significant variation from group to group; not all Amish families send children to Amish private schools.
Progressive Amish Schools (Elkhart and LaGrange Counties, Indiana; Centreville, Michigan)	**(A)** Larger schools, some with three classrooms; indoor plumbing common; up-to-date texts from Amish, Mennonite, and other Christian publishers; many teachers make teaching a career; regular teachers' meetings; singing mostly in English; morning devotions and Bible verse memorization; field trips and nature walks; parents actively involved. **(B)** Homogeneous communities, few schisms; well-integrated economically into the larger, non-Amish community; very progressive in the adoption of technology; considerable reliance on manufacturing in economic base.
Old Order Mennonite Schools (Lancaster County, Pennsylvania)	**(A)** One- and two-room schools; electricity and indoor plumbing common; teachers may belong to a different church than students; career teachers; regular teachers' meetings and teacher training; wide range of subjects offered with interactive activities; may have instruction in music; morning devotions. **(B)** Oldest Mennonite and Amish settlement; considerable social and economic interaction between Amish and Mennonite groups; a diverse Mennonite population; range of lifestyles and use of technology; well integrated into the non–Old Order economy.

Broader Implications

In 1968 the school board in New Glarus, Wisconsin, charged three Old Order Amish fathers with violating the state's compulsory school attendance law. The resulting legal battle, culminating in the 1972 Supreme Court decision in *Wisconsin v. Yoder et al.* that the Old Order Amish could not be compelled to send their children to public high schools, challenged the traditional barriers between church and state. While some asserted the state's special interest in educating its citizens, others asked whether religious groups that saw social isolation as key to their religious survival should be required to send their children to public schools. As John A. Hostetler (1969, 33) put it,

> Is it the purpose of state schools to promote the socialization of all children of all nationalities, of all cultural backgrounds, of all ethnic groups, into one American mold and to promote conformity at the expense of cultural diversity? The state cannot assure an adequate education for all children without setting instructional requirements for all schools, public or non-public. The non-public schools cannot fulfill their distinctive educational goals if these standards preclude them from independently following their own cultural goals. How is balance to be achieved?

Or, as Erickson (1969, 160) asked, "What disparate goals shall we allow and even encourage in education?"[17]

In the twenty-first century, the private schools of the Old Order Amish and the Old Order Mennonites reveal a diversity perhaps unimagined by the U.S. Supreme Court in 1972. For example, Chief Justice Warren Burger, in The Opinion of the Court, characterized Old Order life as "inherently simple and uncomplicated" (in Keim 1975, 158). Today, however, for some Old Order church-communities, the question seems to be how to educate Old Order children to work in the world, an ironic reversal of the problem of earlier generations, who worried about how children educated in the world would remain Old Order.

Hostetler (1969, 20) notes that "schooling in any society is directly related to the value-orientation of a culture." Yet in realizing the core values of their faith and culture, schools in today's Old Order church-communities demonstrate widely varying patterns of interaction with the world and divergent notions of what it means to be Old Order. The Old Order private school presents what Sahlins (1981; 1985, xiv) has termed the "structure of the conjuncture […] the practical realization of the cultural categories in a specific historical context, as expressed in the interested action of the historic agents." In private schools, the Old Orders have attempted to hold to educational practices that, in the era of one-room public schools, characterized for them key values of community responsibility, separation from the world, closeness to the soil, and church-community discipline (Hostetler 1969, 20). Schools have become for Old Order church-communities a means of reproducing and reinforcing their values. In fusing particular educational settings and practices to Old Order beliefs, these private schools support Sahlins' contention that "culture functions as a synthesis of stability and change, past and present, diachrony and synchrony" (1985, 144).

Nevertheless, as Sahlins points out, "every reproduction of the categories is not the same." Kulick (1992) noted, for example, that, in their everyday interactions, villagers in Gapun, Papua New Guinea, use traditional notions of self and personhood in a way that results in language shift and cultural change. Similarly, Old Order private schools help to change the culture of the church-community even as they reproduce it, demonstrating the truth of Sahlins' (1985) assertion that in reproducing culture, people transform it.

Old Order private schools help to preserve a culture in which Pennsylvania German is the language of the group and oral English is the language of the outside, while at the same time, they introduce children to the dominant society and provide them with language and other skills needed to interact with it successfully. In doing so, they have much to teach us about how schools in minority language communities negotiate and maintain boundaries between the community and the dominant society. Old Order schools must serve both the interests of the church-community and the often-conflicting requirements of the state. While Old Orders want their schools to prepare children for a life of service to God and the church-community, the dominant society requires schools to prepare children for success in the workplace and citizenship in the secular state. The struggle for Old Order schools is to limit the effects of English education and so preserve the boundaries between the community and the dominant society, meeting the state's mandate that education enable children to function successfully in the outside world, yet doing so on Old Order terms.

Some might argue that Old Order schools, which reflect the desire of Old Order communities to remain separate from the dominant society for religious reasons, have little to teach us about language and culture maintenance in schools that serve groups that may be unwillingly isolated from the dominant society by race, ethnicity, language, or economic factors. Yet, like other minority groups, the Old Order desire to reinforce cultural and linguistic norms, while at the same time educating children in the language of the dominant society so that they can interact economically with it. An understanding of Old Order schools will contribute to our knowledge of how religious and ethnic minorities negotiate with the outside world to preserve the linguistic, cultural, and religious integrity of the group.

CHAPTER 2

Old Order Schools and Old Order Identities

By fourteen you've pretty much learned all you need to in school.
—A Swartzentruber Amish Bishop

Modern Schools for Twenty-first-Century Realities

A postcard published by American Souvenirs and Gifts shows two schoolhouses and a classroom scene of children lined up by the board for a reading lesson. The caption reads, "As in almost all else, the schools of the Amish are of another century. The one room little red school house with its pot bellied stove and its eight grades together is still the mainstay of the Amish school system."[1] Similarly, in a series of articles for the *Lancaster New Era*, writer E. Klimuska talks about "yester-year learning" and suggests that "in Plain schools, the educational clock stopped 50 years ago. It's as if these schools are outposts, fenced in from the competitive pressures of 20th Century learning, protected from its progress and turmoil. The schools convey images of olden days, when life was slower and easier to handle" (c.1989, 3–4).

The reality is far more complicated. There is little about Old Order education that is nineteenth century, for example. The Old Order Amish and the Old Order Mennonites are quintessentially twenty-first-century peoples, daily confronting modernity and making choices about its relevance in their lives (Kraybill 2001). More importantly, Old Order schools are not all alike, because Old Order communities have made different choices.

In some Old Order communities, for example, young children face a future in which they may be employed as factory workers, laboring side by side with others from a variety of religious and ethnic backgrounds. In others, young children learn early that "working in town for English people" is forbidden by the *Ordnung*. Old Order schools and Old Order education reflect these differences.

Although Old Order communities have largely rejected the authority of the state to determine what kind of education is best for their children, they do not all share the same vision of what schools should be, how children should be taught, and what subjects they should study. As they confront the demands of the twenty-first century, each Old Order group defines for itself what it means to educate its children appropriately.

Education versus Schooling

Old Order schools reflect the church-community's beliefs about the church, the behavior of its members, and the relationship between the church and the dominant society. In structuring the school day, determining the curriculum, setting pedagogical standards, and even constructing the schoolhouse, members of the church-community reveal and reinforce the *Ordnung* and make concrete the community's sense of itself and its place vis-à-vis other church-communities and the secular state. In so doing, Old Order parents help to ensure that their children attend schools that will help them become responsible members of their church-community.

The Old Orders believe that the Bible entrusts the education of children to parents, and they will let neither the educational specialists nor the state usurp parental responsibility for the moral upbringing of their children. Menno Simons, one of the most influential of the early Anabaptist leaders, argued that parents were morally responsible for their children and admonished parents to watch over the souls of their children, for "this is the chief and most important care of the godly, that their children may fear God, do good, and be saved" (1983, 274). "The world," Simons argued, "desire for their children that which is earthly and perishable, such as money, honor, fame and wealth. From infancy they train them up to vice, pride, haughtiness and idolatry. But with you, who are born of God, this is not the case; for it behooves you to seek something else for your children; namely, that which is heavenly and eternal, and hence it is your duty to bring them up in the nurture and admonition of the Lord, as Paul teaches, Eph. 6:1–4" (1983, 274).

In establishing their own schools, Old Order communities have attempted to control the influences to which their children are exposed. As an Amish writer put it, "How can we parents expect our children to grow up untainted by the world, if we voluntarily send them into a worldly environment, where they associate with worldly companions, and are taught by men and women not of our faith six hours a day, five days a week, for the greater part of the year?" (Stoll 1975, 28).

Old Order communities have also drawn an important distinction between schooling and education. Schooling is book learning, the value of which varies in Old Order communities. Education, on the other hand, is the inculcation of values. Writing about the Old Order Amish, Hostetler (1962, 4) notes: "Amish parents want their children to acquire the skills of reading, writing, and ciphering. For this reason they want their children to attend the elementary schools. After completing the grades, however, they believe that Amish youth should get their instruction in farming and management at home. This vocation, they contend, does not require higher education, and such schooling is 'a waste of time.' Too much 'book learning' is not good."

Similarly, Huntington (1994, 78) has noted that "the Amish do not confuse schooling with the larger concept of what the world calls education. Although during most periods in their history they have permitted their children to be schooled by 'outsiders,' they have never permitted their children to be educated by the world."

For the Old Orders, the value of schooling is limited, and indeed, too much of it can have disastrous consequences. "We believe that such time spend [sic] in the schoolroom, beyond the eighth grade or the age of fourteen, will often lead to indolence and an inclination for types of work which require less manual labor, without regard for spiritual and sometimes physical welfare; often resulting in becoming entangled with things that are not edifying." So argued a group of bishops, ministers and deacons before the Holmes County, Ohio, Board of Education.[2] As a Swartzentruber bishop put it, "By fourteen you've pretty much learned all you need to in school, but you can't wait 'til then to start learning what you need to live." An Amish leader voicing his opposition to public schooling put it even more succinctly when he asserted, "With us, our religion is inseparable with a day's work, a night's rest, a meal, or any other practice; therefore, our education can much less be separated from our religious practices" (in Kraybill 2001, 174; Lapp 1991, 321).[3]

The true education upon which the church-community depends for its survival takes place in the sharing of labor; the doing of chores; and the enjoyment of fellowship at church, around the dinner table, and even in silo filling. In establishing a private school, an Old Order community not only ensures that the curriculum taught in school is appropriate for the community, but also that the school maintains its proper place in community life.

Old Order parents do not send their children to school so that they can prepare for a well-paying job or become good citizens. Parents trust that the private school will supplement the efforts of parents and those of the larger church-community to prepare the child "to live for others, to use his talents in service to God and Man, to live an upright and obedient life, and to prepare for the life to come" (Stoll 1975, 31; Hostetler 1993; Hostetler and Huntington 1992).

Reflecting Community Values

As noted earlier, until the middle of the twentieth century most Old Order children attended public schools. Only as state authorities began to consolidate the local one-room schoolhouses and enforce compulsory attendance beyond the eighth grade did Old Order parents resist. The number of Old Order private schools grew as Old Order parents in a number of states were fined or jailed when they refused to send their children to high school or to put them on buses to travel to new centralized schools.

Conflict with state authorities has abated in the years since the 1972 Supreme Court decided in *Wisconsin v. Yoder et al.* that "enforcement of the State's requirement of compulsory formal education after the eighth grade would gravely endanger if not destroy the free exercise of . . . [Amish] religious beliefs" (in Keim 1975, 98). Yet the Supreme Court decision did not result in a unified Old Order response. Instead, Old Order schools have become increasingly diverse as Old Order communities, each attempting to preserve itself from what it sees as "worldliness," react differently to pressures from the dominant society and from other Old Order communities.[4]

All Old Order groups change over time, but they do not all make the same changes, nor are all innovations equally important symbolically. Old Order groups define themselves by emphasizing their differences, not only from non–Old Order society, but also from other Old Order groups (Hostetler 1993, 48). For example, the Swartzentruber Amish, among the most conservative of Amish groups, find the dominant, non–Old Order society to be useful but irrelevant in many respects. Members of the different Swartzentruber church-communities engage in economic exchanges with the "English," or non-Amish. They shop in non-Amish stores; visit garage sales; maintain farm stands, harness shops, and sawmills that attract non-Amish customers; and seek medical help when they must; and they recognize these things as necessary to the survival of the church-community. But the non-Amish world is clearly different from the Swartzentruber world. Other Old Order groups often pose a greater threat, for these groups demonstrate the extent to which a church can "modernize" while still remaining visibly separate from the world.

The Swartzentruber Amish see commitment to the old ways as essential to the survival of the community. In Swartzentruber eyes, Old Order groups that have abandoned the old ways for worldly ones provide clear evidence that the world can be a powerful lure. "There are always some wanting some more modernisms," commented a Swartzentruber Amish bishop about other Old Order groups in the Holmes County, Ohio, neighborhood in which he used to live. "They're all one pack to me." A recent schism in the Swartzentruber community was characterized by one woman in terms of change versus the retention of traditional ways. Her own group, she said, "took a step back when they split," rejecting changes; while the others were "just like kids. The grass is always greener."

The Swartzentruber Amish have made fewer concessions to the demands of technology and modernity than have most of their Old Order counterparts. As Hostetler and Huntington (1992, 10) note, "Much of Amish ritual today consists of maintaining the purity and unity of the church community." For the Swartzentruber Amish, the practices of daily life reinforce this purity and unity, for they have drawn a sharp line between themselves and the world and between themselves and Old Order communities that they deem more worldly—those that, in the words of a Swartzentruber bishop, "want to be Amish but don't know how." Their unwavering commitment to the traditions as practiced by previous generations and their belief that God's way is unchanging makes compromise

Although the Crossroads School and the River View School look similar to those that are not Old Order, the basement in the Crossroads School hints at architectural innovations many Swartzentrubers feel have no place in a schoolhouse.

difficult if not impossible, so the Swartzentruber Amish often come into conflict not only with the dominant society but also with other Old Order groups.[5]

This was particularly evident in Holmes County, Ohio, when the Crossroads School burned down.[6] Old Order and Swartzentruber Amish parents who had been sending their children to this formerly public one-room schoolhouse disagreed about how the school should be rebuilt. Ultimately, the Old Order parents prevailed, and they erected a building that had a basement big enough to serve as a playroom for the children on cold or rainy days. The basement, which has a poured cement floor and cinderblock walls, is lighted naturally and houses a Ping-Pong table and a furnace that heats the classroom through vents in the floor. One enters the classroom through a cloakroom that features small cubbies in which the children can hang their coats and put their lunch pails. On a table in the entryway sits a large insulated water jug and a number of glasses so that the children can easily get a drink when they come in from recess. There is

The entryway to the Crossroads School features individual cubbies for children's belongings. This side is for the girls.

no indoor plumbing or artificial lighting. The floor in the one large classroom is hardwood, and the walls are plain, painted white above tan wainscoting. Single-paneled curtains on each window are pulled back to one side to allow more light. There is bench in front of the teacher's desk for students doing recitation, and hanging from the ceiling near the teacher's desk is a rope that the teacher tugs on to ring the school bell. Behind the school is a playground with a wooden swing set. There are also two cinderblock outhouses that have been painted gray.

The new Crossroads schoolhouse was built to accommodate at least thirty scholars comfortably and is wide enough that the room could easily be divided into two classrooms. In spring 2002, however, there were only eleven students, for members of two of the three Swartzentruber Amish groups that, along with other Old Order Amish families, had been sending children to the school insisted that the new building the others had proposed was too expensive and too fancy.[7] One Swartzentruber father, whose wife and mother had both attended the old Crossroads School, angrily protested the $50,000 price tag "just for one story with a cellar about

The River View School, located within eyesight of the Crossroads School,
is smaller and lacks a cellar.

as big as this house" (not very big).[8] A mother in the St. Lawrence County
Swartzentruber settlement who had attended the old Crossroads School
referred to the new Crossroads schoolhouse and "expensive schoolhouses"
in general as something "we people didn't want."

"One school burned down and they replaced it with two," summed up
a Swartzentruber father. The River View School was built just a short
way from the new Crossroads School. To non–Old Order eyes, the two
buildings are very similar, except that River View has no basement, and
there are hooks and shelves instead of cubbies for coats and lunch pails.
The walls are white, and in the spring of 2002 the wainscoting was still
unpainted, although the teacher suggested that this was because they had
barely managed to get the building done in time for the school year to start.
The curtains in the River View schoolhouse are also single panels of cloth
pulled to one side, but they are a dark navy blue rather than the light blue
used in the Crossroads School. The furnishings in the two schoolhouses,
down to the bench for recitation, are identical; but River View has no

The Swartzentruber scholars of the River View School have only hooks for their cloaks.
The woodstove that heats their school is at the top of the stairs.

playground equipment, just a field for games, and the outhouses are unpainted.

The differences between the two buildings seem minor to outsiders.
Indeed, according to the Crossroads schoolteacher, herself a member of a
Swartzentruber Amish church-community, "all that is different from the
old and new schoolhouse is the new one is a little bigger." But for many of
the Swartzentruber parents, building the larger school, having the furnace
in the basement, and having cubbies for coats were unnecessary and even
prideful extravagances.

Even though the old Crossroads School was large and had a cellar,
Swartzentruber families had sent their children there because they had
not built the school themselves. According to Hostetler (1993, 259),
the old, one-room public school buildings were "generally acceptable to
the Amish, even though they included some things forbidden in Amish
homes." Just as when a Swartzentruber family buys a house built by a non-
Amish carpenter and so must put up with non-Amish design, parents were

able to accommodate elements that were not to the liking of their church because they were already part of the structure. It was another matter for the community to build a school for itself that had elements frowned upon by the church.

In refusing to send their children to the new Crossroads School, two Swartzentruber church-communities rejected what they saw as "drift," unnecessary change in a worldly direction. Calling the new school "a church building" because of its size and extravagance, many implicitly denounced it as alien to their way of life and linked it to a key innovation of groups such as the Beachy Amish, which, in addition to building churches, have adopted automobiles and electricity, use English instead of German in church services, and have modified their plain dress (Hostetler 1993, 95; 283–84).[9]

The Old Order Amish families who built the new Crossroads School are certainly as committed to God's path as the Swartzentrubers, but they have drawn the boundaries around their communities differently. Kraybill (2001, 297) writes that "the Amish view social change as a matter of moving cultural fences—holding to old boundaries and setting new ones. This dynamic process involves negotiating symbolic boundaries in the moral order. . . . Cultural fences mark the lines of separation between the two worlds. Coping with social change involves fortifying old fences as well as moving fences and building new ones." For a number of Old Order groups, increasing economic pressures and the decreasing ability of the church-community to support itself entirely through farming have meant that, as Olshan (1994, 145–46) puts it, "the old patterns [are] no longer viable," and they have begun to permit greater interaction with the non–Old Order world (Kollmorgen 1942). While Swartzentruber church-communities consciously resist moving the fences at all, other Old Order communities, more engaged with the world economically and thus facing different social pressures for change, find in private schools a means of reinforcing the church boundaries. They hope that schools will help to hold off the child's introduction to the world and thus lessen the impact of the world upon the child.

Having defined separation from the world in such a way that members of the church-community are able to work side by side with non–Old Order employees in factories and restaurants, the most progressive Old Order church-communities have come to understand their relationship to non–Old Order society quite differently (Kraybill and Nolt 1995). Spending more time doing the same things their non–Old Order neighbors do, members of these communities have become increasingly difficult to define as "Old Order" in other than a negative way—as having a lifestyle characterized by lack of electricity, of automobiles, of fashionable clothing. As the line between the Old Order and non–Old Order worlds becomes blurred, emphasizing the scriptural basis for Old Order practice can reinforce the community boundaries, enabling members of the church-community to reject assimilation into the dominant society even as they adopt many of the innovations and practices of their non–Old Order neighbors.

Maintaining Purity and Unity

Kraybill and Bowman (2001, 84) note that in Old Order Mennonite schools "religious values permeate the classroom and playground." Similarly, they point out that Old Order Amish schools "play a critical role in the preservation of Amish culture. They reinforce Amish values and shield youth from contaminating ideas afloat in modern culture" (116). In calling the new Crossroads schoolhouse "too big" and constructing a competing schoolhouse across the road, members of the two dissenting Swartzentruber church-communities offered a competing definition of what a school should be like and the role the school should play in their communities. They drew the boundary between themselves and their Amish neighbors differently than did the third Swartzentruber group and encoded a different vision of what it means to be Amish.

Schoolhouses reveal and encode the community's notion of humility, simplicity, and resignation (Hostetler 1975, 106) and so serve to reinforce the community's sense of itself and its relationship to other Old Order communities and to non–Old Order society. Built according to the standards of their respective church-communities, the Crossroads and River View schoolhouses embody different notions of what it means to be Old Order. In their structure, furnishings, and décor, they, like other Old Order private schools, reflect the values of the communities that use them. Thus, a school built by one group might seem woefully inadequate—or wildly extravagant—to another.

Swartzentruber Amish schools are simple, almost meager affairs. Since the first Swartzentruber Amish families arrived in upstate New York, they have built thirteen schools, all to the same pattern. Roughly 20 feet by 30 feet, these wooden structures, like the River View School, lack cellars, electricity, and indoor plumbing, and exteriors are often unpainted. Inside, there is no paneling; the walls and often the floor are made of particleboard and painted, as are Swartzentruber Amish homes, in white and battleship gray. The schools are single rooms heated by a woodstove, and there is a platform on top of the stove on which children can place their lunches to heat them. Often wire is strung from the stovepipe to the wall, both to anchor the stovepipe and to provide a drying rack for wet mittens. The main entry to the building is through the woodshed, and there are hooks on each side of the door for coats and shelves for lunch boxes. There are no lamps: the building is naturally lighted, and windows are covered only by a single curtain that is tied to one side. A blackboard covers the front wall, a teacher's desk faces the rows of children's desks, and a long bench or several chairs at the front serve for recitation. There is a field in which children can play ball games but no playground.

The schools built by the Old Order Amish of northern Indiana present a sharp contrast. Shady Valley School in Topeka, Indiana, for example, has three classrooms, two on the first floor and another at one end of the basement. The other half of the basement is reserved for game playing, and there is a Ping-Pong table. An apartment built over the first floor accommodates teachers. Outside is a large playground with a swing set, a merry-go-round, basketball nets, and seesaws. There is indoor plumbing. Near Shady Valley, Tree Top School in LaGrange, Indiana, has a curtain that divides a single large room into two classrooms. There are bookshelves, shades on the windows, and pressurized gas lanterns. The walls are painted white, and the floor is hardwood. Beside each teacher's desk is a large table around which children sit when their class is called to work. Like Shady Valley and many other schools in northern Indiana, Tree Top has a residence for the teachers in part of the school building. The teachers' quarters at Tree Top consists of a compact but cozy sitting room, with patterned linoleum and scatter rugs on the floor, and a small kitchen. The building is heated by a woodstove in the cellar. While not as large as the one at Shady Valley, the playground at Tree Top also features a merry-go-round and swings.

The Old Order Mennonite schools in Lancaster County offer yet another version of humble simplicity. For example, Hill and Valley School, run by Old Order Wenger Mennonites, is an old public schoolhouse. There is no indoor plumbing, but there is electricity. Plants hang in the windows, and there is a copying machine next to the file cabinet along the wall by the teacher's desk. There is a high table on the other side of the teacher's desk around which students stand when their grade is called to the front for recitation. Maple Hill School in Lancaster County, another formerly public schoolhouse in Lancaster County, has been expanded to two rooms, each housing four grades. The large classrooms have plants hanging from the ceiling, and outside there are swings, a basketball hoop, and a baseball diamond. Renovations to the Maple Hill building have, like the rebuilding of the Crossroads School, caused dissension. According to a Wenger Mennonite woman whose children were attending Maple Hill, "teachers had only gas lights to work late with and that was a problem, so we decided to put in electricity, but the Thirty-fivers [the Reidenbach Mennonite families][10] who sent their children to the school objected. They expressed concerns that electricity would bring in other things like computers."

In determining whether a school will have a basement, indoor plumbing, electricity, a playground, or a room where a teacher might live, Old Order communities make clear the role of this state-mandated institution within the community and the impact it will have on the church and its member families. In short, within the broadly stated goal of cultivating humility, simplicity, and resignation to God, church-communities have incorporated the schools in different ways, each revealing the way in which the community defines its relationship with the world and with other Old Order groups.

Teaching the "Three Rs" and More

The Old Order private school system was slow to evolve (Keim 1975, 15). Old Order Amish writer Uria R. Byler suggests that Old Order communities resisted setting up private schools because they were concerned about their cost and feared that such schools would "offend" the dominant society, that it would be impossible to get qualified teachers, or that the pupils would be ill-disciplined (1969, 9). Yet another reason for their reluctance to create private schools may be that, prior to public school consolidation, the status quo was not threatened enough to warrant a departure from traditional practices. Private schools were established when public schools and schooling began to take the children far from home and displace parental supervision with state control.

In the most conservative Amish settlements, the private school plays a limited role in the life of the church community. It is an outside institution, state mandated, and designed to meet specific, limited needs. A former teacher in a Swartzentruber school, for example, had few expectations for the schools in her community. "You have to go so you can learn to spell and do arithmetic and to satisfy others," she asserted. "And so you aren't stupid," added her sister. Pressed to elaborate, the former teacher acknowledged that the schools did have broader social goals: "You need to go to school to learn to get along with strangers" (cf. Hostetler and Huntington 1976, 198). She went on to talk of one family that lived far from its nearest Swartzentruber neighbors on the outskirts of the settlement. "When there was just one in school, he stayed with his *Dawdis* [grandparents] and went to school, but there are four in school now, so they can't. The mother can teach them at home, but she can't teach them to get along with strangers."[11]

By "strangers," the teacher and her sister mean Swartzentruber Amish children and others in Swartzentruber church-communities outside of the immediate family. In other words, the school is not preparing children to interact socially with the dominant society; rather, the Swartzentruber Amish expect that their schools will socialize children to interact appropriately with others in their church-community. There is little emphasis on other behavioral outcomes.

In Swartzentruber schools, change comes slowly, for the community is unwilling to depart from practices that have worked for generations. For the most part, the Swartzentruber Amish have simply continued the same educational practices they followed when their one-room schoolhouses were public, using the same texts their parents and grandparents found useful. When the Swartzentruber Amish have made curricular or other changes in their schools, they have tended to go back in time rather than accept "modernisms," thereby eliminating features of education not immediately applicable to their way of life. The rejection of the new Crossroads school, for example, is mirrored in the rejection of subjects such as geography or health, which Swartzentruber students studied when they attended public schools, but which are not in the curriculum of the schools the Swartzentrubers have built for themselves. Similarly, few of the Swartzentruber parents in the Heuvelton settlement had used the archaic *McGuffey's Readers* when they attended school in Ohio, but they have adopted these books, used by earlier generations, to teach their children in New York.

In Swartzentruber communities, the private school isolates children from worldly influence and thus provides a safe place for children to acquire necessary social and academic skills. Still, it remains a state-mandated institution, "part of the domain of the outside world" (Hostetler and Redekop 1962, 198). In a number of ways, the Swartzentruber Amish attempt to limit the effects of school by keeping the boundaries between the school and the church-community intact (see chapter 3).

In other Old Order communities, however, the private school has become central to community activities, and its role in ensuring the survival of the church-community is openly recognized. As an Old Order (Wenger) Mennonite teacher put it, private schools should "give the children a good solid eighth-grade education so they can get along in today's world without being a burden to society. No Mennonite from our group draws welfare or Social Security—at least I hope not." Echoing both the emphasis on teaching self-sufficiency and the acknowledgement that earning a living will involve being in the world, a teacher from the Old Order Amish settlement in Fredericktown, Ohio, said, "We expect our schools to provide a basic education for our children that is essential to our way of living and also to be able to communicate and make a living in the outside world. Also to learn discipline and respect to God and fellowmen."

In Old Order communities such as those in Lancaster County, Ashland, Ohio, and Norfolk, New York, the private school has become an educational "firewall," a barrier limiting the influence of the world on Old Order youth. An Old Order Amish teacher from Ashland, Ohio, for example, wrote: "I really don't know anything about public schools, but I just know we don't want Amish children to go there. I don't know do we have different lessons or not, but I know one thing that we do not want and that is we don't want the Amish children among the English too much. You see you [non–Old Order] have many things like radios, phones, etc. that we don't have." This is echoed in the forward of *Standards of the Old Order Amish and Old Order Mennonite Private and Vocational Schools of Penna.*:

Any person even remotely acquainted with the Amish and Old Order Mennonite sect knows that there [sic] way of living differs greatly from others. [...] Tradition to them is a sacred trust, and it is a part of their religion to uphold and adhere to the ideals of their forefathers.... To maintain these principles in the future is of vital importance to the Amish. This has been the overriding reason for the establishment of the Amish schools in the United States during the last decade. (*Pennsylvania Standards* 1969, 1)

For many Old Order educators, private schools should prepare children for work that may bring them face to face with technology and with behavior that is unacceptable in their Old Order worlds, but they should also prepare them to resist the temptations these may offer. After all, as an Old Order (Wenger) Mennonite teacher acknowledges, "Members of our plain church need to be members of our church of their own free will. At one time in their lives a Christian will need to say 'no' to the enticing vanities of the world." By minimizing the world's influence and reinforcing the values and behaviors of the Old Order community, private school education prepares children to say no.

Reinforcing Old Order values does not, however, mean teaching religion. Indeed, one Old Order (Wenger) Mennonite teacher tells of "a family who wanted Bible School taught and the teacher refused to teach it because it was against religious beliefs according to both parents and teacher. These parents finally realized it's not going to be taught so they left the school on their own accord." The school is not the place for religious instruction; rather, the school is to reinforce the teachings of parents and church by reflecting religious values in the pedagogy used, discipline, and subjects taught or not taught. The *Pennsylvania Standards* (1969, 2) states:

With the exception of devotion[s] it is the Amish and Old Order Mennonite theory that the Bible be taught in the home & church[;] however it is further our aim to teach Religion all day long in our curriculum (lessons) and on the play ground.

In Arithmetic by accuracy (no cheating);
In English by learning to say what we mean.
In History by humanity (kindness-mercy)

In Health by teaching cleanliness and thriftiness.
In Geography by learning to make a[n] honest living from the soil.
In Music by singing praises to God.
On the school ground by teaching honesty, respect, sincerity, hum-
  bleness and yes, the Golden Rule.

Is Religion then continuously mentioned? Seldom, just enough to bring
the whole thing to a point now and then.

Or, as an Old Order Amish teacher from Ohio put it, "We expect our
schools to each be like big families by working and playing together, learning to get along & all under a Christian attitude."

Nevertheless, some of the "highest," that is, most progressive Old Order communities do see in Old Order schools an opportunity for more than
subtle reinforcement of religious values and social behavior. Some include
overt religious teaching in the daily curriculum. In a 1958 editorial in the
Blackboard Bulletin, Ervin N. Hershberger argued that "the public schools
are better equipped to teach 'the 3 Rs' than the Amish ones . . . [yet] . . .
the Amish schools must do more." He went on to say,

A Christian school is hardly worthy of its name if it does not in many
ways surpass the present public school.

For example: they teach how to be a good national citizen; we should
train our children to be dynamic witnesses for Christ. They teach social
ethics; we should train for Christian character. They teach fairness; we
should teach second-mile Christianity. Their best schools may teach excellent conduct and refinement; we should teach spiritual regeneration.
They may teach moral virtues; we should teach the new birth. They may
teach the best that man could offer; we should do all of that and more; we
should teach what God has offered. We have no right to fall behind them
in the good things which they teach, but we have the Christian duty of
going beyond that, if our schools are to be truly Christian. (Hershberger
1958, in *Challenge*, 68–69)[12]

As another wrote, the Old Orders "have the privilege of teaching the
regular branches [subjects], and at the same time we can interweave the
doctrine of God, Christ, and the Church in all our studies, even in arith-

metic" (Kauffman 1959; in *Challenge*, 69). Writing in the *Blackboard Bulletin* in January 1961, the editor asserted the need to wage a battle against spiritual decay on three fields: "1. The church, represented by the ministry; 2. The home, represented by the parents; and 3. The church school, represented by Christian teachers" (in *Challenge*, 76). In short, the private school has, in some Old Order groups, become as important as parent and church in the struggle to inculcate in children the religion of their parents and church-community.

Illustrating this redefinition of Old Order education as *Christian* education, two Old Order teachers from Michigan wrote, "We believe the Bible is the inspired Word of God. It is the only Source of true knowledge. We feel the need of acknowledging the Creator in the schooling of our children. As public school instruction moves into the fields of modern progressive education, audiovisual training, sex education, computer programming, the need becomes readily apparent for an educational system that is separate from the public school educational system and based on the words of Paul: 'And be not conformed to this world . . . ' (Romans 12:2).[13] Similarly, an Old Order Amish teacher from Michigan asserts, "I believe our main goal in having our own schools is to be able to implant more Christian morals into our children, to keep them away from (or being exposed to) the many things which aren't good for body and soul." An Old Order teacher from Indiana goes further, arguing that "the purpose of our schools is to teach the basic subjects, then teach them about Jesus Christ, getting along with your fellow man, lead them towards joining church later, accepting Jesus, and then inheriting eternal life. That's what we're after."

Ultimately, the school's role in maintaining and reinforcing cultural, behavioral, and religious norms is shaped both by situational factors, including the size of the community and its proximity to other Old Order church-communities, and by patterns of social and economic interaction with other Old Order groups and the dominant society. For the majority of Old Order children, the school provides the first encounter with the world, plain and non-plain, outside their immediate families and church-community. Therefore, Old Order church-communities have realized the need to reinforce religious ideology and preserve the markers of their particular Old Order identity in every aspect of Old Order education. Schools vary greatly as a result of the choices communities make about pedagogy, curriculum, textbooks, assessment, parent-teacher-student interaction, and even, as noted earlier, school design.

In a sense, the goal of all Old Order private schools is the same: "to prepare the child for the Amish or Mennonite way of living and the responsibilities of adulthood" (*Pennsylvania Standards* 1969, 5) so that they might achieve everlasting life (Huntington 1993). Yet the "Amish or Mennonite way of living," and consequently the responsibilities of adulthood, vary greatly across the spectrum of Old Order groups and so must the schools that inculcate resistance to the world.[14]

CHAPTER 3

The Swartzentruber Schools

If you wish to be seen, stand up. If you wish to be heard, speak up.
If you wish to be appreciated, shut up.
—A hand-lettered saying hung on the wall of Line Road School,
Heuvelton, New York

The Swartzentruber Amish

On cold winter mornings, the teacher must be the first to school so that she can light the fire in the woodstove. When her pupils arrive, she will have some of them fill the wood box and others fetch water. If the pupils are lucky, the pump will not be frozen. Otherwise, they might have to take the bucket to the nearest Amish farmhouse to fill it so that there will be water for drinking and hand washing.

To non–Old Order eyes, perhaps no schools reflect the Old Order desire to remain "strangers and pilgrims" in the world as well as those of the Swartzentruber Amish. Constructed plainly of wood painted white, or sometimes with corrugated tin siding, they are often set in the corner of a farmer's field. During the summertime, a visitor to a Swartzentruber school finds the schoolyard reconverted to cow pasture, with the path to the schoolhouse blocked with barbed wire, cows grazing by the entrance to the woodshed, and cow pies dotting the area where children play ball during recess.

Often untidy and shabby looking, and with no playgrounds, these little schools hardly seem a force for social resistance. Nevertheless, reflecting the community's distrust of those outside the church and dread of "drift" or increasing worldliness, Swartzentruber schools are different not only from their public counterparts but also from the schools of most other Old Order church-communities.

The so-called Swartzentruber Amish, a general term for three distinct groups of Amish, are the plainest of the plain people. The Swartzentruber churches trace their origin to disagreements in the Old Order Amish community in the Holmes County, Ohio, area between 1913 and 1917 over the practices of excommunication and shunning (*Bann und Meidung*). Bishop Samuel E. Yoder of Apple Creek in Wayne County argued unsuccessfully that joining the church was a lifetime commitment and that one who had joined the church and then left must be placed under the *Bann* and shunned until he or she repented and returned to the church. David Luthy notes, "This interpretation is called 'streng Meidung' (strict shunning) and was not held by Sam Yoder alone" (1998, 19). Yet the Yoder faction was in the minority, and by 1917 a permanent division had taken place between the Sam Yoder people and the other Old Order Amish districts. After Yoder's death, when both bishops for the community had the last name Swartzentruber, the Yoder group came to be called "Swartzentruber Amish."

"Not only does the policy of not allowing members to transfer to other Old Order Amish groups (except when a division occurs) separate the Swartzentruber Amish from other Amish," Luthy writes, "so do their more traditional or conservative practices in clothing, buggies, house architecture and furnishings, farm machinery, and employment." (1998, 20–21). Only in an emergency or when there is no bus service available and the distance is too impractical for horse and buggy will Swartzentruber Amish ride in automobiles.

Change, when it comes to Swartzentruber communities, comes slowly and may be in the direction of increasing conservatism. For example, a young Swartzentruber mother in the Heuvelton, New York, settlement refused to accept a baby-food grinder as a gift from a non–Amish friend because, she said, "We don't use those." When asked why a baby-food grinder would not be permitted by the *Ordnung*, even though meat grinders, for example, are permitted, the young woman's mother explained that in Ohio baby-food grinders had been permitted when they had been received as gifts, but in New York "we couldn't have them anymore." Similarly, when the Swartzentruber settlement in the Heuvelton area was first established in 1974, many Swartzentruber farmers took their produce and baked goods to village farmers' markets; however, roughly twenty years later, the Swartzentruber community decided that this practice violated the longstanding prohibition on "working in town" and forbade it. This has led to a proliferation of Swartzentruber Amish farm stands on the back roads.

Since the initial schism in 1917, Swartzentruber settlements have been established in twelve states and the province of Ontario. All share the same *Ordnung*, but schisms have resulted in three non-fellowshipping factions (Luthy 1998, 21–22). Nevertheless, children from the different factions often attend school together, for Swartzentruber schools serve neighborhoods rather than church-communities, and fathers from different factions will sit together on the governing boards.

The Goals of Swartzentruber Education

Regardless of the conflicts that now divide the different Swartzentruber factions, members of the different Swartzentruber church-communities are united in their understanding of how schools should work and how children should be educated. Cooperation between the different factions has helped to standardize Swartzentruber schools and curriculum to a greater degree than that seen in any other large Old Order settlement. In Swartzentruber one-room schoolhouses, children learn English, German, and basic arithmetic—and most importantly, the patterns of social interaction, work ethic, discipline, and obedience to authority that will make them good church members.

A typical Swartzentruber Amish private school is a one-room building flanked by outhouses and heated by a woodstove. It is attended by around twenty students in grades one through eight and is generally taught by an unmarried girl of approximately 17 or 18 years old, rarely over 22. The teacher sits at the front, and when the "scholars" (as school children are called) come to the front to recite their lessons, they sit on a bench or on chairs set in a row on one side of the teacher's desk. Because the Swartzentruber Amish will not make use of school busses, each school generally serves only three or four families. Since it is not unusual for a family to have a child in each grade, schools may serve as many as thirty scholars, and new schools are built as they are needed. Swartzentruber schools have no gas lamps or lanterns, and of course no electricity, telephone service, or indoor plumbing.

When one enters a Swartzentruber school, one is struck by the plainness of the building. The walls are painted battleship gray about four feet up from the floor and then white to the ceiling. The doors and window frames are gray, and the floor, if it is particleboard, may also be painted gray. Often the floor is very muddy. The Swartzentruber Amish do not build walkways to their schools, for the buildings are impermanent, intended only to serve the families in the immediate area. When the families have no more children to send, unless new families have moved in, the school will close. The desks and chairs are generally cast-offs from public schools, often old and made of wood and metal. The Swartzentruber Amish prefer the type of desk on which the lid can be raised up to allow children to put their books inside, and they will not allow desk chairs made with plastic seats or backs. There is usually a small table in a corner of the room on which sits a bucket or a large jug of water, a bowl that serves as a washbasin, and a cup or two for drinking.

All Swartzentruber schools are heated by wood- or coal-burning stoves in the main schoolroom. In Kendrew Corners School near Heuvelton, New York, for example, a large woodstove made from an oil drum rests on metal legs attached to wooden blocks in the back corner of the room. It provides uneven heat, roasting the children who sit close to it, while barely warming the children at the front of the room. Children coming in from the cold North Country weather take off their coats and boots next to its warmth and use it first to thaw the ink in their pens and then to heat their lunches, which, following the morning recess, they place on a metal platform balanced atop the stove. In the recently built Ridgeview School, as in most of the Heuvelton area schools, which are built to a standard design, the stove is against the back wall, directly opposite the teacher's desk and next to the door to the woodshed. In the Swartzentruber River View School in Ohio, the stove is on a side wall, next to the stairs leading to the entryway and woodshed.

Swartzentruber schoolhouses offer children the basics: a roof over their heads during lessons, a desk to work at, and a board to write on. Similarly, Swartzentruber teachers define their role narrowly. As one teacher put

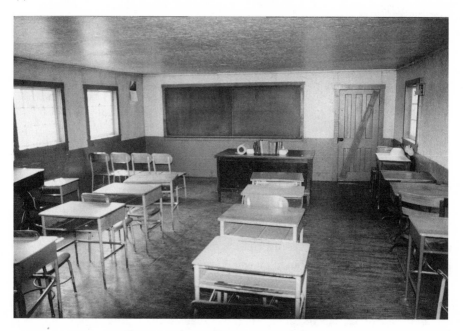

A Swartzentruber school, freshly cleaned and ready for the new school term.

it, children are in school "to learn things, things they have to learn [such as] how to work arithmetic, and how to write." They are expected to play together without conflict, the older ones helping the younger. Teachers provide instruction in the English and "Bible German" necessary for life in a Swartzentruber community and in the practical skills of reading, writing, and arithmetic, which are not easily or efficiently acquired in other settings. As one teacher noted, "If they have to learn them [these subjects] at home, they wouldn't learn them as well."

Furthermore, Swartzentruber communities expect that schools will reinforce the teachings of parents and church. Children learn by doing, through repeated practice and rote memorization in a classroom that downplays individual difference and competition, fosters obedience to authority, and guarantees that school is separate from the real work and pleasures of life at home and in the community.

Swartzentruber schools are plain, and things that hang on the wall must be, in some way, useful. In most Swartzentruber schools, for example, there are charts, usually hand-drawn, showing German "diagraphs" or

A woodstove in the back corner of a Swartzentruber school heats both the classroom
and the children's noon meals. The warmth it provides can be uneven,
and the far windows often remain frosty.

the arithmetic symbols for addition, subtraction, multiplication, and division. There are always charts showing the English and German alphabets in print and cursive, again, often handmade. There are no cute animals on the alphabet charts, no "apple" for "A."[1]

Other charts and pictures that are put up are generally standardized. The teacher at one Heuvelton school, for example, hangs up individual charts so that students can keep track of their spelling, reading, and arithmetic scores, but she colors the charts herself, and they are identical. When she permits scholars to do "freehand" coloring following tests, she hangs the pictures at the front of the room by age, in part so that younger children can see how coloring is supposed to be done.

Coloring itself reflects community values. Scholars are encouraged to draw only subjects appropriate to Swartzentruber life, including barns, animals, and flowers. Drawings of cars, people, or other elements of the non-Swartzentruber world are discouraged because, as teachers tell stu-

A Swartzentruber scholar documents his world in this freehand drawing.

dents, "That's not our way." Moreover, just as in real life behavior must remain within the limits of the *Ordnung*, in coloring the children must learn to "stay between the lines" and to make things appropriate colors. There can be no blue horses or polka-dot houses because that is not how things are in the world. As one teacher explained, "Scholars have to color in the lines. They learn that in first grade, and if they scribble, they don't get to color. Sometimes they don't know what color [to use], so I tell them. If they use strange colors, I tell them not to do so." Swartzentruber first-graders routinely raise their hands to ask what colors to use in their so-called freehand drawings. One first-grader, told to make the pigs in her picture pink, then raised her hand to ask what color to make the trough, and then the barn.

From the beginning of their formal education—in coloring exercises, at recess, in the lunches they bring from home, and in the way lessons are presented and studied—children are made aware of what behavior is acceptable and what is not, and the line between the two is non-negotiable. Corporal punishment is acceptable in Swartzentruber schools, and although the teachers dislike spanking the children, they will do so if they feel it is necessary. As one teacher put it, "If you don't spank the children that need it, you could lose your job. The school board wants discipline."[2]

Viewing education as a way to encourage the child to follow instructions, respect authority, and master basic information, the Swartzentruber Amish narrowly define what it means for a school to be successful. "Keep them [the children] a little straight. That's about the best school," summed up one Swartzentruber teacher. Similarly, asked to define "a good school," another teacher responded, "I just don't know. For me, I would say if they [the children] can come along good with each other—work, play, whatever. They [the children] have to obey the teacher and do what the teacher says."

Teachers are supposed to enforce discipline and make sure the children do the work set out for them. Asked what she would do if a child didn't understand the work, one teacher replied, "I explain it again and again until he gets it. Sometimes he just can't get it or maybe it's not important for him to understand it then and he'll just learn it when he gets older." Similarly, talking about what it would mean for a student to be successful, another teacher asserted that children must simply "try to work and behave and obey the parents. 'Hard to learn' or 'easy to learn,' that's just the way they are. Obeying the rules, that's what counts. To be a successful member of the church, obey the rules." As a bishop noted, getting a teacher who enforces the rules is "half the battle."

To the extent that teachers enforce the rules, they reinforce the teachings of parents and church. Any explicit teaching of religion is unacceptable, however. Swartzentruber children sing hymns to start the day, and they read from the Bible during German lessons, but they do not discuss biblical topics or even pray before the noontime meal. As one bishop put it, "We don't want religion taught in the schools; we want to keep it in the home. This keeps parents responsible." Suggesting that the school keeps parents in line as well as children, the bishop further asserted, "Parents would get away from it [teaching religion] if the schools were to take over. We don't want that. That's for higher class churches."[3] The teacher must help children learn to work together and to do their best, thereby reinforcing the lessons of church and home, but she must not usurp the place of the parents and ministers by teaching those lessons herself.

With success defined as the acquisition of appropriate behavior rather than mastery of a subject, Swartzentruber children are rarely held back.

One teacher, talking of a student with cystic fibrosis, noted that "he just does what he can do. I will pass him even if he doesn't take the test. I will talk to the parents to see what they want to do. He learns easy." Yet, this teacher noted further, it is not only those who are ill who are unlikely to fail: "It's very seldom that [children] don't pass. They have to be very poor that they don't pass. My brother was on a one-year trial. He didn't pass, but the next year he was much better, so he jumped ahead."[4]

Schedules, Expectations, and Community Boundaries

The primary goals of Swartzentruber education are realized through pedagogical practices, texts, and patterns of school-community interaction that ground the school in the values of the church-community, most particularly in the church-community's devotion to the *Ordnung*. While the Swartzentruber schools appear to be nostalgic vestiges of the "little red schoolhouses" pictured on postcards, they are not examples of education misplaced in time but rather evidence of the community's resistance to change and "drift" from the discipline of the church. Every element of Swartzentruber schooling links children to their parents and grandparents, reinforcing the continuity of the present with the past, a realization that God's truth is unchanging.

Swartzentruber Amish schools demonstrate a determination to continue unchanged those practices that define the church-community. All Swartzentruber schools cover the same lessons in the same books at about the same time of day and year, and the school calendar of events and lessons repeats itself year after year. As scholars, Swartzentruber children take part in the same activities, study the same lessons, and learn to obey the same rules as their parents and elder siblings did before them.

Typically, by 8:30 in the morning the scholars are in their seats, and the teacher rings a bell on her desk to announce that school has started. Then first and second graders rush to sit next to older children, sharing chairs and songbooks. Most schools begin the day with three hymns, all from the *Liedersammlung*, a compilation of hymns dating to 1892. Teachers keep track of who chooses the hymns and what hymns are chosen. The child who chooses the hymn acts as the *Vorsinger* for that song, singing the first line and establishing the tune and pace for the others to join in.[5]

When the last note is sung on the third hymn, children immediately return to their own desks, and reading lessons begin. From 10:00 to 10:15, the children enjoy the first recess, after which they have arithmetic lessons until lunchtime at 11:30. The lunch period is an hour long, and the children eat quickly so that they can play. Usually the oldest child in the family (which might be the teacher) parcels out food among the siblings. Following lunch, there is English or phonics, and then, at 1:50, a 20-minute recess. Spelling is the last class of the day, and the teacher dismisses the children at 3:00. On Fridays, grades four to eight have German lessons. In most schools, this is accomplished by substituting German reading for English reading and German spelling for English.

There is little variation from school to school. One teacher noted that she had recess from 9:45 to 10:00 in the morning and from 1:45 to 2:00 in the afternoon, and that she taught the same subjects in the same order except that she often used the time right after lunch to cover any arithmetic lessons she might not have gotten to. The teacher at the Swartzentruber River View School in Ohio noted that she had begun the school year by having arithmetic lessons first but had to change this schedule. "I was used to start[ing] with arithmetic," she noted, "but the people here were used to reading first. I was so messed up." The change brought her schedule into line with that followed by her peers in New York.

That Swartzentruber schools are so standardized is particularly surprising, since there is no central planning committee and teachers seldom meet. Each teacher simply replicates what went on the year before, repeating the same lessons as she herself might have learned them. Given the material that must be covered in each grade, teachers simply take students through a set portion of their books each week. There is little opportunity for innovation, since teachers generally use the books left by their predecessors and the divisions are already marked. It is possible for a child to leave at the beginning of a lesson at one school to arrive at another in time to catch the finish of the same lesson.

Just as teachers know what is expected of them, so too do the children. Following the singing, students immediately begin to work individually. Those who have unfinished lessons will start to work on them; those concerned about an upcoming spelling test might start reading over the words; and those with no work to do will take out unfinished pictures to color, build models of barns or farm machinery out of paper, request permission to get a storybook,[6] or just stare out the window.

When she is not working with a particular grade, the teacher walks up and down the aisles, stopping to talk to students individually, but she rarely tells a student who is coloring or staring out the window to "get back to work." She may ask the child if he or she has completed an assignment. If the answer is yes, the teacher moves on; if the answer is no, the child takes the question as a command to go back to the books. In either case, the child is responsible for completing the work.

Often while the teacher is walking up and down the aisles, children will hold up their books with a finger pointing to words in their lessons that they don't know, swiveling around in their seats to follow the teacher's progress around the room. The teacher stops by each one to read the words aloud. Shortly thereafter, the teacher calls the first class to the front to begin the lesson.

If it is a class in arithmetic, the call to the front provides an opportunity for workbook grading. Sitting on a straight bench or on a line of chairs in front of the teacher's desk or perpendicular to it, children face the blackboard rather than their classmates, and they turn their eyes to the teacher or to their work. There is little discussion of the lesson among the children. After they exchange their work, the teacher reads off the answers, relying on those given at the back of the teacher's edition, and the students check them. Afterward, children call out the number of problems they got wrong, and the teacher, using an "E-Z Grader,"[7] tells them their percentage score as she records it in the grade book. She then briefly describes what they must do in the next section, perhaps talking them through the example problem, and then dismisses the grade. Rarely does she spend more than ten minutes with a class.

Once they begin to work, children often have difficulty, and they quickly start raising their hands to ask questions or even come to the front of the class to talk with the teacher at her desk. The teacher persists in working with individual grades at the front of the class even while children are engaged in a variety of activities all around her desk.

Reading classes present perhaps the biggest challenge to the teacher's concentration and to discipline. Called to the front to read aloud from the assigned pages, each member of the class, in turn, reads a paragraph (or, for first and second graders, a single word or sentence). Within the grade, few appear to concentrate on the student who is reading. Most preview their own paragraph, holding up the book to the teacher and pointing to words

Called to class in the front of the room, children sitting on the bench face the teacher
and the blackboard, not their classmates. There is little else inside the classroom of the
River View School to distract scholars.

they don't know for help with pronunciation. The teacher answers these
questions aloud while the student who is reading continues, seemingly
oblivious to the interruptions. The teacher rarely corrects a student's pronunciation while he or she is reading; only when the student pauses, indi-
cating that he or she does not know the word, does the teacher supply it.

First graders begin school by learning the "A-B-Cs" and "1-2-3s," a process of memorization in which they repeatedly recite the letters and numbers and write them on the board over and over and drill with flash cards.
The goal is to memorize the alphabet and numbers up to 100 as quickly as
possible. Once they know the alphabet and their numbers, they begin with
their books. The teacher points to the word and says it. The children repeat
the word, write it on the board, and memorize it. At this point, the structure of their reading lesson is identical to those of their older classmates.

While the reading class is in session, children from the other grades
are responsible for working on their own without bothering the others.
Often children practice spelling words by writing them over and over on

the blackboard at the front of the room. Those still sitting at their desks demand the teacher's attention by raising their hands for permission to throw paper away or get a book to read from the shelf. The teacher follows all of these activities carefully, giving the correct word to the reader who stumbles over the passage, supplying a correct pronunciation to the one about to read, and attending to the scholars working at their desk and at the board. When she wants a student to carry out a task, such as adjusting the stove, picking up something from the floor, or grading a stack of workbooks, she simply says so, and the student obeys.

Despite the activity, the classroom is quiet and controlled. The teacher is clearly in charge, and she says little to her students beyond giving them assignments, supplying answers, explaining problems, and assigning chores. In response to a student's request for permission to throw something away or to get a book, she simply nods. A sharp shake of her head is usually sufficient to get a student back on task.

School activities emphasize both dependence on others in the school community and the authority of the teacher. All students are engaged in the same kinds of activities, albeit at different grade levels, and older ones may be called on to help younger ones. Teachers expect children to work quietly on their own, but children know that, if they ask for help, the teacher or older members of the classroom community will supply it. When students do not know an answer, the teacher tells it to them.

Mottoes in the classroom and instructions on workbooks further reinforce the lessons of obedience and respect for authority. In the fifth-grade penmanship workbook, for example, children copy the rules for being an interesting person:

1. Be a good listener.
2. Do not talk too much.
3. Do not talk too long at a time.
4. Give every one a chance.
5. Do not interrupt.
6. Talk about things you know and enjoy.[8]

A motto hung on the wall of a Heuvelton school states the lesson more succinctly: If you wish to be seen, stand up. If you wish to be heard, speak up. If you wish to be appreciated, shut up.

While the classroom activities emphasize an interesting mix of self-sufficiency, dependence on authority, and discipline, recess emphasizes cooperation. The games played are generally noncompetitive. Rounders, for
example, is a baseball-like game played without teams. A batter who hits
the ball must make it around the bases during the time it takes for three
additional batters to take their turn at the plate. If three batters hit fly outs
and the runner still hasn't made it home without being tagged, he or she
is automatically out. Older children are allowed only three strikes, but
younger ones have an unlimited number. Children come and go from the
game, which will go on as long as anyone is interested in playing (or until
the teacher rings the bell). Children do play board games, such as *Sorry*
or *Chutes and Ladders*, but these are group contests, for each player will be
guided and encouraged by the other players and by a host of onlookers.
Play is somewhat gendered and age-graded; older girls are more likely to
stay in and play board games than the younger girls or the boys, and boys
are more likely to be dominant in building snow houses during winter. But
all may and do join in these activities.

Informally, a teacher ceases to be a teacher at recess, taking instead the
position of authority rightfully hers, not because of her teaching position
but because of her age relative to the others; in fact, she takes on the role
of big sister to her pupils (which she may well be in real life). She joins
in their playground games, and on Fridays she might spend recess time
braiding the younger girls' hair for church to save busy mothers at home
the trouble. If she has siblings in the class, her lunch is likely to come out
of the same lunch pail as theirs, and she might have the task of dividing up
the contents and pouring the milk. Moreover, she joins in their talk. Before, during, and after school, the teacher is first a member of the community, connected to her students by ties of family, friendship, and church.
Only during lesson time is she the teacher.

Teaching English and Reinforcing Community Boundaries

As the teacher's changing relationship to her students suggests, the Swartzentruber private school is in the community and a part of community life,
but it is certainly not *of* the community, a distinction reinforced in subtle
but important ways. A young Swartzentruber father says, for example,
"We don't talk English to each other except in school when we have to."

The Swartzentruber Amish, like most Old Order Amish and Old Order Mennonite groups, use a dialect of "Pennsylvania German" within the home and with others in the community. English is for use with outsiders. This domain-specific bilingualism—German for insiders and English for outsiders—serves as a constant reminder of the differences between the church-community and the surrounding society. German not only isolates children from non–Old Order culture, but it protects them from it and reinforces their place in the church-community.[9]

Few Swartzentruber children know much, if any, English when they begin school at age six.[10] Generally, children of school age or younger are not taken along when parents go shopping or make other forays into the non–Old Order world, so the only encounters they have had with people outside their homes and immediate family have taken place at church or when visiting Swartzentruber friends and relatives. These interactions have all been in German; any meetings with the "English" take place in settings well controlled by parents, and young children are rarely included in the conversation. Non–Old Order customers for Swartzentruber products, for example, are kept at the farm stand and are waited on by the older siblings, and during visits to a doctor's office the child is expected to be seen and not heard.

Ironically, however, since Pennsylvania German is not a written language (Johnson-Weiner 1997), an Amish person wishing to write to someone in another community must use English. As a result, for the Swartzentruber Amish and other Old Order groups, while spoken English is identified with the outside world from which they separate themselves, written English plays a vital role in intra-group communication. For the six-year-old entering school, the English language, heretofore largely unknown and little heard, is an introduction to a much larger world in which the child has never participated and to which the child has been unconnected.[11]

Thus, when Swartzentruber children enter school and are addressed in English by the teacher, who is, in most cases, a neighbor they know well or a sibling who has never before spoken English to them, they enter an institution that is both a "normal part of life" and yet "part of the domain of the outside world" (Hostetler and Redekop 1962, 198). Swartzentruber schools are, in short, ambiguous space; and even as teachers help their scholars to become fluent in English so that they can read and talk to outsiders, they limit the effects of language education in a variety of subtle ways. For example, when school is not formally in session, teachers generally use Pennsylvania German (Johnson-Weiner 1993). As one teacher noted, "We learn Dutch [Pennsylvania German] at home. In school it's time to learn our English, but the only time we talk English is during lessons." German is the language of the playground, lunchtime, joking—the times when the teacher relates to her students as community member and not as teacher.

Even in school, if English proves too difficult, children turn to German to ask questions and get help and support. In a second grade phonics class, for example, the teacher read the workbook instructions in English but then explained what was required in German and answered all the children's questions in German. Similarly, another teacher routinely read the English instructions printed in workbooks to her first and second graders and then explained them in German. A year later, a different teacher in the same school routinely used German to answer the questions about arithmetic posed by eighth graders. Another teacher asserted that she "talks only English after fourth grade," but then acknowledged using German "when [I] really need to explain something." As a teacher of several years experience put it when asked why she tended to use German to explain problems to her scholars, "[It] still comes the handiest for me to talk German because that's the language we use the most." Another teacher read the answers to the arithmetic problems and assigned the next day's work in English, but then she explained the assignment and answered questions about it in German. In this way German, the language of the community, also becomes in school the language of security, the one used to provide help, support, and friendship.

Swartzentruber schools further distance children from community-inappropriate uses of English through the very exercises that encourage its acquisition. Most striking is in the "oral performance" of reading aloud. Most reading material in Swartzentruber homes, including the *Budget*, local newspapers, and letters from friends, is in English. After chores are done at home, children might sit and read silently to themselves those texts that parents consider appropriate, just as, at school, after their work is done, children are permitted to get a book off the shelf for silent reading. Parents seldom read stories to their children at home, and teachers use oral reading in English only to reinforce vocabulary and to evaluate students' progress.

Called with their grade to the front of the room to read, children take turns reading paragraphs. Swartzentruber teachers make no attempt to equalize the amount read; a paragraph is a paragraph, whether it is a hundred lines long or one. Oral reading begins in first grade when the teacher models the text for the student one word at a time. Standing over a child, she points from word to word with her pencil, stressing each item equally in a monotone that ends on a falling note only with the last word. In one lesson, the teacher modeled a sentence in this way for a first grader and then instructed the child, "Try and say it [the English sentence] quickly." Like the teacher, the child produced a monotone string of syllables, each receiving the same stress, distinguished at the end only by a falling tone on the last syllable. Teachers instruct the children to read "Bible German" using the same technique and with the same result. When they read aloud, children render the text in a singsong chant that is difficult to follow or comprehend; indeed, at times it almost seems as if the children become lost in the singsong and cease to produce any language at all.[12]

Often the contrast between oral reading and conversation is striking, as when the teacher models the sentence in a chant-like monotone to the children and then translates it into conversational German. One teacher, for example, introducing a new passage to a fourth grade class, read the sentence, "See-how-the-goats-pull," one word at a time, each word evenly stressed and uttered in a monotone that fell only at the last syllable. The children repeated each word as the teacher read it. She then gave the Pennsylvania German translation, "[seənč vi di ges tsiə?]," in a cheerful tone while pointing to the picture. In the next highest grade, she again read the sentences in a monotone, one word at a time, with the children repeating each word as it was read, but this time children supplied the translation in German, and the teacher repeated it in a conversational tone.

The monotone oral production of written English is reinforced in board work. In copying sentences on the board, the majority of children put a dash between each word, a practice also followed when writing spelling lists on the board. In another variation of "chanting orthography," other children write sentences and word lists with no spaces between words, some even linking the last letter of one word to the first letter of the next (e.g., *sorroworganize*).

The chant-like quality of oral reading in Swartzentruber schools, evident in both English and German reading, links this activity to other ritualized language use, particularly to preaching. Like "Bible German," English becomes a language restricted to particular domains, and there are limits on its use; it is not meant for general communication.

Only English reading and spelling are taught as separate subjects after the fourth grade. This means that, since grades one and two have phonics, only grades three and four engage in the study of language structure. The texts used, *Practice Exercises in Basic English*, Books C and D, provide basic instruction in sentence structure, word choice, subject-verb agreement, and punctuation. After completing these texts, children gain further expertise in English only as they use it to do other work. In other words, English is learned and used as a tool to complete necessary tasks, and there is no attempt to teach children to use the language like native speakers. By the end of the eighth grade, children have a functional competence in English and an active vocabulary that will enable them to shop, deal with customers at their roadside stands, and engage in casual business interactions with their non-Amish neighbors. In Swartzentruber schools, children are not learning English so that they can interact more fully in the world around them. They must, however, be able to deal with that world in its language.

In their pattern of language use, Swartzentruber schools reinforce community values and protect children from the values of the outside world. Pennsylvania German becomes further identified as the language of community, of fun and group activities, of support when things become difficult, of being Swartzentruber. Bible German is linked to reading the Bible and singing hymns. Children learn to read English in the silent, passive way that they will use to read the Old Order newspapers, and they learn to write English well enough to correspond with others. Oral English remains the language one uses to communicate with the unfamiliar and often difficult world that is outside their own.

Textbooks, Curriculum, and Community Conservatism

The daily schedule of lessons, relationships between teacher and students, school activities, and the pattern of language all serve to mark the school as a "different" space, but these are only a few of the ways in which Swartzentruber schools keep the outside world strange and unfamiliar and reinforce community-sanctioned means of interacting with it. There is, for example, little pedagogical innovation. William Riddle, writing of his visit in 1854 to a Lancaster County public school that had only Amish students, noted that "the branches taught, as I was informed, were confined to the four fundamentals—reading in the German Bible, spelling, writing, and a little arithmetic [. . .] The other branches—geography, history, and grammar—were tabooed as in no way necessary to make good farmers out of the boys and good housewives out of the girls" (1910, 143–44; Luthy 1993). Following a curriculum that is limited and standardized by tradition, Swartzentruber children study almost exactly the same subjects as their Amish counterparts of a century and a half ago: phonics, spelling, reading, and arithmetic, and, beginning in fourth grade, "Bible German."

The extreme conservatism of the Swartzentruber Amish and their determination to remain separate are reflected in and reinforced by the use in schools of texts from the nineteenth and early twentieth centuries. First graders begin to learn English with *McGuffey's Eclectic Primer*, which was first copyrighted in 1881 and most recently in 1909. In second grade they begin to use the 1919 *Essentials of Spelling*. For arithmetic, Swartzentruber schools use Clifford Upton's 1933 *Arithmetic Workbook* series for the first two grades. Third graders then move on to the first of the three books in the Strayer-Upton *Practical Arithmetics* series, which first appeared in 1928 and was most recently copyrighted in 1934.[13]

Much of the vocabulary of these archaic texts, particularly that introduced in the older grades, is of little use to the Swartzentruber Amish in their correspondence with each other or in their business dealings with the non-Amish world. For example, in sixth grade, children memorize for spelling tests such vocabulary words as "luncheon," "telegraph," "madam," "trolley," and "piano," terms that have no cultural cognates in Swartzentruber life and will not often be used in their interactions with non–Old Order society. By eighth grade, their spelling lists include words no longer used by their English-speaking neighbors, including household terms such as "emetic," "gimp," "chiffonier," and "poultice"; industrial terms such as "magneto" and "adz"; urban terms such as "jitney" and "linotype"; and rural words such as "Bordeaux," "sulky," and "whiffle tree."[14]

Even more than the speller, the *McGuffey's Readers* used in grades one to four present English from bygone days. There is archaic vocabulary; for example, lesson XIV from the second reader (used in third grade classes) introduces "Henry the Bootblack," who, unlike his modern counterparts, does not polish shoes but "blackens" them, and lesson XXIX introduces a tiny "rill" and talks of a deep pool "where wild flowers fringe the brink" (63). Other stories are about "jolly" things such as "hour glasses" and "silver dollars" and feature children with names like "Ned" and "Herbert" and "Nell." While *McGuffey's Eclectic Primer*, through which children are first introduced to the ABCs and to reading, presents "slate exercises" for penmanship practice, the discussion of punctuation in *McGuffey's Second Eclectic Reader* presents "Alas, my noble boy! That thou shouldst die!" as an example of how to use an exclamation point.

But the archaic is not restricted to reading and spelling texts. In arithmetic too, children learn much about numbers and little about the world outside their communities. The first book of the *Strayer-Upton Practical Arithmetics* series, for example, features story problems with street car conductors, jackstones, and miles and rods. Book three introduces them to an electric calculating machine. Using these turn-of-the-century texts, children in Swartzentruber Amish parochial schools memorize vocabulary words and sentence structures no longer used in everyday American English conversations, learning an English no longer spoken by their non-Amish neighbors.

In his survey of German texts used in Old Order Mennonite communities in Ontario, Jakobsh (1993, 171) points out numerous deviations from standard German and suggests that these remain in the school texts because "there is not the slightest intention among these 'plain folk' to emulate the writing or speaking conventions of people in Germany." Similarly, the Swartzentruber communities are not bothered by archaic texts because they have no interest in following the conventions of modern-day non-Amish society. Simply put, Swartzentruber children are not expected to learn about the world; as far as parents are concerned, the less exposure to the world the better. Rather than acquire cultural knowledge about the surrounding society, children must acquire the skills of reading, writing, and arithmetic, and for this, the currency of the language and examples is unimportant. When children are learning how to figure out compound interest, it is just as easy to work with numbers from another time—Mr. Cox borrowing only $6,000 from the bank at 6 percent interest to buy his dream house on the installment plan, for example—as it is to work with twenty-first-century prices.

Passed down from older sibling to younger, from parent to child, these archaic texts reinforce a sense of continuity in the community. As one mother put it, "That's [McGuffey's Readers] all we used. That's all I know. It's nice, it's not so strange, when children have the same books as parents." Thus, textbooks, like other symbols of Swartzentruber life, including distinctive dress, horse and buggy transportation, and the schoolhouse itself, serve as a physical bond uniting generations (Johnson-Weiner 1997). Moreover, archaic texts both maintain the distance between contemporary non-Amish and Swartzentruber communities and, by demonstrating that the skills required to lead a Swartzentruber life remain the same across time, reinforce the notion that the important values—God's truths—are unchanging.

Not all Swartzentruber families were used to the McGuffey's when they moved to northern New York. In Ohio, some had attended school with children from other Amish churches and had used readers developed by the Pathway Publishing Company, an Old Order Amish—owned business, in all grades. One Swartzentruber mother, who had taught school both in Holmes County and in the Heuvelton area, noted that in Ohio, where she taught children from different Old Order Amish churches in the same school, "they had had English in all the grades" and used only Pathway Readers for reading classes. "We had the McGuffey's when we moved up here," she noted, adding by way of explanation, "I think some parts of Ohio had the McGuffey's, and people that moved up here from there wanted them."

For the sixth through eighth grades, Swartzentruber schools use the Pathway series, and teachers seem to prefer them, largely because of perceived deficiencies in the McGuffey's. Some teachers suggest, for example, that the McGuffey's simply become too difficult. One complained that the McGuffey's stories were too short. As the mother and former teacher mentioned above put it, "I don't like the McGuffey's because I think they're harder and not as interesting." In explaining the Swartzentrubers' adoption of Pathway texts for the sixth through eighth grades, however, it may also be important that, by this time, the children are starting to take responsibility for waiting on customers at roadside stands and are close to taking on adult responsibilities that necessitate fluency in "the world's" English. The Pathway Readers are written specifically for Old Order schools and are careful to limit and guide children's introduction to the world both in their portrayal of farms and other unchanging elements of Old Order life and in their selection of readings by non–Old Order authors. However, the language of the series is by design the modern English spoken by English neighbors and customers, the language needed for business transactions with the dominant society.

It may also be important that, by the time children are in fifth grade and starting to use the Pathway texts, they are old enough to recognize the differences between their own community and the Old Order Amish world of the *Pathway Readers*, which are published by members of an Old Order Amish church that is "higher" than the Swartzentruber churches. They can find the Pathway stories enjoyable, yet they can also recognize that the Readers neither present nor represent their own world. As one teacher noted, "The Pathway books are more interesting. If I would like to read, I would read out of those." Nevertheless, she added, the readers are "all about English people," and despite the Pathway emphasis on stories about Amish life, "they [the Pathway characters] are different kinds of Amish; they ask questions. Some of the things wouldn't really be called Amish. Their [the characters'] clothes are different." Using both *McGuffey's* and *Pathway Readers* allows the Swartzentruber schools to be both traditional and practical, to protect their children from worldly influence and reinforce community values while giving them the English skills they need. In comparing the two series, one teacher noted, "I like my [*McGuffey's*] readers; the scholars like the pictures, but they're pictures from long ago. The stories are a lot of the time a lesson for them [scholars]; they learn things about the stories, things that happen. We like the Pathway too because they're interesting and a lot of Amish." As this same teacher noted later, "We got the *McGuffey's* first, and maybe they're easier. The Amish in Pathway aren't like us, but they [the scholars] like them."

Ultimately, Swartzentruber teachers think little about why they use these texts. Commenting on the books in her school, one teacher suggests, "The reason why I think they choose these is because we had them in Ohio. We're used to them. I just use whatever books are in here."

Pedagogy and Behavioral Norms

The *Pathway Readers* have sets of questions at the end of each story and workbooks that require students to think about the story and analyze events. These seem to encourage children to question not only the vocabulary and the events but also the story's application to their own lives. Yet the Swartzentruber schools do not use the workbooks, and the teachers rarely ask questions about the reading selections. As one teacher put it, "I wasn't ever learnt to use them, and I don't think they [Swartzentruber teachers in general] ever use them."

Continuing the pattern fostered by the use of archaic texts divorced from both the non-Amish world children see around them and the Old Order world in which the children live, Swartzentruber teachers encourage rote learning, a mastery of basic information, and respect for authority; and they downplay, at the same time, engagement with the material, critical thinking, and questioning (Keim 1975). There is little discussion of the content; children must simply do the lesson without talking about it, just as they must do their chores at home without discussion.

Swartzentruber pedagogy reinforces a hierarchical power structure. Children ask their teachers questions, but they never question their teachers. Following a schedule that varies little from school to school or from year to year, children learn early on to depend on their teachers to tell them what to do and how to do it. Although children are expected to work quietly on their own, they continually raise their hands to ask the teacher how to pronounce a spelling word or to do an arithmetic problem. The teacher generally responds, not by encouraging them to think for themselves, to sound out the word or figure out the problem, but by giving them the answer. Children learn by rote; there is little attempt to teach patterns. Counting on fingers to figure out arithmetic problems is acceptable and even encouraged. As one teacher put it, "I like it if they can count their fingers. I think it's better for them."

Even spelling is learned by repetition, not by sound correspondences. As noted above, teachers commonly move from desk to desk as children hold up their readers and point to a word they do not know. Often child after child will point to the same word, and a child may repeatedly ask the same word, seemingly as much for reassurance as for information. In each case, the teacher simply supplies the word in question. A child may ask the pronunciation of "ring" and then of "bring," and the teacher supplies both without pointing out the relationship between the two words.

Indeed, in doing phonics, teachers and children treat the sound that is the focus of the lesson as just one more item to be memorized, and children recite lists such as "a" [æ], "cat," "rat," never analyzing the words to see their phonetic similarity. Prior to spelling tests, children stand at the blackboard to write the spelling words over and over, erasing the list with their hands when they finish. Often the children do not know the meaning of the words they are memorizing, for spelling words are generally not presented in context, and there is little discussion of meaning and appropriate use.[15] Some teachers require students to write sentences using the words. One Swartzentruber teacher admitted to me that she didn't know what all the words in the upper-grade spelling lists meant, so she picked only words she knew for the sentence exercises. "Otherwise," she said, "I wouldn't know what the sentence means." Another teacher had the students write sentences in English but then tell her in German what the sentence said. She made no attempt to analyze the English sentence for grammatical correctness or appropriate use of a word.[16]

The teacher's lack of familiarity with English vocabulary and pronunciation reinforces distinct Swartzentruber pronunciations for many less-familiar words and reinforces the distance between Swartzentruber English and that of the non-Swartzentruber world. One teacher, for example, helping her students pronounce new vocabulary, supplied [éliəns] for "alliance," and [élgəns] for "allegiance," and another rendered "Phoenix" as [foníks] and "centered" as [kantərd]. "Stomach" is generally pronounced [stomǎč] with the second syllable stressed and the final *ch* pronounced as in "*church.*"

Swartzentruber pedagogy is grounded in a belief in the efficacy of repeated actions. At home Swartzentruber children are instructed through example and repeated practice. In short, they learn by copying and doing; and given little opportunity to vary from the model, they do a task repeatedly, each time doing it better. Rather than telling her daughters how to make a pie, for example, a mother will hand them dough, and they will copy her actions as she rolls it out and twists the edging. Over time and with practice, the daughters will come to make pies in the same way as their mother and as well (Johnson-Weiner 2001a). Similarly, in Swartzentruber schools children learn by repeatedly copying what the teacher tells them. They will ask the pronunciation of the same vocabulary word over and over, write their spelling words on the board numerous times, and recite their multiplication tables until they "know" the answer to any multiplication problem.

Like individual lessons, the school day and the school term are routinized, and there is little change from one day or one year to the next. Teachers spend little time outside of class preparing lessons. As one said, "I don't spend time at home preparing [for school], just at test time figuring up averages. The first year I did a lot more work. I never thought the first year I would teach again." Another commented, "Every day is alike, most of the days. I don't have to prepare at night." A teacher with three years of experience noted that now she spent no time outside of school hours preparing lessons or grading students' work. "The older scholars help grade," she said.

As this last example demonstrates, teachers, like their students, have learned by observation and repetition. There are no teachers' meetings at which new teachers can receive tips from more experienced counterparts, no lessons in pedagogy, and no formal evaluation before a teacher begins to teach. Substitute teaching is the only advance training a girl receives for teaching. One teacher noted that the first time she was in the classroom as a teacher was for a week of substituting. In talking about her preparation for teaching, she pointed out that as a student she had seen good teachers and bad ones, so when she started teaching, she just tried to follow the example of the good ones. In the classroom, then, new teachers consciously teach in the same way, covering the same material, using the same books as the teachers they had when they were children.

On the Margins of the Community

As child after child goes through the same books and learns the same lessons, school is a rite of passage for Swartzentruber children. Parents and the other adult members of the broader church-community, having completed their own formal education, are no longer involved in the school's activities. Indeed, parents often dread the start of school in the fall. "I lose my help," one mother complained, a sentiment echoed frequently by other Swartzentruber mothers. Parents will routinely keep children home from school if they need them to perform chores.

Although children spend a considerable amount of time in school and acquire skills that are necessary to full participation in the economy and social life of the community, schools are marginal in Swartzentruber life. In part, this may be because none of the children and few of the teachers are baptized, so although the church-community is concerned that school reflect its values, church members are not involved in school activities. More likely, however, schools remain at the periphery of church-community life because children learn the important lessons—how to manage the farm and the house or how to care for children—at home, and they gain the knowledge one must have to join church through parental and ministerial instruction.

As a result, school is not permitted to impinge on the more important activities of home and church. Swartzentruber teachers give no homework, for example. Children are expected to finish their assignments, but parents expect that school work will be done at school and do not encourage their children to use time at home to study or review their lessons, even at test time. While much might be made of a young child's first day of school, little note is taken of his last at the end of eighth grade other than to joke with him about how nice it is not to have to go any more. Only the teachers recognize the eighth grader's graduation, generally giving each graduating child a special gift, glassware for girls and tools for boys.

Parents seldom visit school, and there is no special place set aside for visitors to sit. Swartzentruber schools rarely offer a guest book for visitors to sign, and there is never a chart hung on a classroom wall recording visitors to the school.[17] There is no special program for visitors, and children do not introduce themselves. One Swartzentruber mother commented that "it might be good if parents did visit some time to see what they're learning." Her husband noted, however, that as far back as he could remember, his own parents had never visited school. Needless to say, this couple had never visited the school their children attended, and in fact, the mother was not sure precisely where it was and had to ask her daughter to give me directions.

Teachers generally handle discipline on their own. Asked about cheating and bullying in the school, for example, one teacher noted, "Yeah, sometimes there are some that do it more than others. If it gets too bad, I talk to the parents, but I like to take care of it myself. I don't like to bother the parents."

This lack of community involvement extends to special school events. Parents do not attend school picnics, and children do not put on special programs for parents and community members. Teachers are expected to supply special treats, usually small candies, pencils, little erasers, or other inexpensive items, at Christmas and Easter, prepare valentines for the students on Valentine's Day, and recognize with special little gifts any extra contribution made by older students (e.g., helping to clean the schoolhouse at the end of the term). Teachers are also expected to supply a special lunch on the last day of school. At one school, this meant that the teacher supplied all 32 students with large bowls of ice cream and piles of potato chips, pretzels, and popcorn. The only outsiders who attended the party were the teacher's sisters, who had brought the bowls, spoons, and treats from home. The mother of another teacher commented that generally the only visitors on the last day were older children who had graduated a year or two before, but she didn't expect that any of her older children, the teacher's siblings, would go.

The lack of communication between parents and teachers goes both ways. The mother of a girl who had broken her collarbone skating during recess told me that the girl had stayed at school until the day was over: "The teacher didn't send her home. She [the child] didn't get much done with the rest of the classes that day, though." Following the incident, the teacher did not speak with the parents, nor did the parents make a special attempt to talk to the teacher, although, according to the mother, "the teacher's mother said later that now the teacher knows she should better send a hurt child home."[18]

School Administration

The marginalization of schools in Swartzentruber church-communities is further evident in the lack of parental involvement in school governance. Each school has a three-member board, one member of which changes every year. Members are voted in by the fathers of children attending the school, and only men serve. Ministers do not serve on the board because they are considered to be too busy with their other duties. One mother noted that, since only three families used their children's school, "there aren't enough families at the school to vote." Her husband, she commented, "was number one on the school board this year. He's number one for one year; usually they take turns." While the boards are supposed to meet every month, just to see if there are any problems, many don't. Commenting on school board activities, the woman quoted above said, "If they had to have meetings then we'd really think we had trouble." Another mother concurred. She noted that the board of her children's school had met before the start of the term and then again six weeks later. She didn't expect them to meet again until the term was over.

Teachers have little contact with the board, attending meetings only if they have something to bring up. The teacher at the River View School in Holmes County, Ohio, for example, said that her school board met every month, but she had met with them only once. Although her father was the school board treasurer, she had little idea about what went on at meetings. Similarly, a Heuvelton teacher noted that she had little conversation with the board and did not really have to see them. Asked in late November how often she had met with the board of her school, another teacher replied, "Not yet this year." She then acknowledged that she had met with the board members before the term started, when she was "told how they have it in this school, when school starts and when it closes." That meeting also guaranteed that there would be plenty of wood for the woodstove and set up the rotation of families who would take turns driving the teacher home after school on Friday; the rest of the week she would board with the family of some of the pupils.

The board generally sets the calendar, deciding when the term will begin and end and making sure that school meets the required 160 days. All generally agree that school will not meet on Good Friday, Easter Monday, Christmas Day, Old Christmas (Epiphany), New Year's Day, and Thanksgiving. Other days must be negotiated. One teacher reported, "In four years I only met with the board once, when I wanted to hold school on Easter Monday to get done [with the term] earlier."[19] When a teacher needs to have a day off, she is responsible for getting a substitute (often a sibling) and for paying the substitute out of her own wages. The teacher is responsible for keeping attendance, but only she looks at her records.[20]

Teachers are responsible for cleaning the classroom, particularly at the end of the school year, and they must turn in to the school board an order for books for the following year. On the last day of school, before their special lunch, children help teachers pack up songbooks and textbooks. Worn-out pages and parts of books are saved as well because, as several teachers told me, a child might need a page if a book is missing one.

The board must meet in the spring to hire a teacher for the following term. Generally, potential teachers, whether new or returning, are asked in July whether they will teach in the fall. The hiring of a teacher for a school is a much-whispered-about event, and the choice is kept secret from school children until as close to the first day of school as possible. If the teacher is under 21, then her father will negotiate her salary for her, with the amount determined by the teacher's experience and age and the number of pupils she will have to teach.

Swartzentruber salaries are low, another indication of the marginal place of schools in Swartzentruber society. One 18-year-old teacher earned $800 for the 2001–2002 school term, or $5.00 a day. "That's pretty good for a girl," another commented when she told me that she too was earning $5.00 daily. Upon turning 21 and so becoming, in Swartzentruber eyes, independent, another teacher commented, "Some get $5.00, others get $6.00. I heard of one who gets $4.75. Dad got $5.25 [for me], but now that I'm 21, I want to see if I can get a little more. I have to pay for shoes and all now." The River View School's teacher earned approximately the same as her New York counterparts, $150 per month, but she had to pay for school cleaning supplies. All teachers are responsible for duplicating their own tests, and many depend on English neighbors for photocopying and for scrap paper for the children to use in school.[21]

The low salary virtually ensures that there are no male teachers, which, in turn, further marginalizes the schools. Even underage young men can generally earn more doing farm labor. Since children do not learn the most important lessons in school, a female teacher, generally underage, with no special training, and isolated from governing boards that meet infrequently at best, is considered sufficient.

Schools are funded by the entire settlement. A Swartzentruber bishop noted that the Heuvelton, New York, settlement had 127 families in six church districts and three (non-fellowshipping) church-communities.[22] Money is collected from all in a free-will offering. "Sometimes," the bishop said, "an older couple ain't got no children, so they can afford to give a little more, but a younger family can't give so much." The total amount collected is divided to meet the costs of teachers, whose salaries have been determined in negotiations with individual school boards.

Although costs for textbooks and other school expenses are met by the individual school communities, books are ordered centrally. Each teacher must tell the board what is needed after the school year ends, and the board then forwards the order to the central dealer, who may or may not be involved with the school board.

There are no Swartzentruber bookstores. Individuals who sell books generally sell only a few titles in which they have a particular interest (e.g., family genealogies or health books). The Heuvelton-area schoolbook seller noted that he had gotten involved in selling textbooks "when all the girls were still at home, not yet in school [the oldest is now 27 and married; another, at 22, is a teacher]." He got the job, he thinks, because he had a central location and "they didn't want to go too far." He also notes that he was willing to help: "Some need to spend some time when they order. They need to know how many scholars, and how many grade cards and penmanship books to get." His wife added, "We ask all the teachers to let us know in the first six weeks if they need to order more; then we can send in one big order and save money." Acknowledging that there are always some who order late, she added, "We always get extras."

In all but one Swartzentruber school, the books are owned by the school. The board replaces texts too worn out to be used and buys necessary workbooks. The teacher hands out books to the children at the beginning of the term. One mother noted that this sometimes leads to complaints of "favoritism," that the teacher gives certain students books in better condition. Also, she added, it is harder to make children take care of books. In her children's school, she said, individual families buy a complete set of books for all eight grades and hand them down to their own children. There's a high initial expense, and "a new family will have quite a burden, over $200, but it's only once." Moreover, she said, "You can make sure children take care of them."

Success and Swartzentruber Education

A number of studies have suggested that graduates of Old Order Amish parochial schools perform as well, if not better than, their non-Amish counterparts at rural public schools on tests of spelling, word usage, and arithmetic (Hostetler 1969; Hostetler and Huntington 1971; 1992). Lacking fluency both in the vocabulary of modern English and the pragmatics of language use in the dominant society, Swartzentruber graduates would probably not do as well, even if they were willing to adopt such standard measurements of achievement. Swartzentruber families, for example, often ask non–Old Order neighbors and acquaintances to explain a variety of official (and official-looking) mailings. One young woman, recently married after teaching for several years, was worried about a letter from the local hospital and unable to figure out what it was asking her and her husband to do. A non—Old Order friend found it to be a patient satisfaction questionnaire.

Nevertheless, the private schools have sufficiently educated this couple and their peers for life in their Swartzentruber community. Working as a carpenter, the husband can make measurements, figure the amount of material needed for a project, and talk with non-Swartzentruber clients. The wife can read recipes and letters from friends, wait on English-speaking customers at the farm stand, write to order items from catalogs, and measure fabric to sew. Both can make change and shop. As one Swartzentruber man noted, "Your people [non-Amish] would be lost without calculators. We learn to do arithmetic in our heads." Everything else they need to know to live as Swartzentruber Amish, they, like their siblings, learned in the family and community activities of Swartzentruber life.

In short, in every way, from the plain architecture and undecorated walls of the schoolhouse to the marginalization of teachers and school activities, Swartzentruber communities have structured formal education to provide enough book learning for children to earn a living, while at the same time separating them from the dominant society and reinforcing group norms and obedience to church discipline. By the time children graduate after eight years of schooling, they will have finished the last pages in the textbooks, a clear physical sign that the school has no more to offer them. They will have learned to speak English, but not in a way that has taught them very much about the English-speaking world around them. They will have acquired practical skills in calculation—not enough to become involved in high finance, but enough to figure out how much wood or fabric they need for a particular project and to keep their checkbooks balanced.

Far more importantly, they will have learned the boundaries of their community and how community members must act to support each other and the church. Studying the same textbooks, playing the same games, and following the same rules as their parents and grandparents before them, they will have learned to maintain the status quo that represents God's unchanging truth.

For the Swartzentruber Amish, the child's real education takes place more outside the school than in it, and there is often the sense that, when the child has completed eighth grade, he or she can get on with learning the important lessons of life. On leaving school, the young boy or girl is able to take on major tasks and responsibilities at home or as a hired hand on a neighbor's farm and so begin the final phase of a more important education.

CHAPTER 4

Small Schools in Small Settlements

Remember, school is not meant to be a child-training center.
It is merely a supplement to the home.
—*Blackboard Bulletin*, November 1966

Smaller Old Order Amish Settlements

People used to seeing pictures of the Amish in tourist centers such as Intercourse, Pennsylvania, or Berlin, Ohio, tend to think of the Old Orders as living in crowded semi-rural settings, their buggies choking traffic as they wait to make left turns onto busy highways. Yet there are many smaller, more isolated and rural Old Order settlements. Away from tourist eyes and cameras, these Old Order communities tend to be homogeneous, members of the community sharing a common *Ordnung*; seeing other church members frequently in community events, frolics, and at work; and interacting daily with their non–Old Order neighbors in stores and on the job.

The Old Order Amish community in Norfolk, New York, is only 40 miles from the Swartzentruber Amish settlement in the Heuvelton-DePuyster area, yet the Norfolk community differs from the Swartzentruber settlement in size, *Ordnung*, and community lifestyle. Founded in 1974 by families from Allen County, Indiana, and southern Michigan, the Norfolk community was at one time much larger, with two church districts and a two-room schoolhouse. Now it is very small, with only seven families. The old schoolhouse has been abandoned, and in the spring of 2002 the teacher met her 15 scholars in the cellar of an unfinished house.[1]

Norfolk is not a wealthy community, and many of the men have turned to carpentry to supplement farm income, some working as builders and others making furniture or mini-barns. In the past, a number of the young girls and women in the Norfolk community worked for non-Amish employers, cleaning houses or babysitting. There is less of this now because there are fewer young women who are both out of school and unmarried, and so able to work away from home. Several of the married women have started businesses, including an organic produce business and a greenhouse.

Norfolk is a small community, and its members often interact with those in Old Order Amish communities in western New York and in northern Pennsylvania. Some from the Norfolk community were among the founders of the Old Order Somerset settlement in Perry County, Ohio, which was started in late fall 1990. With only ten families, Somerset, like Norfolk, is quite small. Although a number of the men are involved in construction work, the community remains agricultural, with most families raising and selling produce.

In some ways, the Somerset settlement is a "higher," or more modern community than Norfolk, for it permits the use of natural gas and coal for heat and may soon permit iceboxes. In other ways, however, it is "lower," for Somerset women always wear the cape over their dresses, while Norfolk women often leave it off except for church and visiting. Moreover, Somerset women wear longer dresses in darker colors, and the pleats on their caps are not ironed.[2] The Norfolk and Somerset settlements are not in fellowship; they have different *Ordnungs*, and ministers from one community will not preach in the other. However, the communities continue to be connected through family and social ties.

Both are connected as well by family and social ties to the larger Fredericktown and Ashland settlements, little-known neighbors to the world's largest Amish settlement in Holmes and Wayne Counties, Ohio (L. Miller 1992, 58). The Fredericktown settlement, founded in 1973, has seven church districts spread across Richland, Morrow, and Knox Counties, Ohio. There are ten schools, the last built for the 2002–2003 term. The Ashland settlement, founded in 1954, has eight church districts and nine schools, and encompasses large areas of Ashland and Richland Counties, Ohio.

Ashland and Fredericktown are in fellowship with each other, and they also fellowship with the Norfolk settlement, although their *Ordnungs* differ. The Fredericktown and Ashland communities are both higher and lower than the Somerset and Norfolk communities. As a member of the Somerset church put it, "Ashland and Fredericktown think Norfolk is higher because Norfolk has chainsaws, but [in Ashland and Fredericktown] the women wear suits [that is, their capes are the same color as their dresses] and in Norfolk they don't, which makes Norfolk lower." Ashland and Fredericktown also permit indoor plumbing, an innovation resisted by the Somerset and Norfolk groups.

Yet, despite some variation in dress and in their use of technology, these four settlements share important similarities. Linked socially and religiously, they are also homogeneous settlements. All of those living within the settlement are members of the same church-community, so children will go to school with others whose families have accepted the same *Ordnung*. Moreover, although these different settlements are largely agrarian, members of each settlement have close economic links to the dominant society. In each church-community, men and women work away from home for non–Old Order employers, the men in construction and other kinds of day labor and the women doing housecleaning or fruit picking. Thus, far from tourist centers, these Old Order Amish are in daily contact with their non–Old Order neighbors, not as objects of curiosity but as fellow laborers. In addition, many in these settlements have started small businesses, including harness making, blacksmithing, engine repair, and bulk food and variety retailing, which also serve a clientele from outside the Old Order community.

Like the Swartzentruber Amish, these Old Order Amish church-communities continue to define themselves and what it means to be Old Order in opposition both to other Old Order communities and to the worldly society around them. However, these groups have begun to redefine the separation of the church from the world to permit members to engage in wage labor outside the community. Their proximity to, and dependence on, the surrounding society has fostered a close working relationship between members of the church-community and outsiders. Moreover, unlike the Swartzentruber Amish, who see themselves as quite different from other Old Order groups,[3] these homogeneous, self-contained Old Order church-communities feel a connection to other Amish communities, even those with whom they are not in fellowship. Relatively isolated from other Old Order groups, and thus less threatened by differences in *Ordnung*, they foster links to other church-communities through visiting, correspondence, and the reading of Old Order publications.

In short, these Old Order Amish church-communities have drawn the boundaries between themselves and the world differently than have the Swartzentruber Amish. Children in the Somerset, Norfolk, Fredericktown, and Ashland Old Order church-communities, and in similar settlements such as those in Clyde and Prattsburg, New York, and in Berne and Vevay, Indiana,[4] grow up in homes that make greater use of technology, some with indoor plumbing, for example, or kerosene refrigerators. Their parents lead working lives that are more involved with non–Old Order neighbors, some even working for wages in non–Old Order businesses. They read Old Order Amish publications ignored by the Swartzentrubers, and these tie them to Old Order communities distant from their own and often differing in *Ordnung*.

Education for a Different Amish Life

Although members of the Norfolk, Somerset, Fredericktown, and Ashland church-communities desire, like the Swartzentruber Amish, to educate their children for an Amish life, they do not educate them for the same kind of Amish life, and the private schooling that has evolved in these communities reflects different and broader educational goals. As one parent put it, "Times change and so education must change for the times." Schools must prepare children to interact with the world but give them the wherewithal to remain separate from it.

At first glance, the one-room schoolhouses of these settlements do not give the impression of "changing for the times"; from the outside, they seem as plain looking as any Swartzentruber school. However, a closer look reveals that schoolhouses in these communities are located on land maintained year-round as school grounds, and some have playground equipment. The schoolhouses are therefore a constant physical presence in the community.

Inside, the schoolhouses contrast sharply with those maintained by the Swartzentruber Amish. For example, when I visited the Brook Private School in Norfolk, New York, during the spring 2002 term, there were

With the door open to catch the breeze, lessons go on in a small Ohio school. The lunchboxes left on the playground perhaps hold a snack for recess.

paper chains hanging from the ceiling, and on the front wall behind the teacher's desk was a picture of flowers in a pot with the title, "Visitors Make Us Bloom." Like other visitors, I was expected to write my name and the date of my visit on a flower petal, which would then be added to the bouquet. That same term, the Grove School in the Somerset settlement of Perry County, Ohio, sported paper cardinals, made by the students, hanging from the ceiling.[5] Both of these schools have battery-powered clocks,[6] shelves of storybooks for students to read in their free time, and tables around which the children sit when the teacher is "taking their class."[7] The schoolhouse walls are filled with pictures the children have colored, and alphabet charts, English and German pronunciation guides, and posters explaining arithmetic functions.

Although the Ashland and Fredericktown settlements are older and larger than the Somerset and Norfolk communities, the schools are similar, with all eight grades in the same room, generally with only one teacher. While wood- and coal-burning stoves in the cellars of the schools heat

A visitors' chart at the beginning of the school year. By the end of the term the teacher hopes it will be filled with cutouts of farm animals, flowers, and buggies, each bearing the name of a visitor to the school.

some Fredericktown schools, other schools in these communities have the stove in the classroom itself. Most of them have only a swing set and/or a seesaw on the playground, and a space is set aside for ball playing. Inside each classroom there is a globe, a clock on the wall, and numerous charts to welcome visitors, to reinforce values of hard work and friendship, and to remind children of parts of speech.

Ideally, children in these Old Order private schools will receive, as one teacher put it, "enough learning to go on in life and make a living." "We expect our schools to provide a basic education for our children," asserted a Fredericktown teacher, "[one] that is essential to our way of living and also to be able to communicate and make a living in the outside world." Moreover, she added, children ought "to learn discipline and respect to God and fellow men."[8] Similarly, a teacher in the Ashland community asserted, "Above all else, [we] try to prepare them [the children] for living a life pleasing to their Creator, which gives hope for Eternal Salvation through their Redeemer. And then to be prepared to make a decent living while going through this life." Similar sentiments are expressed by teachers in New York. As one put it, "The goal of having our own schools is preparing for usefulness by preparing for eternity." Another from the same community noted more simply that "the role of the Old Order schools is to be separate from the world and for education on the basic needs for survival."

In short, these communities expect the private schools to help prepare children for this life in a way that augments and reinforces the attempts of church and parents to prepare them for the next. Asked what Amish private schools should do, one mother in the Norfolk Old Order Amish community answered, "Education. But that wouldn't be the main thing. We want them to learn spiritual values besides their arithmetic." As one teacher put it, "We expect our schools to each be like big families by working and playing together, learning to get along and all under a Christian attitude." "It's more than just the lessons, it's teaching them right from wrong. You're like a mother. You're with the children all day," commented another.

In these small church-communities, schools play a central and acknowledged role in the rearing of children for the economic and spiritual demands of life in the church-community. In characterizing the school as a big family and casting the teacher as parent, the church-community expects that teachers, like real parents, will daily provide children with a good example of how they should behave as adults. According to one Old Order teacher, "a teacher plays a role in teaching the children to be Christian by example and with discipline." Notes another, "I already heard say [that] a teacher has it a lot like the leader of a church. [She] has so many young souls entrusted in her care to love and discipline [. . .] the teacher's example is a big influence to the children." No Swartzentruber teacher would make such an analogy.

A Curriculum to Prepare Children for the World

Teachers in these communities take on a larger task than their Swartzentruber counterparts, for they must, as one teacher put it, "enforce what the parents teach the child at home, and to this add the education that is necessary for the child." This education will give them Old Order values and also prepare them to interact regularly with others outside their community. In Swartzentruber schools, children do not study geography, history, or health because, as a Swartzentruber teacher said simply, "We don't need them, we don't use them." But the Old Order Amish children in church-communities like Somerset and Ashland will interact with the surrounding, non–Old Order society far more than their Swartzentruber counterparts, so it is not surprising that "the education that is necessary" is more broadly defined than it is in Swartzentruber schools.

Schools in Norfolk, Somerset, Ashland, and Fredericktown have begun to add other subjects, including art, health, geography, and history, to the basic curriculum of arithmetic, spelling, penmanship, English, and reading. These additions to the school curriculum provide students with a more up-to-date and realistic view of life outside the church-community, better preparing them for interaction with non–Old Order society and even emphasizing that, while belonging to an Old Order church-community, they are also citizens of the United States.

With an expanded curriculum and broader educational goals, the schools in these communities are not as standardized as Swartzentruber schools. The curriculum, the daily schedule, and the textbooks used vary from school to school. In the Fredericktown settlement, for example, different geography textbooks circulate between the schools. Since grades five through eight at each school do geography as a single group, a different book is needed each year. Thus, while one teacher is using *You and the Americas*, her counterpart at a neighboring school is using *Ohio History and Government*; the next year they will switch. Enough different texts are circulating that children have a different book every year that they study geography.

Teachers in the same settlement do not necessarily cover the same subjects, and they may construct very different teaching schedules. "Not all schools do health," reports a textbook dealer in the Ashland community, although "they're supposed to in the second grade." One Ashland teacher noted, for example, that at her school they do not teach geography, and that while they have health textbooks, "we don't work at them." This same teacher saves Friday for German study. Another Ashland teacher, however, noted that she would have liked to restrict the study of German to Fridays in order to have more time for her other classes, but that at her school families were used to having German study every day.

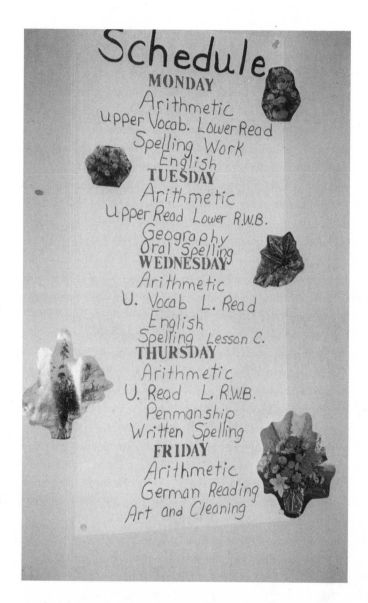

Schedule

MONDAY
Arithmetic
upper Vocab. Lower Read
Spelling Work
English
TUESDAY
Arithmetic
Upper Read Lower R.W.B.
Geography
Oral Spelling
WEDNESDAY
Arithmetic
U. Vocab L. Read
English
Spelling Lesson C.
THURSDAY
Arithmetic
U. Read L. R.W.B.
Penmanship
Written Spelling
FRIDAY
Arithmetic
German Reading
Art and Cleaning

A schedule posted on the classroom wall reminds students what they need to be working on. Students are expected to have their work ready when the teacher calls their class to meet.

Even in the same school, a change in teachers can bring about radical changes in the daily routine. One year, for example, a Norfolk teacher reserved Mondays and Wednesdays for arithmetic, spelling, reading, and phonics, but on Wednesdays and Fridays she also taught German and health. On Tuesdays she taught geography, and on Wednesdays she found time for history. Some years later, a teacher at the same school substituted extra recess periods for history and health.

Just as they do in Swartzentruber schools, textbooks help to isolate children from the surrounding non–Old Order society, yet in these more outward-looking communities, they also provide a link to that world. In an interesting juxtaposition of tradition and change, many schools use both archaic textbooks from the turn of the twentieth century and other texts more recently discarded by public schools, many dating to the 1950s and 1960s, a period during which a large number of private schools were founded. While the former reinforce isolation from the world, the latter emphasize continuity with a past in which the parents and grandparents of children in today's Old Order private schools attended school with non–Old Order neighbors. Thus, through their texts, children are prepared for a more complex future in which, as members of an Old Order church-community, they will also be participants in a larger society whose culture is not their own and whose values are different.

For example, Norfolk, Fredericktown, and Somerset, as well as certain grades in some Ashland schools, are using the 1951 *Learning to Spell* series from Ginn & Company, reprinted by the Old Order Book Society.[9] The majority of Ashland schools, however, have retained the archaic 1919 *Essentials of English Spelling*, but they have also provided students with a more up-to-date and extended history curriculum. While fourth graders use material that, according to one teacher, was "duplicated from some smart teacher," fifth and sixth graders use the 1965 Laidlaw Brothers' *Our Country*, a public school textbook now reprinted by the Gordonville Print Shop. Seventh and eighth graders use texts by Old Order Amish authors, *Seeking a Better Country* by Noah Zook and *Our Better Country* by Uria R. Byler, respectively. These texts, both published by the Gordonville Print Shop, introduce Old Order children to American history told from an Old Order point of view to emphasize, as Byler wrote, "the importance to a minority, or a small religious group, such as the Amish, of living in a country such as ours" (1963, 9).

Nearly all of these schools are using the Strayer-Upton *Practical Arithmetics* series for grades three to eight and the *Arithmetic Workbook* from the Gordonville Print Shop for grades one and two, this last a reprint of workbooks written and copyrighted by Clifford B. Upton in 1933. As noted earlier, while the Strayer-Upton texts give children a solid grounding in arithmetic skills, they teach them little about the world in which they live. There have been some recent changes, however, with the Somerset School now using Schoolaid's "Spunky" books for the first and second graders.[10] Published by Old Order Mennonites, the Spunky texts still provide little information about the non–Old Order world, yet in the pictures used and the prices quoted, they provide a much more realistic indication of what the child is likely to encounter at a nearby store.

Yet change does not come easily in these communities. For example, several Fredericktown schools experimented with the Spunky texts for the first and second grade, but the school discontinued their use following a very close vote ("nearly 50-50") by the board members for the ten Fredericktown schools to retain the Strayer-Upton texts. As one teacher noted, although the teachers who used the Spunky texts favored them overwhelmingly, the board members were less willing to change what had worked well in the past. Fredericktown schools also continue to use old public school readers, in particular the *Dick and Jane* series, originally published by Scott, Foresman, and Company and now reprinted by Gordonville. One Fredericktown teacher, commenting that "our English, arithmetic, and spelling [books] have been the same for years," noted that the school had just switched from the 1930s *Alice and Jerry* readers to the 1950s *Dick and Jane* series only because "our Alice & Jerry books were getting old, and, if I'm correct, they stopped printing them."

Many fear that by changing the texts traditionally used in their schools the school boards are lowering educational or doctrinal standards. According to some Ashland parents, for example, the decision by some Ashland schools to replace the *McGuffey's Readers* with *Pathway Readers* was a sign that teachers were no longer able to teach more difficult texts. Arguing that the Pathway texts were easier for inexperienced teachers to use, one parent argued, "When we started our own schools, we had teachers that had been to public schools, but now we don't," suggesting that public schools had prepared teachers in a way their own private schools did not. At least one teacher saw the change as indicative of decreasing standards in the private schools. "We used to have McGuffey's, but they lowered the standards and now they're too hard." This teacher also regrets how quickly the change was made, noting that "a large percentage of the scholars don't have comprehension of what they read and can't do the workbooks." Worried about the ability of teachers to instruct reading with the new Pathway texts, he noted how afraid he was that "we spent a lot of money if children aren't helped [to use the books]."

Like the other schools, the Norfolk school relies on reprints of old public school readers, yet the community has not been as consistent in its choices as the other settlements have been. The Norfolk community has been particularly concerned that some texts have a doctrinal slant. In 1993, for example, all but first graders were using *Pathway Readers*,[11] but in 1996, fifth and eighth graders were using texts from the *Dick and Jane* series and *The Road to Safety* series, respectively. By 2000 none of the grades were using Pathway texts because some parents were worried that the Pathway books were too moralistic and had too much religious content. The departure of some families for other settlements helped to resolve the issues, and by the start of the 2001–2002 school year and at the teacher's request, all grades had the *Pathway Readers*. In a letter written following the end of the school term, the teacher asserted, "I feel the choice of textbooks makes a big dif[ference]." Pointing out that the *Pathway Readers* have "very true to life stories and examples of other young children," she argued that these "can be a big help to the children in my opinion. [It t]eaches them some more on what they learn at home & in church on the importance to obey the parents & our Heavenly Father."

Although most teachers report that they simply use the textbooks that were in the schools when they began teaching, and several note that these were the same ones in use when they were students, changing textbooks does not seem to present a problem if board and parents agree. "I don't believe there's really a problem here about changing text books . . . if the teacher has a good reason for it. The 3 terms [my] sis-in-law taught she changed quite a few things," noted a Somerset teacher.[12] She had herself replaced the German reader *Biblische Geschichten* with the German language New Testament because "we really want to live by the New Testament and I felt it very important that the children learn how to read it and try to understand it." Moreover, she said, although *Biblische Geschichten* "was more or less a German Bible story book about the Old Testament which is good to read and had many good lessons in it," it also had some pictures that "were not really fitting for little eyes (or so I thought)."

Learning to Play Life's Rough Game

As choosing texts "fitting for little eyes" suggests, teachers in these schools are not only teaching more subjects, but they are teaching them quite differently from their Swartzentruber counterparts, using pedagogic strategies that, while acknowledging the teacher's authority, emphasize a parental bond between the teacher and her students. The language of instruction is inclusive rather than imperative. "*Let's* make our books beautiful," encouraged a teacher after instructing second graders to color the pictures in their phonics workbook. "*Let's* say all the pictures, and then you can do the page by yourselves after that," said another who was working with first graders. "Do you understand? *Let's* do the next one," suggested another teacher to her fourth grade arithmetic class. Working with an older girl who was helping to correct third grade workbooks, the teacher commented on a child who had missed many problems, "Well, maybe *we* should just erase it and have her do it over again." The older girl immediately began erasing.[13]

Unlike teachers in Swartzentruber schools, who appear to expect children simply to do work because it must be done and so make little attempt to involve children actively in the lesson or to present the exercises in a more interesting way, teachers in these schools feel it is necessary to engage the children actively in their education. Teachers often approach problems as if they were games to be played. "I'll put a problem on the board, and you see which of you can get the answer first," said one teacher working with a class at the blackboard. It is not enough for children to know how to do arithmetic; they must learn to think for themselves about the operations they need to carry out in order to solve a problem. "How would you find out how many feet in ten yards?" asked a Fredericktown teacher, for example.

In each of these schools, grades called to the front for recitation sit around a table. The children face each other, the teacher sits with them, and they become a separate class within the larger schoolroom. Seated with the group at the front, the teacher's attention is focused on the children sitting at the table with her, and while she is certainly aware of what is going on in the schoolroom, she does not answer questions from the other children, and no children come to her for help. Asking questions, the teacher guides children around the table through the lesson, often having them work through problems while they are together before dismissing them to work at their desks.

At their seats, children often listen as other grades are called to the front, but unlike their Swartzentruber counterparts, they do not raise their hands to ask questions or otherwise interrupt the teacher when she is working with a class; the children know that they are expected to work on their own and to figure things out for themselves. When the teacher is not taking classes for recitation, then she will go around the classroom, check on children's progress, and give assistance; otherwise the children work independently.[14]

Although they are seldom fluent in English when they start first grade, children in these communities are likely to know some, so from the beginning, English plays a greater role in classroom interaction than it does in Swartzentruber schools. Moreover, since the schools in these small communities are preparing children for a life in which they may well be working outside the church-community, there is a strong emphasis on the correct use of English. A teacher of many years experience in Norfolk and later in Michigan argued that "if school is going to give them enough learning to go on in life and make a living, you want them to learn English" and asserted further that she wanted her students "not just to speak it but to speak it properly." Commenting on the importance of good pronunciation, a Norfolk mother and former teacher in the Norfolk school told how difficult it was to get children to pronounce the "th" sound, to say "three" and not "sree." "I'd write 'sree' on the board and say 'sree to get them to say 'three' right." When her husband moved to Norfolk, she said, "he said 'sree.' They all do down there where he's from. But he doesn't do it now. I guess in the young folk he learned not to.'

For teachers in these schools, learning to use English well means more than simply giving words a standard pronunciation. Although acknowledging that she didn't know why English would be important "except to make your living," a former Norfolk teacher asserted, "I'm always after my children to use it properly. That word 'ain't'—we don't want them to use. They ought to use English right." Often unsure about their own language use, many of the teachers in these small schools rely on dictionaries and other reference sources. After writing a number of vocabulary words on the board in phonetic transcription (including "camouflage," "hypocrite," and "intercede"), one teacher noted that "sometimes, many times" she has to look up definitions, and "that's what makes it hard." Nevertheless, she argued, it was important to do so. Children needed to learn such words, she asserted, because "it will help them if they have outside work, they may be in contact with the outside. Anything they need to do with the outside, they need to know a little about what they're talking about." This emphasis on preparing children to *use* English is widespread. Another teacher explicitly tied the grammar lesson to the children's own use of the language. Addressing first graders, she advised them to "use *is* when you talk about one thing and use *are* when you talk about more than one thing."

In these schools, reading is an extension of conversational English use, a further example of the assumption that English will be the children's second language, not simply a foreign language that they will use on isolated occasions to talk to worldly others. "I don't like them to read in a singsong," noted a mother and former teacher. "I always told my scholars, 'That's not the way we talk, is it?' And I'd talk to them like that and show them." Her own children's teacher echoed her views. Asked how she liked her scholars to read, this teacher replied, "With expression. They should read it like they think. It's hard for the first grade because they can't read ahead, but I wouldn't like it in a monotone." Taking the third grade reading class, which consisted of one student, this teacher took turns reading aloud with the child. Both used normal intonation in their reading. Reading a dialogue, the child even altered his voice to portray the different characters. At one point the teacher corrected his pronunciation, saying "that's 'clap,' not 'clamp.'" Another time the same teacher corrected a second grader saying, "That's a question." The little girl reread the sentence with appropriate intonation.

Believing that the children must come to use English as naturally as they use Pennsylvania German, many teachers stress the use of English for all classroom interaction. A teacher in Fredericktown, for example, working with first graders to teach them the English names for the days of the week, wrote them on the board and pointed out the similarities between them. After erasing them, she encouraged the first graders to name the days on their own, one at a time. All of her instructions were in English.

Similarly, an Ashland teacher quizzed first graders on measurement, asking how many inches in a foot, minutes in an hour, and days in a year; again, the lesson was entirely in English. A Norfolk teacher encouraged her first graders in English to read their spelling words out loud and to "study them good so you can get 100 on the spelling test."

In these schools, phonics is an analysis of language, and teachers stress phonics as a means of acquiring new vocabulary and greater facility in reading. Teachers regularly point out patterns in word structure and encourage children to sound out words. At the Norfolk school, for example, the teacher asked her first graders what new word they would have if they took "she" and added the sound "p" to the end. Pressing them further, she asked them whether the "sh" sound was at the beginning or the end of the new word and then proceeded to ask them to find the sound in a word list. Finally, she sent them to their seats to circle the sound as it appeared in the list of words in their workbook.

Nevertheless, as in Swartzentruber schools, children are reminded that English has its place. A New York teacher, for example, stopped using the book *Learning German* for German lessons "because the children had to do so much translating, and the parents were concerned that writing all these things in English would detract from their German heritage." "Now," she added, "the children just answer the questions at the end of each German story. The parents were the ones who raised the issue." As another New York teacher put it, the use of English had to be controlled. "I guess we want to be different from the world, that's why. English would lead us into more things." The children should only speak English at school, she asserted, but "parents should make them speak just German at home."

As children work, they are surrounded by numerous posters, mottoes, and poems that not only serve to remind them of school rules but also reinforce community values.

In a school in the Fredericktown settlement, for example, in addition to a posting of the Golden Rule, the teacher had hung a poster with a poem that read, in part

> So let's be like the postage stamp
> For playing life's rough game,
> And just keep on sticking
> Though we hide our heads in shame.

For the stamp stuck to the letter
Till he saw it safely through;
There's no one that could do better
Let's keep sticking and be true.

In an Ashland school, the teacher had posted a number of rhymes to instruct the children, including "B1 and B2 are for the children's diet / But what I use the most is B-have and B-quiet."

In making posters and wall displays for their classrooms, many of the teachers have found creative ways to present basic information or encourage their students. For example, one teacher hung sheets of construction paper, each one presenting a different part of speech, like clothes on a clothesline across the front of her desk. Another put up a poster likening people to various pieces of farm and sports equipment: "wheelbarrows," for example, need to be pushed; while "canoes" "need to be paddled." Implicitly, children were asked what kind of people they would be. In yet another school, the teacher hung a poster that featured large paper lollipops, which had been labeled with the different chores that needed to be done around the schoolhouse and arrayed as a bouquet under the title "lick the job."

In contrast to the plainness of their Swartzentruber counterparts, the schools of Norfolk, Somerset, Fredericktown, and Ashland highlight children's artwork, though there is generally little in the way of freehand drawing, unrealistic colors, or the early, beginning scribbling of the first graders. Instead, one sees on schoolhouse walls beautifully colored versions of the same flower or horse or farmyard, evidence that children have learned to color appropriately and to stay within the lines. Often teachers hand out pictures for the children to color when they have finished tests or assignments, and, subtly preparing children to fill different gender roles, girls are likely to be given different pictures to color than boys. In one school, for example, boys colored pictures of a large decorated Easter egg, while girls colored a picture of a basket full of eggs. Often girls will color pictures of flowers or bunnies, while boys color pictures of horses.

The arrangements of children's pictures and teachers' posters are symmetrical and orderly. No picture hangs over another, and brightly colored flowers are evenly spaced. As in Swartzentruber schools, art and its placement in the classroom reinforces the community's expectations that children will be orderly, careful, and respectful in their work.

The emphasis on learning to work and play together appropriately is further realized in playtime activities that reinforce conformity to community expectations. For example, many, though not all, of the schools in these small communities have swings for the children to use, so recess becomes a time when children must learn to take turns as they wait to use the limited playground equipment, an extension of the turn-taking reinforced in classroom interaction. Moreover, as in Swartzentruber schools, children learn by doing. In one school, for example, the children held an auction at which they sold to each other crafts they had made. Each child had made something, and items for sale, which included pillowcases, birdhouses, wooden guns that shot rubber bands, houses made from notebook paper, beeswax candles, and a doll dress, reflected skills they were learning at home. The only eighth grade boy was made auctioneer, and while he received coaching from the teacher ("Tell them what it is"), he quickly established his authority by announcing that "anybody that bids that don't have the money goes in the snowbank." As at the auctions attended by their parents, the children had numbered cards to hold up when they bid, and the two eighth grade girls kept track of sales and numbers. Older children were assigned to help younger ones.[15]

Order and Authority

Teachers in these smaller, homogeneous communities use play and classroom activities to model appropriate patterns of interaction, emphasizing the importance of acting as a responsible member of the community and stressing the need for obedience to authority. Giving the teacher parent-like responsibility for reinforcing church teaching and community values implicitly structures the teacher's relationship with her pupils. As in Swartzentruber schools, during class time the teacher and students are in a hierarchical relationship, and the teacher is to be obeyed because she is the teacher. At recess, like the Swartzentruber teachers, who assume the informal authority of older siblings, teachers in these small schools command the obedience due them because they are older. In this way, authority and obedience are modeled and reinforced. In short, teachers in the Somerset, Norfolk, Fredericktown, and Ashland settlements, like their Swartzentruber counterparts, have authority because of their position and age, and they must certainly keep order.

In contrast to Swartzentruber teachers, however, teachers in these small settlements also deserve the children's respect and attention as moral guides. Even outside of school, although the teacher may be an older sister, cousin, or fellow worker in the field, she is still "Teacher," and children must heed what she says. Implicitly defining respect as obedience, teachers often argue that lack of respect is a major reason that a teacher might lose control over a classroom, so a child's failure to respect the teacher calls for immediate discipline. One new teacher, finding school "nerve-wrecking," saw the source of her difficulties as the failure of previous teachers who didn't have the children's respect. Asked how she was approaching her task, she said simply, "I'm trying to get their respect and have order."

"There always were a few who thought they were the boss and then would give arguments as each one had their own opinion," noted one teacher. "I tried to really work on that by talking to them, making them stay in their seat a while to think their things over, etc." "Of course," she added, "if misbehavior was bad enough, the paddle was used." School influences the community, not only in the person of the teacher but also in the patterns of interaction it fosters between children. The teacher provides no shortcuts, and even when children come together as a class, they must answer as individuals. Each child learns that he or she alone is responsible for the work that must be done.

Children also learn that individual differences must be accepted. Some children are slower to learn than others, and to do one's best is what is expected. One teacher notes the particular challenges posed by "easy to learn" children, who finish their work quickly and so have little to do: "This is where good teachers try to come up with creative ideas, and others hope they ["easy to learn children"] will amuse themselves, and/or stay out of mischief. I tell them—write 50 things you'd like for sure to see before going blind or what can a dog do that you can't. (Their paper has to show effort or a harsh order is imposed.)" He suggested further that teachers could "make a 'think and do' puzzle for younger grades," and any child could "check lower grade's work." Another teacher also acknowledged the particular challenges of working with children of different abilities:

And what [did] I do with the easy learners that always finish their lessons before others? Sometimes I had to rack my brain but I got them (mostly first grade) to do blackboard practice and sometimes that urged the slower workers to hurry more so they can also go to the blackboard. Then other times I let them give each other flash cards. Then the same thing happened. The slower ones also wanted to do flash cards. Or I'd interest them in reading a book, as [I] thought that would be good practice.

Bullying or teasing is considered unacceptable behavior. According to one Ashland teacher, "We always have problems with misbehaving. I often made 'em sit in their seats for a while and sometimes they need harder punishments." Her co-teacher noted that he swiftly tried to correct unacceptable behavior, first by having the offending child apologize. Then, "if it happens again—it is serious; and can end up with a sound spanking." A Fredericktown teacher said, "[I] didn't have a problem with bullies, but I had plenty [of] teasers and pranksters to go around! My punishments aren't always [the] same. Sometimes they have to stay in their seats in recess, or write (100 or 50) lines. Anything that cures the problem!"

Still, the Fredericktown teacher asserted, "The hardest parts [about teaching . . .] are the punishments—the discipline." She acknowledged her gratitude for "a terrific set of parents," noting that "if I have a problem with one of their children [. . .] they are always willing to listen and try to help."[16] Similarly, an Ashland teacher writes, "The hardest [part of teaching] is probably keeping an order which I believe would be in harmony with God's order, and to the ultimate well-being of the child, and to the satisfaction of all parents involved."

As parent-figures, teachers must, as they exercise authority, reinforce the spiritual values of the community. This, in turn, necessitates greater parental involvement in the classroom, for parents must ensure not only that the teacher is, in fact, teaching appropriately, but also that when the teacher disciplines children, the children know the teacher speaks for the community in general and their parents in particular. A Norfolk mother argued, for example, that parents should support the teacher in discipline and "not listen just to children." As she put it, "They [children] need to be punished every now and then. You have to keep after them always and can't let things go one day and punish the next. The day-to-day atmosphere [at the school] is a big influence." A teacher friend who was visiting from the Old Order Amish settlement in Clyde, New York, agreed. "Their [the children's] characters need to be molded. Spiritual values is [sic] the main thing." Elaborating together, they defined these spiritual values as getting along with each other, being honest, giving in to authority, and learning that one can't always have one's way. "It's a day-to-day thing," the teacher reiterated. "They [the children] need a good example. The role of the school is to provide the example and the daily reinforcement."[17] A former Norfolk teacher notes, "Teachings in our schools go hand in hand with what is taught in our homes and church. The morals and values are the same."[18]

Thus, parents and teacher are partners in the children's education, each supporting the other in discipline and the instruction of values. Ultimately, then, parents and teachers work together to evaluate the success of the child. Generally, 69–70 percent is considered a passing score, and children with averages below 69 percent may be kept back at the end of the school year. This is never, however, a decision made by the teacher alone. "I've never had a child repeat a grade," notes one teacher, adding, "the parents are okay with it, if they see it's necessary." Another teacher said, "If a pupil is too poor in arith[metic], it doesn't do any good to just push him on and on." Still, she added, "I never held any back. Parents don't really like if their child has to go to school longer."

In larger communities, teachers may have the assistance of a helper several days a week. According to one Ashland parent, all the teachers in that community had helpers; one teacher noted that she had been given six weeks to decide if she wanted a helper or not.[19] In some cases, as noted above, the helper assists with discipline. Other teachers receive help if they have large classes or several slow learners. Said one new teacher in Fredericktown, "This school has too many slow learners, and I don't have time to help them enough and they get poor scores." Her school board, too, had given her six weeks to decide if she needed a helper.

Reinforcing the Religious Foundation

A teacher from New York suggests, "The teacher should *help the parents*, by teaching the children (by example) how to be good Christians. The teacher doesn't need to have special classes to teach the children this—it will show through in every area of her life if the teacher is a devoted Christian." Unlike teachers in Swartzentruber schools, teachers in these small communities make their Christian faith an overt presence in the school room, holding devotions, leading prayers in the schoolroom, and hanging posters on classroom walls that highlight particular Bible verses.

As in Swartzentruber schools, teachers begin the day with singing, but in these schools the songs are just as likely to be English as German. As one teacher put it, "We choose wholesome material for Christian life. We sing both English and German songs in our schools." Other teachers reported singing mostly in English, while one teacher said that her school sang in German one week and English the next, and that she enjoyed the Gospel songs.

In all of these schools the teachers lead devotions at the start of the school day. In some schools, these are short. For example, a Fredericktown teacher noted that "for devotions we recite the Lord's Prayer in German every morning. Every Friday we read out of the German Testament." Another Fredericktown teacher commented that she began her day with the roll call, followed by the Lord's Prayer in German and, on Wednesdays and Fridays, reading from the German New Testament. A New York teacher also reported that her school day began with the Lord's Prayer in German, followed by a short Bible study, in which "every now and then we memorized Bible verses."

Teachers and students also pray silently before the noon meal. The teacher tells the students to put their books away, and then she rings a bell, a symbol for all to bow their heads. Another ring of the bell sends children hurrying to grab their lunch pails.

Despite Bible reading and classroom prayers, however, teachers are careful not to preach or to usurp the duties of ministers and parents. The New York teacher who had her students memorize Bible verses noted that she would often have a question and answer session after reading a Bible story in English, and that when children had questions about a particular verse, she would have them look it up and then she would tell them what it meant. Nevertheless, she asserted that she "really wouldn't want to explain the Bible or anything. That's for the parents. I'm just a young girl." It is the parents' duty, she added, "to be the child's main teacher in this area." Another teacher, whose sixth to eighth graders read the New Testament on Wednesday and Friday mornings, said she had them do so "mostly to teach them to read. I don't ask questions. We read out of the Bible and sing in German, but, as for teaching and explaining, I don't do that."

In each of these schools, the children and the teacher are, as one teacher put it, "under the same *Ordnung.*" While they may be in different church districts and therefore may not see each other in church, all follow the same discipline, the same rules for interacting with each other in the church-community and with others Amish and non–Old Order outsiders. A parent and former teacher noted that he "would be very hesitant to say or feel that mixing children in with a more liberal *Ordnung* wouldn't have a detrimental effect." But, he added, "this in no way is meant to judge, or condemn a more liberal group. Birds of a feather flock together, and we spiritually weak humans, especially children, are attracted to whatever is more pleasing to the flesh if we associate with it." However, another parent in the same community was less convinced that having their children go to school with children from churches with different *Ordnungs* would be a threat. "Children are children," he asserted. "All they want is something to play with."

To Be a Good Teacher

Casting the teacher in a parental role and investing her with responsibility for the moral and spiritual well-being of children means that communities must think more carefully about who will teach. It is not enough that the teacher simply keep the children orderly and take them through their books efficiently. Swartzentruber school boards look for someone who did well in school and might be willing to teach. School boards in these small communities also want someone who exhibits the qualities of a good parent and church member.

A number of the teachers in these communities had dreamed of becoming teachers long before they were asked to teach. One teacher said, for example, that as a child she often "played school." "I had a schoolroom and I named it 'Valley View' and I had imaginary pupils. It seems a little silly now, but I liked it." Yet while many had thought of becoming teachers, all had waited to be asked; and once hired, they had assumed their positions with a great sense of responsibility and with the belief that teaching would be a God-given challenge. "What led me to become a teacher?" one wrote. "Actually it was through the need of having a teacher that I started and not because I really wanted to. I had many struggles through my years of teaching trying to adjust my mind to it and trying to enjoy it, and trying to see the reason God had for me."

Generally, the school boards begin the process of staffing the private schools early in spring when they ask current teachers whether they plan to return in the fall. One new teacher notes, for example, that she was asked to teach in March and given two weeks in which to make up her mind. The children find out who their teacher will be a month before school starts.

Like their Swartzentruber counterparts, new teachers in these small communities generally receive little or no formal training for teaching. One teacher remembered that, apart from two days as a substitute, she had had no previous teaching experience and that the first thing she did after making the decision to teach was to start making the different charts she would hang up in her classroom. A mother and former teacher argues that a prospective teacher "has got to have an education. Not like your people [non–Old Order] and all, but she has to learn good in school. Then, when she's a few years older and teaching, she goes through those books again, and she learns it better with the scholars."

Sometimes, perhaps anticipating the offer of a teaching position, a young person will visit schools. An Ashland teacher said, for example, that, before she started teaching, she had visited a number of other schools, although she hadn't been to any since she became a teacher. Others suggest that such preparation may only have limited value. A New York teacher asserted that giving advice to teachers before they began teaching was pointless: "The advice I received before teaching I couldn't comprehend it really. Truly 'experience' is still the best teacher."

While many argue that being a good teacher is something one can't learn from a book, others have suggested that some teacher training is necessary. As one teacher noted at the end of the school term, "It is still not final on how we will try to give our teachers training to better prepare them for their awesome responsibility. I don't want to push this issue for fear it will appear as if I feel I'm qualified to train our teachers, and yet at the same time, I see a tremendous need for such. I try to place such in the Hands of a Higher Power, and let Him work it out however He sees best." Even the New York teacher who argued that experience was the best teacher lamented, "I do wish someone could've made me realize that children need to be reminded, to repeat things over and over as they tend to forget and also how to deal with different behaviors."

Teachers in some small settlements do attend teacher meetings during the summer at which they discuss a number of issues related to private schools, including discipline and special education. The Norfolk teacher, who is from a small settlement in western New York, urged beginning teachers to "go to a Teachers Meeting if possible. I gleaned a lot of tips there." Several of the Fredericktown and Ashland teachers attended the Ohio State South District Teachers' Meeting held in Holmes County in early August, before the start of the fall term. In 2002, a total of 670 attended this one-day event, during which, following the opening prayer, they heard speakers on "How to benefit most from our schools," "Why we have board members," "Parents keeping a healthy relationship with the teacher," "The teacher finding success in failure," "Providing for our special children," "Mockery and its effects," "What creates boldness in teaching," and "What is teaching?" As the topics suggest, the primary focus of the meetings is on social concerns rather than pedagogical training. This is perhaps not surprising, since only a third—234—of the 670 participants in the one-day event were teachers; the rest were board members and parents, mostly fathers, according to one who attended.

As a parent and former teacher in Ashland put it, the big meetings have a lot to do with new state rulings, and somebody needs to go to keep informed. Teachers are welcome, he agreed, "but most don't go. Usually it's just board members and committee men, especially new board members." There is, he pointed out, a concern about the influence teachers and others from "higher" settlements might exert. Although he did not wish to suggest that there would be a danger in teachers going for a day to the regional meetings "to pick up good parts," he asserted that there should not be too much contact "to guard against drift."

Nevertheless, out of concern for what they saw as declining standards in the schools, several parents and former teachers in the Ashland community presented a case for a local teachers' meeting to the Annual School Meeting, which is held regularly at the beginning of the new calendar year. At this meeting, governed by three "committee men" drawn from across the settlement, members of all the local school boards in the settlement meet together to debate issues that affect all the schools. This ensures that, as a former Ashland teacher put it, "we're all alike."[20] Anxious not to suggest that they had superior knowledge of teaching, the group of parents and former teacher argued, nevertheless, that the community was "losing out in our schools" and that there were things the community could do that would be helpful.

In summer 2002, the Ashland community held its first general teachers' meeting. Organized as a day-long session for all the teachers of the Ashland community, the meeting provided the organizers—three men who, as one of them put it, "have a number of years teaching experience"—the opportunity to talk about discipline and the spiritual role schools should play. A former teacher and one of the organizers wrote, "The meeting was unable to cover everything, but we touched briefly on many subjects, and possible problems, and what might work as solutions. We talked a bit on keeping order and discipline. I hope, and have a trust, that our efforts were not in vain, but can be a help for better fruits in our educational system, and above that; for Eternity." Later he commented, "We have at least made a start." A teacher who attended this first meeting noted that the sessions seemed to focus on teaching first graders and that "they said how we have to keep order and stuff." It was helpful, she added, "but they tell you too much stuff. You can't remember it all and can't do it all."

This general meeting may lead to further attempts on the part of more experienced teachers to work with beginners. In fall 2002, Ashland teachers, fresh from their first community teachers' meeting, were preparing for a change in the usually informal teachers' get-togethers. The organizers of the general teachers' meeting had asked if they could attend the first teachers' gathering of the term and had requested that all teachers copy a verse from the German-language songbook, the *Liedersammlung*, using their best German *fraktur* script. One teacher, working on this assignment, said that she thought at least some of the men would come often to teach the teachers, something that she thought would be useful. A beginning teacher also thought the organizers would be back. "They'll come to the first teachers' meeting," she suggested, "and then they'll write and ask if we'll have them back."

In addition to formally organized teachers' meetings, when there is more than one school in the settlement, teachers often get together with each other to exchange ideas and just to talk. Fredericktown teachers, for example, get together every six weeks, while Ashland teachers meet every month. Meetings generally rotate from school to school and provide teachers a time to relax and exchange ideas. Preparing for the first meeting of the fall term, one Fredericktown teacher was putting all her various pictures and charts in order so that other teachers could copy them for their schools. One Ashland teacher said, "Most times we sit or walk around and talk about lessons and sometimes we do some duplicating, like pictures to color and work sheets."

Involving the Community

In instituting the community-wide teachers' meeting and continuing informal teacher training through the monthly teacher get-togethers, members of the Ashland settlement are acting on their belief that strong school standards are necessary for the continued survival of the community. The notion of the school as family, the teacher helping to train children to be both good Christians and able workers in much the same way parents must do, breaks down the boundaries between what goes on at school and what goes on at home. As a result, school activities are much more central to community life than they are among the Swartzentrubers. Parents, individually and through the actions of the school board and the community as a whole, must become more involved in the day-to-day activities of the school, both to support the teacher as she works to reinforce parental lessons and to ensure that she is doing so effectively.

In these church-communities, there is a general consensus that regular board meetings are necessary to avoid problems in the schools or to keep minor problems from becoming serious ones. In keeping with Old Order belief that Scripture places man in a position of authority as head of the household (cf. Johnson-Weiner 2001a, b), school boards generally consist of three men, each the father of a child or children attending the school, who meet regularly with the teacher and interested parents. In most districts, meetings take place once a month. A Fredericktown teacher explains, "In my board meetings only the fathers come. The board usually asks me if I'm having any problems, and if there are any repairs, etc. needed. [. . .] It's the school board's duty to keep up with the repairs and maintenance of the school building and property. Also to keep towels, soap, etc. supplied." Another Fredericktown teacher says that her school board meets once a month along with the other parents. Similarly, an Ashland teacher reports, "We have a board meeting every month, the board and I. There are usually three of the fathers on [the] board. If I have problems or things need to be fixed, I tell the board." She later noted, "The board comes to see if we need some advice or to fix anything that's necessary."

In other church-communities, mothers might also attend. One teacher noted that mothers usually attend school meetings and just visit quietly with each other, but "they would say something if they had something to say." Another noted that "her parents" were "pretty much involved. I meet with them once a month; then they usually all take a turn to visit school, too. I think I have a terrific set of parents."

Some of the smaller church-communities, such as Norfolk, do not have regular meetings because, with the small number of families that have children in school, every father is *de facto* a board member. As a Norfolk mother and former teacher put it, "We didn't have regular parents' meeting, but I would see them in church and many were relatives. I didn't have regular meetings with the board, but I was right there beside them. Mothers were as involved as fathers. One mother was very quiet until it came to her children. Then she could talk. She was really supportive. She really did a lot." A teacher from the Somerset settlement also noted that her community was too small "to appoint anyone as school board." But she said, "If a problem arises or things need to be repaired or discussed, the fathers (mostly) get together and decide what's to be done."

Even in communities in which mothers seldom attend board meetings, they are nevertheless frequent visitors to the schools. Indeed, parents, relatives, friends, and visitors from out of town visit schools and are a welcome interruption to the day, an event to be celebrated. Asked whether she thought parents and friends would visit her school, one new Fredericktown teacher asserted, "I hope they do!" A focal point in her classroom was a large freehand drawing of a lane going past an Amish farm. Visitors are asked to put their names on pictures of flowers or various farm animals that would be pasted into the fields. She had made cutouts of horses pulling buggies for board members to fill in when they came to visit.

"It doesn't bother me much anymore to have visitors in school, as I had so many of them already," comments an Ashland, Ohio, teacher. "Here we think parents should visit their schools, so they can see how things are going." Even in the small community of Somerset, where, the teacher reports, "visitors are not a 'too common' sight in our school because of our small community," they come from far and wide. "I think I can say we had out of state people every year. This year we even had people from Canada!"

As school activities prepare children to encounter the world outside their church-community, the community reinforces its presence and its influence in the children's lives through school visits. "PARENTS: Have you visited your school yet?" asked a February issue of *Der Kirche Brief*, a newsletter published in the Ashland settlement. "If not, now is the time to do so. An accompanying hot lunch would make your visit extra special," added the announcement, which was signed "your school."

Even on days when there are no visitors, visitors are a presence, for there is always a bench or row of chairs along a back wall ready for any who come, and prominent in each classroom is a chart that notes visitors' names and the dates of their visits. One school chart, for example, had "Welcome Visitors" across the top, and each visitor was asked to write his/her name and the date of the visit on a paper heart, which was pasted below. Another chart featured a large, hand-crank popcorn maker under the slogan, "Visitors. Thanks for poppin' in," while a third pictured a giant apple under the slogan, "Always Room for One More." Happy worms were stuck onto the apple, each featuring the name of a visitor and the date of the visit.

In addition, every school has a visitor's book to record who comes to the school and when. Signing the visitor's book and filling in the sign that will hang on the visitor's chart are important rituals of every visit, and the same names will appear repeatedly in the book and on the chart, demonstrating the regularity of visits from parents and community members. Finally, children in each school acknowledge the visitors by introducing themselves and singing songs.

After singing, the formal part of the visit is over, and guests must sit quietly at the back of the classroom while school resumes. Sometimes, however, visitors bring treats. Often mothers or friends of the teacher will work together to surprise the teacher and the children with something special. The visitors' book often notes not only who came but the fact that the visitors brought cookies, candy, or even a hot meal.

In communities with more than one school, the schools themselves often interact socially with each other, and teachers visit other schools whenever they can, further demonstrating to children that schooling is a community endeavor. Moreover, while visits to schools bring the community into the classroom, special programs for holidays and end-of-year parties to which all members of the community are invited bring the school into the community. In recounting her last day of school, a Fredericktown teacher spoke of a "carry-in dinner and a softball game."

The last day of school in the Somerset settlement was similar. The children arrived at the normal time to begin school, and together they packed up their desks, cleaned the schoolroom and received presents from their teacher. At 11:00 a.m. parents arrived with a potluck lunch, and after setting the food on the front table, mothers, babies, and little girls sat at the back of the room on one side, fathers and little boys at the back on the other, and the school children at their desks. As soon as all were settled, the teacher called "all who passed" to the front of the room, so all the children, graduating eighth graders first, followed by seventh graders, and so on to the youngest, arranged themselves in rows at the front of the classroom.

In a clearly rehearsed program, the children sang three songs in English and then five in German. After the singing, in which some parents and younger siblings had quietly joined in, the teacher announced that school was dismissed, and the entire community gathered to eat sloppy joes, salads, and cake, to give the teacher presents, and to play ball in the schoolyard.

Those finishing school are not finished with their education, for they will go work for parents and others in the community, learning to be contributing church members. Like the Swartzentruber Amish, these different church-communities measure success in the discipline and willingness of the children to do their best in school, and in the performance of the children as they leave school and become community members.

The members of these church-communities remain apart from the dominant society that surrounds them, yet in their growing dependence on that society, they are faced with change. Hostetler has argued that Amish communities face "two ways of life [. . .] competing for fulfillment. The one is maximizing material prosperity, comforts, protection, and status. The other way looks upon the maximization of material prosperity as a disease, deeply destructive of the way humankind was meant to live" (in Testa 1992, ix). While these communities remain isolated from many of the demands and temptations facing larger communities in more populated regions, in their growing economic dependence on the non–Old Order world and in their willingness to work with it and in it, they are beginning to confront the choice Hostetler describes.

"Teaching is different than what it used to be," says an Ashland teacher, now retired. "The overall trend, in the world, or wherever we choose to look, is change, and much of it is not for the better. Our schools are not isolated from this, and I cannot put my finger on any one issue, and say, 'this is the cause.' But maybe an answer straight from the heart—as our faith becomes more lukewarm, the undesirables show up more and more. Children harder to discipline, less interest[ed] in lessons, parents more unconcerned. I still see a strong future for our schools. We are not that weak yet. Our schools are very important. How they are today is in a large part how our church will be tomorrow."

CHAPTER 5

Mainstream Amish Schools

The trend in education was toward television, evolution, sex teaching, and other modern worldly ideas in child instruction. These changes were certainly not conducive to the Amish way of life.
—Uria R. Byler, *School Bells Ringing*

Defining the Mainstream

Talking about the Amish in the Holmes County settlement an hour away from her own, an Ashland Amish woman commented, "We always thought, 'They're Holmes County people, they're higher than us,' but they're common [not so different]." The earliest settlers in the Ashland community moved west out of the Holmes County area because they were concerned about "drift," or increasing worldliness in the settlement. Today, home to the largest settlement of Amish in the world, Holmes and neighboring Wayne County offer challenges to Old Order Amish residents that church-communities in more isolated areas do not face. First, there is the large Old Order population. The *Ohio Amish Directory* lists 183 church districts, 5,275 families, and 24,101 Amish individuals. And the numbers are growing. As the editors of the newest edition of the *Ohio Amish Directory* (Wengerd 2000) note, the previous edition, published in 1996, listed only 156 districts; in the four years between editions, the number of families has increased 12 percent and the number of individuals 20 percent. Moreover, given that the *Ohio Amish Directory* does not include the Swartzentruber churches, the growth is likely much greater.

As population increases, the difficulties of maintaining an agrarian life-style multiply. Land prices have risen steadily, causing increasing numbers of Amish to search for employment off the land in various agriculturally related businesses and in enterprises that cater to the growing tourist presence. Indeed, according to one report, at least 60 percent of the Amish in Holmes County are involved in work off the farm.[1] The "Directory" section of *The Guidebook to Amish Communities & Business Directory* (Garrett 1996) lists a wide variety of Amish-owned businesses in the Holmes County vicinity, including a manufacturer of hydraulic and cable brakes for horse-drawn vehicles, several country stores and bakeries, furniture makers and wood workers, an axel manufacturer, a dealer in chainsaws and logging supplies, and dry goods dealers. The chapter in the *Guidebook* on "Communities" labels the Holmes/Wayne settlement "tourist friendly" (Garrett 1996, 96). Levi Miller (1992, 58) concurs, noting that Holmes County has become the second largest tourist attraction in Ohio and that some Amish families have even started hosting dinners for tourists within their homes.

The growth in the Old Order Amish population has led to disagreements within the settlement and a diversity of lifestyles that are labeled Old Order. Each church-community has chosen for itself where to draw the boundary between the church and the world and how to define non-conformity. From the main body of the Old Order Amish, schisms have resulted in the Swartzentruber Amish, the Andy Weaver Church, Dans Gmee, the Beachy Amish-Mennonites, and the New Order (Kraybill 1994). As Kreps, Donnermeyer, and Kreps note, "These groups differ on many issues, including clothing, use of farm and shop machinery, indoor and outdoor plumbing and other household conveniences, safety devices on buggies, and conditions under which members may interact with the non-Amish" (1997, 28). There are Old Order Amish homes with indoor plumbing, kerosene refrigerators, linoleum floors, and battery-powered living room floor lamps next to Amish homes that have none of these things. While the Swartzentruber Amish do not permit their members to work in town or to work as wage laborers in the regular employ of a non-Amish firm, members of other groups can be found staffing and running businesses that serve a wide variety of commercial needs and Amish and non-Amish clientele. All are devoted to the Anabaptist ideals of their forebears, yet all have realized these differently as they continue to define themselves in opposition to non–Old Order society and to the groups with which they are not in fellowship.

The multiplicity of Old Order Amish identities exacerbates the tendency on the part of many, both Amish and non–Old Order, to look at the different groups and to identify some as more "traditional"—even more "Amish"—than others. This is understandable, for as groups have split from the main body of the Old Order Amish church, they have tended to characterize themselves as keeping more to Anabaptist ideals than the group from which they have broken. Schismatic groups are quick to establish differences between themselves and other church-communities. Less progressive groups often point to what they see as "drift" in the higher church-communities, and more progressive groups chide the lower churches for what they perceive as devotion to "man-made tradition" rather than to true spirituality.[2]

In the Preface to the *Ohio Amish Directory*, the editor, Marvin Wengerd, ends with a plea: "And finally, I would be pleased if somehow the Ohio Amish Directory would help all of us see ourselves more together. Yes, there are differences, and there always will be. God has an interest, though, in having us build bridges, not burning them, *to be repairers of the breach, restorers of paths to dwell in.* (Isaiah 58:12). Jesus said, *"And that they may be made perfect in one, and that the world may know that Thou hast sent me."* (John 17:23)." In Holmes County and vicinity, it is the private Amish schools that offer the best opportunities for bridge building between the different church-communities, or at least for different groups to work together.

Historically, the diverse Amish communities of the Holmes County region came together in opposition to attempts by the secular state to change public education. For example, the first Amish private schools in this large settlement were started in Wayne County as a result of the East Union Board of Education's decision to enforce the 1921 Bing Law, which made school attendance compulsory until age 16. Luthy (1986, 513) notes that, although this was but another step in a campaign by the state of Ohio to strengthen educational standards, "the Amish, who already felt that their children were getting more classroom education than was needed for farming, were getting quite upset with the new law." With a lengthened school year and more years of compulsory schooling, schools were offering more subjects, and as Hostetler and Huntington (1971; 1992, 37) put it, Amish parents objected "to having their children trained for a way of life contrary to their religion."

"The Amish in Holmes and Wayne counties longed for the time when only the basics had been taught—reading, writing, and arithmetic. Some of the bishops and ministers decided that it would be better if the children did not study history, geography, and hygiene. Some of the parents told their children not to study those certain subjects," according to Luthy (1986, 513). Eventually, faced with the charge of neglect, the Old Order Amish decided that it would be better to have their children study certain subjects than for the parents to lose their parental rights (Luthy 1986; Hostetler and Huntington 1992), and, with that compromise, children returned to public schools.

This was not the end of the conflict, however. In order to avoid having their children attend high school, it became the Amish practice to have children repeatedly enroll in eighth grade until they had reached age 16. With the consolidation of many of the smaller public schools, this became increasingly difficult, and many children just began staying home. In 1944, the East Union Board of Education began to enforce the compulsory education law, and eleven Amish men were ordered to appear in court (Wengerd 2000, xviii). The Amish community responded by forming a committee to develop Amish private schools. In a resolution to the Holmes County Board of Education in 1954, a group of Amish bishops and ministers argued: "We believe that such time spend [sic] in the schoolroom, beyond the eighth grade or the age of fourteen, will often lead to indolence and an inclination for types of work which require less manual labor, without regard for spiritual and sometimes physical welfare; often resulting in becoming entangled with things that are not edifying." The resolution continued, "No parent of our faith shall cause his or her child to attend school of an advanced grade in the Public School System, other than the elementary schools."

Two Old Order private schools opened in the fall of 1944, and by 1958 there were six Amish private schools in Wayne County and another six in Holmes. The Ohio Amish Directory of 2000 lists 130 schools in Holmes, Wayne, Coshocton, and Tuscarawas Counties (cf. Blackboard Bulletin, November 1999). As one teacher noted, "Our forefathers who started these schools had many hard struggles till they had it going. I am sure they did it for the sake of their children and generations to come."

Today schools in this settlement reach a geographically defined population, not one defined by *Ordnung*. They are, according to one Old Order woman, "neighborhood schools, not church schools." The one-room schoolhouses, often with a curtain down the middle to create two classrooms, welcome children from a variety of Amish backgrounds, including Old Order, New Order, Beachy Amish, and Swartzentruber, where they are often taught by a teacher who may be from a different church district or even from a non-fellowshipping group. Fathers from different groups serve together on school boards.

The result, according to one Holmes County mother, is that children know others who dress differently and whose homes are not the same, "but in the school it doesn't really make a difference [. . .] it doesn't matter in making friends." As a Swartzentruber Amish mother affirmed, mixing with Amish children from different churches does not blur the boundaries that separate one group from another. "Everybody's the same in school," she commented. "There was one boy rode a bicycle home. A lazy one [boy]. We used to have neighbors, and they had an indoor bathroom, and we thought it was so easy. It was really easy. But we knew they were different people." Another Swartzentruber woman, whose family was about to move to an area of Holmes County where her son would be one of only two Swartzentruber children in the school, said, "As long as they are all together Amish, it's OK." She added, however, that she wasn't "crazy about the idea" of her son going to school with so few others like him and would be happy after the move if more Swartzentruber families were to move into the area.

As one Holmes County woman put it, "It's attitude that matters. Some want more things; others think it's [a potential change or policy] not spiritual. But they can all get along. It's attitude." A Swartzentruber teacher, none of whose students are Swartzentruber, said, "You are right about no[ne of] our kind of people going there in my school. Yes, there are about two different kinds of Amish. I can't really say that it affects my teaching. Of course sometimes they would want to do some things, but they know that I'm not allowed to so they don't say much." She noted further about board members and parents: "We work with each other and try to keep working together. So far we didn't have any trouble about that [church differences]." Disagreements such as those that led Swartzentruber parents to build the River View School are rare.

In the heterogeneous Old Order Amish world of the Holmes County area, Old Order private schools define a middle road, reflecting no particular Old Order church-community. They are not as progressive as the most progressive communities would like, nor are they so progressive that they cannot serve the children of the most conservative groups. At the same time, while they do not always offer all the subjects more progressive parents might wish for, they are not so conservative that parents in more progressive communities will not enroll their children.

Old Order schools in the Holmes County area allow Amish parents to ensure that education remains like it was before school consolidation. Nevertheless, simply because Old Order private schools serve only the Old Order, however diverse they may be, some Amish parents have declined to enroll their children. Levi Miller (1992, 28–29) asserts that "many older Amish regret that public schools did not maintain their smallness and usefulness to the Amish. Although the Amish want to maintain their own ways, they do not want to be cut off from their non-Amish neighbors." In the Holmes County area, many Old Order families have, in fact, chosen not to take their children out of the public schools. The most recent *Ohio Amish Directory* suggests that a third of the Old Order Amish in the Holmes County vicinity continue to send their children to local public schools, some of which have predominantly Amish enrollment. Indeed, over half of the students in the East Holmes School District are Amish, and the district has maintained a number of smaller "Amish" elementary schools that Old Order children attend until they leave school after eighth grade (Miller 1992). One member of the East Holmes School Board notes that six schools have a predominantly Amish student body, and one of these is maintained entirely by the Amish community, although the East Holmes School District supplies the faculty.[3]

Because teachers in these public schools must be accredited and meet state standards, and because these schools use the same texts as other public schools in the district, Amish children who attend these schools receive an education comparable to that received by their non–Old Order peers attending other public schools in the district. As a result, the public schools continue to influence the private ones. As they have evolved in the Holmes County area, the Old Order Amish private schools are mainstream in the most basic sense of the word. They do not aim to be different from the public schools so much as they aim to provide a basic education similar to that offered by the public schools in a way that reflects the commonalities of Old Order Amish life and supports Old Order and values.

Schools Grounded in the Past but Adapting for the Future

An East Holmes School Board member observed that there was sometimes tension between younger parents who wanted to send their children to public schools and older members of the community. Younger parents were concerned, she suggested, that their children acquire the education they would need to work in an increasingly industrial environment.[4]

To meet the needs of a diverse student population and at the same time ensure that children in private schools receive a basic education comparable to the one they would get in public schools, Old Order educators in the Holmes County vicinity have defined private school education in such a way that it is like public education but different. In other words, while the subject matter remains similar to that of the public schools, the Old Order schools provide a context in which these subjects can be presented in an Old Order way, in an atmosphere that, ideally, reinforces common Old Order values of humility, cooperation, and obedience and eschews worldly values of competition and delight in individual achievement. In this way, children will have the book knowledge to engage the world economically as well as the values to be strong members of their Old Order communities.

The private schools that prepare Holmes County area Old Order children for the future are grounded in the past yet adaptable to the changing demands of the present. For example, many of the private schools in the area were one-room country public schools bought by the Amish as the buildings were vacated in school consolidation. The Millersburg School near Mt. Hope in Holmes County is an old building built of glazed yellow cinder blocks, with a cellar that houses the wood-burning furnace. Remodeled in the summer of 2002 so that the classroom could be separated with a curtain, it now features slanted dry-erase boards instead of the old blackboards. The desks are bolted to the floor, and there are outhouses at the edge of the schoolyard, but the playground offers a softball diamond, a swing set, and a volleyball net. Many of the children ride bicycles to school and park them by the cellar door. The Forest View School nearby, built in 1937, is a two-story yellow brick structure with a furnace in the basement and indoor plumbing. The large main classroom on the first floor is divided into two smaller classrooms with a curtain, but for several years a special education class has met in a basement room. There is a shed in the back for horses but also a basketball court, a softball diamond, a swing set and seesaw, and a large wooden ship with a yellow slide off one side built for the children to play on.

As more schools are needed, communities have built them to meet general community specifications. The Crossroads School, built in 2000, offers an example of new school architecture: wood with vinyl siding, no indoor plumbing, a wide and airy classroom that, if necessary, can be divided with a curtain into two smaller classrooms, and a large basement in which children can play when it rains. The desks are arranged in rows facing the teacher's desk. Children in each grade sit together, although the desks of first graders may be next to those of eighth graders.

Old Order schools began by preserving what school consolidation threatened to take away. Initially, schools used the same texts as the public schools and relied on the same teaching schedule and pedagogical practices. In contrast to Swartzentruber schools, which over time have narrowed the curriculum and now offer only phonics, reading, spelling, penmanship, arithmetic, and German, the majority of Holmes County area Old Order private schools continue to offer the curriculum set forth in "The Education Program" outlined by the *Minimum Standards for the Amish Private or Private Elementary Schools of the State of Ohio* (hereafter *Ohio Minimum Standards*):[5]

The graded course of study shall consist of the following subjects:
a. The language arts including reading, writing, spelling and English.
b. Mathematics.
c. Geography and History.
d. Health and safety rules.
e. German writing, reading and spelling.
f. Vocal music.
g. The English language should be spoken at all times by the teacher and pupils while school is in session, except in German classes. (Buchanan 1967, 233; Hershberger n.d. 4)

Once public, one-room schoolhouses still serve Old Order students in the Holmes County region. These scholars have a basketball court, a ball field, and a Noah's Ark jungle gym. Behind the school are swing sets.

The *Ohio Minimum Standards* ranks the subjects in order of importance: "reading, writing, spelling and English," and notes further that "reading is [. . .] one of the most important subjects in our schools today, and should be stressed as such," while "mathematics will be the subject most extensively used 'in adult years'" (Buchanan 1967, 239; Hershberger n.d., 8).

Still, the curriculum varies from school to school as school communities decide to add other subjects. One school, for example, recently added health. One of the teachers explained, "This year was the first term we taught 'Health.' We asked the board if they think it would be OK to teach Health and get the books. They agreed that if we think it's something useful, or something we would enjoy teaching, we can go ahead and get it." At this particular school, children study arithmetic, English, penmanship, reading, vocabulary, spelling, health, German, and "a little geography," a curriculum common to many of the schools in the Holmes County vicinity.

The *Ohio Minimum Standards* also guarantees that "no parents or guardians shall be obligated to have their children taught the elements in these subjects that are conscientiously opposed" (Buchanan 1967, 239; Hershberger n.d., 8). Although the above school added health to the curriculum, students do not cover the chapter in their text on human reproduction. Similarly, children at a school in Wayne County, near the Holmes County border, do not study geography or health because the teacher, a member of a Swartzentruber Amish church-community, will not teach these subjects.

Textbooks and pedagogy reflect the community's belief that schools play a key role in preparing children for the future. For example, the majority of Old Order Amish in the Holmes County region appear to feel that the quality of textbooks signals concern not only for schooling but also for child rearing. Writing to a counterpart in Ashland, one Holmes County teacher argued that up-to-date textbooks and other teaching materials are important because "the less quality material a school has, like out-dated workbooks or the teacher not having the material she needs, the more likely it is that the pupils are misbehaved to the extent of being rude."

Having "up-to-date" textbooks, however, does not simply mean having the most recently published. It means rather having the "best" or most suitable books for an Old Order audience, for the values expressed in the materials are far more important than the date or even the coverage of particular topics. Some Old Order parents, for example, have considered history to be an unacceptable subject for Old Order schools "on the grounds that there is too much glorification of war in the history textbooks of today." As Old Order writer and teacher, Uria R. Byler asserted, "There are many books on the market that are almost worthless, from the standpoint of what we want our children to learn."[6]

Although the texts used vary from school to school, many are using books supplied by Old Order presses. The *Pathway Readers*, for example, are found in all the Holmes area private schools, as are the Pathway workbooks and vocabulary books. In some schools, geography and health texts replace the readers in the upper grades. The Strayer-Upton arithmetic workbooks, published by the Gordonville Print Shop, continue to be found in a number of schools, although Schoolaid's Spunky books are widespread in first and second grades, and a number of schools are replacing Strayer-Upton with the *Study Time Arithmetic* series, which was designed for use with the Spunky books and is published by Study Time Publishers, an Old Order Amish publishing firm in Topeka, Indiana.

One teacher in a school using many Gordonville publications expressed

her wish that all the books be from Study Time, an Old Order Amish publisher, or Rod and Staff, a conservative Mennonite press. She noted that
her sister was using Rod and Staff texts in her school and was very pleased
with them. However, the most conservative Amish groups generally reject
Rod and Staff texts for use in the classroom because they feel the texts are
too overtly religious. Several teachers noted, for example, that Rod and
Staff emphasized the lives of missionaries in the geography texts. Nevertheless, the religious tone of the Rod and Staff books does not appear to
pose a problem for most Holmes area teachers, perhaps because the largest Old Order Amish church-community is involved in mission work and
cooperates to a limited degree with Mennonite aid groups. Currently, for
example, several Old Order Amish teachers in the Holmes County area are
involved in training Old Colony Mennonite teachers in Mexico, a number having gone to Mexico to work with teachers during the summer.[7]

Many schools augment the "book curriculum" in a variety of ways. One
school, for example, had a working beehive in the school, sandwiched between pieces of glass so that children could watch the honey bees leave
and return to the hive and make and store honey. Often in good weather
teachers take students on "nature walks" that not only allow schools to
transcend the physical space of the schoolhouse and enter into the community but also give children the opportunity to apply classroom lessons
to the outside world.

The blurring of boundaries between school space and community space
works in both directions. In contrast to the Swartzentruber Amish, who
mark the boundary between school and community by language use, one
Holmes area school has "German Day" on Fridays, when students, required to use only English during the rest of the school week, are allowed
to talk German during recess. Another teacher, anxious both to draw on
the expertise of the community as a resource and to involve parents further
in the schoolroom, asked the fathers of his school children to take turns
coming into the classroom and speaking for 15 minutes to an hour on a
subject of their choice. Among the topics presented one year were wood-
working, health, Down's syndrome, the Hochstetler Massacre, planets,
weather, the old *Alice and Jerry* books (used to discuss the need for obedience), and the celebration of Easter in different countries.

Other activities emphasize creativity in a way that the schools of less
progressive groups do not. For example, there are different kinds of stu-

dent artwork on the walls, such as food group mobiles, name charts, and charts for spelling.[8] Charts are often more elaborate than those found in the Somerset, Fredericktown, or Ashland schools. At one school, for example, under the motto "Fill Up the Bank with Good Reading," students had colored pictures of piggy banks to serve as their reading charts. First-graders at the same school glued on Cheerios to outline brightly colored yellow stars.

One of the early compromises reached as a result of the compulsory education laws was the agreement that the Amish private schools would hold vocational classes through which students who had completed eighth grade but had not yet turned 16 would fulfill the state's requirement. They would attend school for three hours a week and keep a journal of their studies, which would be available for inspection by school authorities. This practice has gone by the wayside. In the Holmes County area, as in the schools of the smaller settlements in Fredericktown and Ashland and in the Swartzentruber schools, children attend school until they have satisfactorily passed the eighth grade and are 14 years old (Wengerd 2000).

Students who have completed eighth grade but are not yet 14 generally remain in the classroom as "teacher's helper" until their fourteenth birthday. As one teacher put it in describing her students for the coming school year, "And then there is one of the last year eighth grade girls that has to go till October 11, as she is not quite 14 yet. They are supposed to go till they are 14. But those usually just work arithmetic, then help hands [go around to children whose hands are raised to answer their questions]. That sure helps a lot out."

A Good School

The section on "The Amish Private School Movement" in the *Ohio Amish Directory* ends with an expression of thankfulness to God "for the privilege of having our own schools" and a plea that "we be faithful to conduct our schools in a manner which will prepare our children to be a benefit to God and our communities" (Wengerd 2000, xviii). In his study of Amish and Conservative Mennonite education in Ohio, Thomas Newcomb (1986) reports that parents saw public schools to be weak because of the lack of religious instruction, discipline, and parental involvement. Holmes County teachers today continue to see the primary difference between the private schools and the public schools as one of "attitude." "Public schools are very different from private schools," one teacher said. "I believe a lot is their attitudes. There is a lot more mockery and such in the public schools."

Considering the private schools to be characterized chiefly by different attitudes allows individual teachers greater freedom in pedagogy and material covered, and thus, as one teacher put it, "schools are all different or schools vary from one place to another." Another teacher, commenting on why he enjoyed visiting schools, noted that he liked "to see the different ways of going about to achieve the same goal."

In testimony before the Ohio Legislative Service Commission "Amish School Study Committee" on November 22, 1960, Uria R. Byler, an Amish school teacher from Geauga County, Ohio, argued that "the term 'adequate education' is not a narrow term, under which all the American children must be educated to become useful citizens. [. . .] the Amish minimum standards were also formulated [. . .] to provide instruction to the Amish community of Ohio that would prepare the Amish child for its particular way of life. It is absurd to insist that there is only one system that can produce an adequate education, regardless of religion, creed, or occupation" (in Buchanan 1967, 230–31).

Private schools in the Holmes County vicinity reflect community concerns that they not abdicate responsibility for providing children an adequate education—that is, an education that will reinforce the teachings of home and church, prepare children to earn a living, and instill in children the discipline and devotion that will enable them to be good church members.[9] For example, at one school, a large room divided into two smaller classrooms, a "Welcome Back to School" bulletin board display in the classroom in which first graders sit presented the alphabet with each letter offering pertinent advice:

A—Always choose right.	O—Obey your teachers.
B—Be honest.	P—Play fair.
C—Come on time.	Q—Quietly do your work.
E—Enjoy your lessons.	R—Respect others.
F—Finish your work on time.	S—Sit and stand straight.
G—Give joy to others.	T—Take turns.
H—Help one another.	U—Use your time wisely

With a new "dry erase" board at the front of the classroom, a phonics flip chart, pictures, and mobiles, children in the lower grades of this two-room Holmes County school have much to draw their attention.

I—In games, join in.
J—Joyfully sing.
K—Keep trying.
L—Listen carefully.
M—Make friends with everyone.
N—Never cheat or mock.

V—Visit kindly.
W—Welcome visitors.
X—Examine your work.
Y—Yield to the ways of others.
Z—Zealously do your work.

Children in the classroom housing older grades were greeted by a "Welcome Back to School" sign that listed five rules for classroom behavior:

1. Remember the Golden Rule.
2. Use language that pleases Jesus.
3. Leave school only with permission.
4. English is required at all times.
5. Sharpen pencils and use restrooms at recess.

Similar charts in other schools reinforce the same messages: children are to work hard, be disciplined, and treat others fairly.

"True education, according to the Amish, is 'the cultivation of humility, simple living, and resignation to the will of God'" writes Hostetler (1975, 106). Emphasizing discipline, moral values, cooperation, obedience, and *Gelassenheit*, or the "yielding to others," a key virtue in Old Order life, charts such as these explicitly tie schoolwork to values shared by all the Amish churches in the community.[10] The message is further reinforced in pedagogy, teacher cooperation, and parental involvement.

Most schools in the Holmes County area, for example, have two teachers, and as one teacher noted, "With more than one teacher we have to work together. Communication is very important." Another teacher said that she and her co-teacher meet together before the students arrive to "decide who will pick songs, who will help the upper graders play, and who will help the lower graders play and things like that. We try to be outside at all times and help them play if possible." In the classroom, teachers eschew rote learning and memorization, relying on questions to encourage students to arrive at the correct answers. For example, reading a Bible story to the class at the beginning of the school day, the teacher paused frequently to ask questions about events in the story. Another teacher, working with a third grader, encouraged him to sound out words. He was the only child in the reading class, and the teacher took turns with him as they read through the assignment.

In the eyes of most Old Order Amish, discipline and order help to define "a good school." Indeed, the *Ohio Minimum Standards* recommends "that the teacher's attitude shall be one favoring strict discipline. No school can be successful if discipline is lax" (Buchanan 1967, 236; Hershberger n.d., 3). The "Rules for a Good School," compiled by school children from an Old Order Amish school in Sugar Creek (Holmes County), Ohio, and sent to the *Blackboard Bulletin* in 1965, stress what pupils should and should not do. According to the list, pupils should not

1. Whisper in time of school.
2. Turn around in their seats.
3. Slam their books and make loud noises.
4. Have paper lying on the floor.
5. Run to class.

6. Copy from another pupil's work.
7. Sharpen pencils in time of school.
8. Have their feet out in the aisle.
9. Sit and Watch Visitors.
10. Run in the school room.
11. Laugh when they are reading.
12. Stand up and look out of the windows.

On the other hand, they should

1. Be kind to one another.
2. All help sing.
3. Play together and not argue or fight.
4. Sit up straight in our seats.
5. Be friendly to visitors.
6. Walk along the aisles, and not through the seats.
7. Read aloud in class.
8. Never cheat.
9. Write neatly and not scribble in their books.

Clearly, these lists do not emphasize mastery of particular subject matter, nor do they speak to the importance of the work itself. Similarly, a list of teacher's duties defines a pedagogy, a way of teaching, that is focused on attitude in teaching rather than subject matter. The teacher should simply ·

1. Live by the Golden Rule.
2. Treat the children all alike.
3. Punish a child if he cheats.
4. Make pupils behave, but not be too rough.
5. Be kind, happy, and joyful.
6. Try to get the pupils on her side.
7. Explain the lessons to the children.
8. Help the children play.
9. Try to do things to please the children.
10. Not get "mad."
11. Give rewards for good grades.

12. Teach the children to do what is right.

13. Have rules. [11]

Emphasizing not only the importance of discipline but also the importance of discipline undertaken in the proper spirit, one teacher commented, "A quiet orderly classroom is a must for children to study effectively. That is not always easy to acquire. I experienced that if I do not discipline with love, the results are rarely positive." Despite the warning expressed in the *Ohio Minimum Standards* that "no teacher, regardless of his or her other qualifications can be considered a successful teacher if discipline is lacking and the school allowed to become disorderly. Therefore, the saying of Solomon, 'Spare the rod, and spoil the child,' should apply to all teachers" (Buchanan 1967, 238; Hershberger, n.d., 7), his co-teacher (and former pupil) suggests that discipline in their school is seldom corporal:

> When the children need discipline, we usually have a good talk with them somewhere away from the rest. We usually try to explain to them why we need to punish them, what they did wrong, what would happen if nobody ever punished them, and so on. [. . .] After that some have to keep their head on their desk for a recess period or such. It is the best to do something about such a problem right away, and not wait till it's so big that you're afraid to do something about it yourself.

Another teacher expressed similar aversion to corporal punishment: "I did not have much teasing in school this term. Can always be thankful for that. Those who misbehave I usually make stay in recess or noon. Or sometimes make them stay after school."

Ultimately, the child's mastery of the subject matter appears to be less important than his acquisition of good work habits and good moral character. It is not common for children to repeat grades. According to one teacher, "a passing grade is 69 percent. The students that have to repeat a grade, that's if they don't have good scores all the way through or don't understand their lessons good that you think they couldn't do their next grade. I passed all my students this term. If I would have one that I would think isn't ready for the next grade, I would talk to their parents about it and see how they feel. [. . .] If they would want to try it in the next grade I would do so." As in other Old Order schools, grades are given for achievement only. Classes are too small to be graded on a curve, and students are not evaluated against each other, for this would lead to unacceptable competition for grades. At the same time, it is effort that matters (see also Hostetler and Huntington 1992, 83).

Acknowledging the centrality of schools to the training of children for adult life means ensuring that all children receive an education. In these schools, not only do parents and teachers accept that some children are "harder to learn" than others, but they also feel the need to provide them with a learning environment suited to their needs. Therefore, a number of Holmes County area schools provide regular "special education" classes.[12] As one teacher put it, "If students have a problem with English or some other subject, sometimes we just give [them] an English book on a lower level or a grade behind. Yes, if they can't keep up with that, that's where special ed. comes in." Children are evaluated by the public schools for inclusion in the special education program. Three board members make arrangements for the special education classes. Once a child has been admitted to the special education program, the board members arrange for his transportation to a school with a special education class.

Parents and teachers have been concerned that children placed in special education classes not be isolated from their peers. In his address to the Special Needs Session at the 1999 Teachers' Meeting held in Aylmer, Ontario, Pathway Publishing founder and former teacher Joseph Stoll asserted that "the term 'normal' should be understood to mean—just as God made you. 'Special needs' pertains to everybody. Every child has special needs, but also has basic needs that should not be neglected. These are the need to be accepted, loved, and be made to feel a part of. [. . .] Special children can be special blessings. The level of needs are different."[13]

One teacher explicitly acknowledged the difference in a booklet he handed out to visitors to his special education classroom. Containing the names of the pupils for that term, it also features a poem entitled "Our School" that reads, in part,

> *Some people think these special ones*
> *Cannot be taught a thing,*
> *They think they are quite stupid*
> *And don't know anything.*

Dear Friends you do not realize
How much these children know,
For they quite often understand
But they are very slow.

In this teacher's special education classroom, as in others in the Holmes County vicinity, the special education children sit with their grades for events involving the entire school, including morning devotions, singing, prayers before the noon meal, and recess. The rest of the day is spent in the special education classroom, where the school day begins with a Bible story and exercises. There is, another teacher notes, "usually no problem to get them mixed in with the other children in games. [They receive] discipline, same as any other child."

Special education classes are labor intensive and thus more costly than regular classes. To help defray the expense, one special education teacher sells a coloring book of freehand drawings made by students in the class. "My goal," says this teacher, "is to teach them [his special education students] good morals, happy carefree days, so they can look back on their school years and say I enjoyed my school years."

The School and the Community

Standard three of the *Ohio Minimum Standards* outlines a system of school administration in which each school district and, in practice, each school[14] is to be administered by a board of three or five elected members. Also, to record business transactions, each board must have a clerk, either as one of the members or as a nonvoting participant in board activities. Defining eligible candidates for office and eligible voters as "members of the church of the respective school district," the *Ohio Minimum Standards* leaves it up to the voters in each district to set the length of the board members' terms of office. In contrast to the practice in Swartzentruber communities and in the smaller, homogeneous settlements such as Ashland and Fredericktown, ministers in the Holmes County area might serve on school boards "if they have scholars going in that school."

School boards are held responsible for hiring teachers, maintaining the schoolhouses, and purchasing needed school supplies. Each board must also set the school tuition and devise the means of raising the money. It must also appoint someone to keep track of school attendance records. Together, the boards are also responsible for electing a school superintendent to advise the private schools.

Yet while school boards administer the schools and pay the bills, teachers generally decide what supplies the school needs. Teachers also inform the boards what workbooks and other single-use books are necessary for the following term, and they may request a change in the textbooks used. In this last, however, while the teacher seems to exercise considerable influence if she chooses to use it, it is the parents who are ultimately in charge. As one teacher put it, "A teacher may make small changes in getting books that she wants. When it comes to major changes, the parents are notified because they have to pay for them." Similarly, another teacher said, "The books belong to the school. If I want new or different books, I have to have permission from the parents before we get them. I let it up to them." Another teacher noted that teachers just ask the board to buy new books, and the board checks with the parents. This particular teacher, expressing the desire to have *Study Time* arithmetic texts for her students, acknowledged sadly that, since the parents had just purchased new Strayer-Upton texts, it would be "kinda dumb to buy new ones."

Although the board and the parents must approve major expenditures, frequent interaction between the board, the teachers, and parents for each school ensures that teachers are generally able to proceed with curricular changes confident of community support. At school board meetings, usually held once a month, teachers have the opportunity to talk about events in the classroom, express opinions on school discipline and other school issues, and lobby the board and parents for necessary funds. According to one teacher, "We have our monthly board meetings. Every other month [we have] parent meetings. Not all schools do the same." Indeed, another teacher noted, "We have parent and board meetings every month at the schoolhouse for both parents [both mothers and fathers attend]. We get to talk with each one individually." According to a third teacher, the school board meets once a month, and parents are welcome although "usually just the fathers come." She added, "That's usually the time they settle up things. I usually get my paycheck. And if something is not going right, we usually bring it up then."

As in schools in smaller, more homogeneous settlements, parents and other community members are also expected to be informally involved in

A fun game of ball reinforces social bonds. Recess brings children outside in all but the most inclement weather. (Ronald N. Wilson Photograph)

the day-to-day life of the school. "Mothers take turns to bring in a hot lunch every month or so," noted one teacher. "Besides that, the parents sometimes drop in to visit for half a day. They show concern and are willing to help drill their pupils at home if they have a problem in math or something." Her co-teacher suggested that "sending a child to school and not going visiting or taking an interest in his work or think[ing] 'now he is in the teacher's hands, now she can take care of him,' is very much like chasing heifers to the back pasture in the spring and not going to check on them until fall. Would a farmer do that? No telling what might happen in that time with them." This same teacher went on to note how "blessed" he felt "with the parent cooperation at our school."

All schools have benches where visitors can sit, charts prominently displayed giving the names of visitors, and guest books. Most teachers have their students sing to welcome strangers. "We had a lot of visitors this term," noted one teacher at the close of the school year. "Quite a few van loads and besides some others."

That parents drill pupils at home, mothers supply regular hot lunches, and visitors are not simply welcomed but expected suggests that in a number of ways the school reflects the larger community in microcosm and reinforces the bonds between individual community members, neighbors, and churches. Sometimes children at one school go off to play ball and have a picnic at another school. "They like to do that," a school visitor noted when she arrived at a neighboring school only to find all the students and teachers gone. Often teachers, sometimes with older pupils in tow, attend classes at another school. One teacher reported, "We went school visiting Monday the 14th. We were in three different schools." Another teacher noted, "We take our 7th and 8th graders to visit other schools for a day. They enjoy that, just to take a look at other people's schools and notice the things they do differently." According to another, writing to a teacher in Ashland, "Something that helps me a lot is visiting other schools. I am sure you would be welcome to bring a vanload to our [Holmes County area] schools to visit. Our schools are far from perfect, but that is what makes them interesting to visit."

Religious without Teaching Religion

Having community members involved in the schools subtly reinforces the values of the different church communities. In his testimony before the Ohio Legislative Service Commission "Amish School Study Committee," Uria R. Byler responded to an assertion that the Old Order Amish had reasons other than religion for establishing their own schools by asking whether "anyone can conceive of any other reason for undertaking a project as expensive as establishing and maintaining a school if it were not the powers of religious conscience." He went on to assert that it was "a matter of religious conscience on the part of the Amish in which we sincerely believe that we can train our children better for our way of life, better in our schools than in any other school" (Buchanan, 1967, 231–32).

Although the schools are grounded in religious conscience, the teaching of religion is frowned upon. Perhaps in part because they must accommodate children from different church-communities, the Holmes County area Old Order schools leave religious instruction for the church and the home.

Even in these schools, however, there is more overtly religious and moralistic instruction than in the schools of less progressive groups, such as the Swartzentruber Amish or the Fredericktown and Ashland communities. The school day begins with devotions. At one school, the teachers began the day with a roll call and memory verse recitation. Students then lined up, the boys on one side and the girls on the other, and sang an English song similar to those one might hear in mainstream Sunday schools. Following the singing, the children returned to their desks in an orderly fashion in order of age, and one of the teachers read them a Bible story. Children then stood by their desks to recite the Lord's Prayer in German. Another school alternated English singing from the *Let's Sing* book with German singing from the *Liedersammlung*.

Moreover, although there is no lecturing about theology, moral values are omnipresent in the lessons and the classroom. For example, in his eighth grade health lesson, one teacher gave his students situations such as this: "One Sunday afternoon all the boys decide to go swimming in the pond. What about Ezra, who has a wooden leg? What should you do?" The point was to discuss how the children could make "a handicapped person feel welcome." The ensuing discussion focused on "doing what God wants." In this same classroom, the teacher had hung a poster of a painting by "invalid Amish Artist Sarah Weaver" that depicts the "way of decision" or the wide path to destruction and hell and the straight and narrow path to paradise. The Golden Rule is ubiquitous on Holmes County schoolhouse walls.

In this school, as in nearly all Holmes County area schools, children follow Mrs. Norman Kauffman's *Bible Theme Memory Course*, a graded sequence of booklets for Bible verse memorization. Although not offering religious instruction as such, the lessons offer Bible verses (in both English and German) and poems that highlight particular behaviors or values to be cultivated. Each booklet begins with a message to "Dear boys and girls," telling children in first grade, for example, that "God wants us to memorize Bible verses! [. . .] We cannot think about God's Word just anytime unless some of it is memorized." Eighth graders are asked: "Have you ever stopped to marvel how wonderfully God created you with a mind that is able to memorize and store up knowledge? And what is better to store in your mind than Bible verses? A verse such as 'Thy word have I hid in mine heart that I might not sin against thee' teaches the valuableness [*sic*] of memorizing. Think of it [. . .] having Bible verses buried in your mind will give you strength that you may 'not sin against God.' How wonderful!" Having successfully completed each lesson, children color the picture for that page. First graders are encouraged to "do your very neatest in coloring these pages and you will have a valuable keep-sake to look at, and enjoy in later years!" There is little discussion of the memory course lessons, but children are expected by the end of each week to be able to recite the assigned verse, and their success at Bible verse memorization is noted in charts on the wall, along with their spelling and arithmetic scores.

The Teachers

The *Ohio Minimum Standards* recognizes that "the teacher is the hub on which the entire school revolves" and emphasizes the importance of choosing teachers with "first of all, good Christian character" (Buchanan 1967, 235; Hershberger n.d., 3). In talking about their decision to teach, instructors often give religious motives. A special education teacher writes, "God led me into the regular classroom to get me ready to teach his Special Children now." Another notes, "It takes a lot of prayer and guidance to be a teacher, and see all the innocent little feet that follow you whenever told to do so. I often pray as David did in Psalm 144:12 'that our sons may be as plants grown up in their youth: that our daughters may be as corner stones, polished after the similitude of a palace.' With God's help nothing shall be impossible."

An early editorial in the *Blackboard Bulletin* argues that "teaching is not a job. It is a calling. A job is for earning money. Pity the school that has a teacher who is there for that purpose. Of course, teachers must eat. And their families eat, too. And wear clothes, and have doctor bills, and rent to pay. But a Christian teacher accepts his or her salary for what it is—a means of paying expenses. He does not consider it as his objective in teaching. He feels it is entirely the responsibility of the school board to see that he is paid a fair wage."[15]

Holmes County area teachers, like their counterparts in Swartzentruber communities and in more isolated, homogeneous settlements, did not apply for their teaching positions. Rather, they were asked by school board members. Their wages, which are considerably higher than those paid teachers in Swartzentruber schools, remain less than what many could earn working in other businesses. One teacher, now in her second year of teaching, earns $400.00 a month. Male teachers earn more. As in other communities, if the teacher is not yet 21 years old, his or her father will negotiate the salary with the school board.

Unlike their Swartzentruber counterparts and many of the teachers in the smaller, homogeneous Old Order communities, the majority of Holmes County area teachers receive some training before entering the classroom. They are encouraged by the *Ohio Minimum Standards* to do so, for, as the *Ohio Minimum Standards* points out, "While the formal education of a teacher need not be carried further than the eighth grade, a self-imposed course of research in the school's accepted subjects is necessary to provide and maintain that 'margin of knowledge'" (Buchanan 1967, 238; Hershberger n.d., 7).

Teachers' Meetings are held every fall prior to the start of the school year. Holmes County area teachers participate in the Ohio State South District Teachers' Meeting, which, as noted earlier, drew 670 participants in 2002.[16] One teacher reported that she had only attended once, when they had one for beginners. As she described the meetings, "They just start in just a little like other schools. They [. . .] have two teachers there. They explain [to] you a little how to do things, explain a little how to work some things. We also had recess and noon [break]." Emphasizing how overwhelming she found the experience, she added, "I really don't remember how it all was." Other teachers attend these larger meetings regularly.

In addition to the large teachers meetings, area teachers gather frequently both to share ideas about teaching and to socialize. One teacher noted that "the teachers sometimes get together to get things ready for the next term." Later she reported that "we had a teachers quilting. [. . .] There were 24 teachers and we got 2 quilts out. It was very interesting."

Private School Education and the Larger World

Some parents continue to send their children to public schools for financial reasons or because, with a predominantly Amish population, the schools remain sensitive to Amish values. For other parents, however, sending children to public school may be an easier way of confronting the diversity of Old Order life in Holmes County. In public schools, Amish children can see that non-Amish children are different and can understand that because they are not Amish they will have a different lifestyle. The boundaries of the church-community are daily reinforced. It is harder for Amish parents to explain to their children in private schools why they cannot do nor have the same things as their classmates who also identify as Amish. Certainly, in the early days of the Old Order private school movement, keeping children away from their non–Old Order peers was not a primary concern for many parents. Asked whether having companions who were not of the Amish faith was a good reason to keep children out of public schools, more than 60 percent of parents said no (Buchanan 1967).

That so many of the Holmes area Amish children are in public schools exerts pressure on the private schools to offer a comparable education. Many parents feared sending their children to the Old Order private schools at first because they were concerned that "no matter how much they [the schools] were spiritually motivated, [they] might not give their children a sound basic education through the first eight grades" (Buchanan 1967, 134–35). Holmes County area parents are aware that their children, if they remain in the area, will likely be earning a living outside the immediate boundaries of the church-community because the scarcity of land threatens the agricultural basis of Amish life. Schools must prepare children to participate in a world in which they might well be hourly wage earners and not farmers, a world in which, increasingly, the routine of their daily lives is not very different from that of their non-Amish neighbors, and in which innovation, technological change, and the reaction to both will likely yield new definitions of what it means to be Old Order Amish.

The majority of Holmes County area church-communities have come to see connections between themselves and the larger Anabaptist world. For example, a number of Holmes County area Amish, including some Amish schoolteachers, are actively working with Old Colony Mennonite Support (Baltic, Ohio) and Mexico Mennonite Aid (Nappanee, Indiana) to support agricultural projects and assist in education in Old Colony Mennonite communities in Mexico. Others work with joint projects of Mennonite Christian Aid, while others have joined with Amish across Holmes, Wayne, and Tuscarawas Counties to sponsor projects as Hoffnung Heim, a shelter for those needing psychiatric and counseling help.

Although not all Holmes County area Amish church-communities are involved in such projects, the main body of Old Order Amish demonstrate a willingness to be involved in efforts that realize and put into practice Old Order religious values, even when these projects take them outside their community or bring outsiders in.[17] As one Amish teacher wrote upon returning from Mexico, "Often I must think, what if I was born in this very setting. I should be thankful for what we have and help where I can."

At the same time, the main group of Old Order Amish, although in fellowship with the large Old Order Amish settlements of Michigan and Indiana, live as neighbors with those who have broken away to establish their own church-communities, some more progressive and some less. Crowded together in the largest area of Amish settlement, these Amish interact with the non–Old Order world but are grounded in Amish communities that must constantly reassert their boundaries. While striving to meet the educational standards set by the public schools, the Old Order private schools provide a place in which all Amish children, regardless of church affiliation, can come to learn. Teachers and school board members of different backgrounds work together and make compromises for the sake of their children, and their decisions about curriculum, pedagogy, and even the art on the walls reinforce common Old Order values while preparing children to face a world in which the values are different.

In defining the middle ground and remaining flexible and open to the needs of different church groups while upholding educational standards, the Holmes County area schools have established a set of educational practices that diverse groups are able to accept. As a result, the Holmes County area Old Order Amish schools have become central to shaping the settlement's survival.

CHAPTER 6

Progressive Amish Schools

One of the greatest advantages of our own school system is . . .
our children will be learning Christian morals in between lines.
—JOHN M. BORNTRAGER, "The Challenge Before Us"

Redefining Community Boundaries

L ike many of their Old Order counterparts in Holmes County, the Old Order Amish in Centreville, Michigan, and Elkhart and La-Grange Counties in Indiana face a world in which their children are as likely to work as wage laborers as farmers. This is an affluent region. As in Holmes County, many in the Centreville and Elkhart-LaGrange settlements operate businesses that provide a non–Old Order clientele with a variety of goods and services, including appliance sales and repair, vinyl products, wood finishing, and taxidermy. Others work in factories where, side by side with non–Old Order employees, they can earn annual salaries of $30,000 and more.

Yet the Centreville, Elkhart, and LaGrange area communities have responded differently to changing social and economic circumstances than have their counterparts in more conservative church-communities. Their wealth and increased interaction with the non–Old Order world have made them more tolerant of technological innovation and activities often identified by other Old Order groups as "worldly."

The churches in Centreville and the Elkhart-LaGrange area are redefining what it means to be Old Order Amish in ways that are anathema to members of lower church-communities. According to a retired Centreville teacher, "The last year or so they allowed phones, you can have them right in the shops, just so they're not so handy. They [the church-community] didn't want them [members making phone calls] to keep bothering neighbors. One church had them in the schoolhouse or in shanties at the end of the lane. Now they can have them right in the shop. I don't know of anybody that has them right in the house, although some have voice mail or answering machines." The Centreville churches also allow rubber tires on large wagons such as those used to move the church benches, and several of the districts now allow bicycles. If the Amish family is living in a home belonging to someone who is not Old Order, then the family may have electricity. In the Elkhart-LaGrange area, many of the children now ride bicycles to school, and a number of Old Order church members carry cell phones.

The Old Order schools along the Michigan-Indiana border reflect these changes, offering a curriculum that prepares children to compete economically with their non–Old Order counterparts on a playing field that may be only marginally, if at all, in the Old Order world. Children in Centreville and Elkhart-LaGrange are exposed to a variety of cultures outside the boundaries of their church-communities. Emphasizing the diversity of the world in which they live, one teacher posted a map of the world that announced: "Five-and-a-half billion people live in more than 175 independent countries on six of the seven continents."

As they have come to lead lives very similar to those of their non-Amish neighbors, the Old Order Amish in the Centreville and Elkhart-LaGrange communities increasingly see the world, not in terms of Old Order Amish and non–Old Order Amish, but as Christian and non-Christian. Old Order schools have become Christian schools, and the goal of Old Order Amish education along the Michigan-Indiana border is as much to prepare the child for "a life of Christian discipleship" broadly conceived as it is to ready the child for an Amish life and adult responsibilities, according to the *Regulations and Guidelines for Amish Parochial Schools of Indiana (Indiana Regulations* 2002, 3).

The Old Order private schools in Elkhart-LaGrange and Centreville, unlike those in more conservative communities, bring religious instruction actively and overtly into the classroom to reinforce church teaching. God is the foundation of Old Order education, asserted one Old Order Amish bishop addressing a group of Indiana teachers: "The closer one adheres to God's word and God's principles when administering a system of teaching honor, respect, and discipline, the greater one's probability of success." He added that there is "no neutral position with respect to good and evil. [. . .] Without exception, our allegiance is with one or the other, and this is as true within the classroom as anywhere else. The classroom is no exception."[1]

In short, in these settlements, as Old Order lifestyle grows increasingly similar to that of the non–Old Order world, it is through their identity as Christians that the Old Order distinguish themselves. Public schools are secular, so the Old Order schools have become Christian. As a result, these communities share a sense that schools have an impact beyond the eight years students attend, and that teachers perform work of great importance. As the Amish bishop noted in his address to the teachers, "A teacher's work affects eternity, you can never tell where your influence will end."[2] As one teacher put it, "Religion is the basis of our schools. In order to preserve it for all generations, [our] forefathers started parochial schools. Without the Amish, Christian religion, there would be no parochial school for the area. What is its role? The church builds on it and schools are a branch of the church. It is the vitality of the school."

Overtly religious, the schools of the Old Order Amish in Centreville, Elkhart, and LaGrange are as unlike those of their Swartzentruber counterparts as any public school. In structure, size, curriculum, and expectations for both students and teachers, the Old Order Amish schools of this border region are at the forefront of change in Old Order education.

Community Schools

The Old Order Amish communities along both sides of the Michigan-Indiana border are well established. The first Amish settlers to the Elkhart-LaGrange area came from Holmes County, Ohio, in 1841. Now, of the approximately 18,000 Amish living in northern Indiana, about 15,000 live in the Elkhart-LaGrange area (Kauffman 2002, 9). The first family to settle in the Centreville area, the Jacob Schwartz family, arrived in 1910 from Allen County, Indiana. Today the Centreville and Elkhart-LaGrange settlements are in constant communication with each other.

Invitations to weddings in a Centreville district give "Indiana time" as well as local time, and many of the teachers in the Elkhart-LaGrange area go home on weekends to Centreville.

The first Old Order private school in the Centreville area, the Spring Creek School, opened in fall 1974, with all eight grades and 21 students. School met in a farmhouse until the schoolhouse could be built. The second school in the community, Mountain Top, opened in 1981. Today there are five schools serving the settlement.

Across the state line, the private school movement in the Elkhart-LaGrange settlement had an earlier start. Plain View School, the oldest Old Order Amish private school in Indiana, was established in 1948. Nevertheless, the Amish school movement caught on slowly in Indiana, and the second school, Pleasant Ridge, wasn't established until nine years later.[3] In the next ten years only six more schools were started (J. E. Miller 1995, 14), but in 1967 the number of Old Order Amish private schools doubled when, with the completion of the new Westview High School, all the local public one-room schools in the Westview Corporation closed.[4] As of 2003 there were 45 Old Order Amish private schools in the Elkhart-LaGrange area.

Physically, the Old Order Amish schools in the Centreville area are much like the newer schools in smaller, more isolated settlements like Ashland and Fredericktown. The Pine Trees School, built in the early 1970s, is an "approximately 28′ x 32′ ground level, one story, one room" structure, with hardwood floors, according to the *Michigan Amish Directory 2002*.[5] Pine Trees School is heated by a woodstove at the front of the single classroom; there is no electricity or indoor plumbing, and in the back of the classroom is a sink with a hand pump. Mountain Top School, built in the summer of 1981, is similar, "a single story wooden structure with white masonite siding measuring 28′ by 44′." (A front entryway, which also serves as a cloakroom, was added several years later to meet state requirements mandating particular square footage per pupil (D. Miller 2002, 63). Again, there is no electricity or indoor plumbing, and a woodstove at the front of the single classroom heats the school.

More recently, however, school construction in the Centreville community has become more elaborate. Hill Tops School, built in 1998, has indoor plumbing, and the floor is linoleum. Each desk sits on a piece of carpeting. Although, like the older schools in the settlement, Hill Tops is heated by a woodstove in the main classroom, there are gas lights. There is a basement in which children can play on rainy days, and unlike schools in Ohio or New York, there are quarters for the teachers on the second floor above the classroom. Moreover, unlike many of the schools of less progressive communities, all of the Centreville schools provide students with a playground featuring such equipment as basketball nets, swings, tether ball, merry-go-rounds, and seesaws, as well as a field on which to play ball. In the yard of the Grove School, built in 1982 with gas lights, wood heat, and hardwood floors but no indoor plumbing, the community created a shallow pond on which the children ice skate in winter (D. Miller 2002, 64).

Most Centreville schools are small and are served by only one teacher. Where there are more students, and community members feel that two teachers are needed, they divide the classroom with a curtain drawn down the middle. In the Elkhart-LaGrange area, however, schools with more than one teacher are the rule rather than the exception. Most of the Elkhart-LaGrange schools have large main rooms that, like the larger Centreville schools, can be divided down the middle with a curtain to form two classrooms, and they generally have special quarters in which the teachers live.

With a student body numbering nearly fifty, Tree Top School, built in 1988, is typical. Two teachers, who live in quarters built over the front entryway, divide the large main room with a curtain during lessons but leave it open during devotions, singing, story time, and other events that involve the whole school. Although it has outhouses, the school also has running water for drinking and hand washing. In addition, there is a full basement, which serves as a play area and houses the woodstove that heats the schoolhouse. Outside, there is a large shed in the back to shelter the horses, for most children drive to school by horse and buggy, and as many as eight buggies are parked by the side of the school during the day. The playground features swings and a merry-go-round as well as a net for volleyball.

Both of the Tree Top teachers live at the school, sharing comfortable quarters that provide them with a cooking area with a kerosene stove, a sitting area with two easy chairs, and bedroom space with dressers. There is even a small bathtub (often used to store newly washed dishes so that they can drip dry). The teachers at the nearby Brook School have even more

With state-of-the-art basketball hoop and cement court, children at this Indiana Amish
school don't let snow get in the way of their game. (Photograph by Doris Kauffmann)

luxurious quarters, with a full kitchen featuring a gas stove and refrig-
erator, indoor plumbing, and full-size bathtub. Brook, like Tree Top, has
one large room that is divided by a curtain to make two classrooms. The
building is oil-heated, and the furnace is in the basement near the Ping-
Pong table. Outside, the playground has seesaws, swings, and a basketball
court.

There are much bigger schools as well. One local school board member
in Indiana argues that the ideal school would have four teachers: "They
then would only have two grades to prepare for and would make their
jobs easier, which would make more teacher prospects. Hunting for teachers is not the board's most fun job. Also the [cost of] building [one] school
would not be as high as two small ones. More parents could make it tougher
for the board, but one parent can cause problems, whether you have ten or
thirty." Shady Valley School, built in 1967 near Topeka, Indiana, is one
of the largest, with two large classrooms and a full basement that houses
a third classroom. Again, the teachers' quarters are built over the front

With three classrooms and special quarters for the teacher, this school in Indiana
accommodates over 60 pupils.

entryway, and there is a playground with swings, seesaws, basketball
court, tetherball, and merry-go-round. More than sixty children attend
Shady Valley School, which has indoor plumbing. There is propane heat
in two of the classrooms and oil heat in the third.

School as an Extension of the Church

Although the Elkhart-LaGrange schools are larger than the schools in
Centreville, the similarities between them inside the classroom—in curriculum, teacher training, and role in the community—are obvious. This is
hardly surprising, for the Centreville and Elkhart-LaGrange communities
fellowship with each other and have similar *Ordnungs*. Moreover, many of
the teachers in the Indiana schools come from the Centreville community,
and teachers from both sides of the state line meet together regularly.

Equally obvious, and more striking, are the differences between these schools and those of Old Order communities elsewhere. As in the Old Order schools of Holmes County, the walls of the classrooms in Centreville and Elkhart-LaGrange are filled with student artwork; commercial and handmade posters highlighting arithmetic operations, prepositions, and spelling rules; as well as maps and displays welcoming visitors. There are alphabet charts, always English and sometimes German, over the blackboards.[6] But in contrast to the schools in Holmes County and to Old Order schools in less progressive settlements, there are also numerous, often commercially produced, inspirational posters, banners, and wall displays, challenging students to have a good attitude and extolling the value of learning. At one Centerville school, for example, banners proclaimed, "Attitude is the mind's paintbrush. It can color any situation"; "We can all learn from each other"; and "The most important tool for success is the belief that you can succeed." A LaGrange school bulletin board featured a large bottle of Elmer's School Glue and the motto, "Together We stick, Divided We're Stuck." At a neighboring school, a motto over the stairs leading to the main door exhorted students: "Be responsible. Actions have consequences." Other mottos, some hand-lettered, graced the walls: "Hardships color all of life . . . you choose the colors"; "You'll always miss 100% of the shots you don't take"; and "You're about to enter a learning zone. Only positive attitudes allowed beyond this point." A hand-made wall display in the entryway to the school showed a gingerbread man holding up a steaming kettle, labeled "education," on a platter, with the words, "Welcome to a feast for the mind. Food for thought served here free. All you can eat."

Most striking of all, the school walls in Centreville and Elkhart-LaGrange are overtly Christian. Charts tracking children's progress at Bible verse memorization hang next to those recording 100s on spelling tests. Bible verses are obvious on wall displays. For example, a poster at one school, designed to keep track of the songs that had been sung during the year, featured a musical staff with notes, two singing children, and Psalm 104:33: "I will sing unto the Lord as long as I live. I will sing praise to my God while I have my being."[7] Maps drawn by the children, which located their county and state in the Western hemisphere, were posted under the title, "Our part of God's Great World." On the blackboard at another school, a handmade poster reminded students, "Faith is remembering I am God's Priceless treasure when I feel utterly worthless. God made you as you are in order to use you as he planned." At another school, signs posted on every wall urged children to "Trust in the Lord." At a school in Howe, Indiana, Psalm 23 was posted over the door, and on one wall was a construction paper display of books on a shelf, each with a child's name on the spine, and the motto, "You are writing a Gospel." The accompanying verse challenged students:

> *You are writing a gospel*
> *A chapter each day*
> *By the words that you do*
> *And the words that you say;*
> *Men read what you write,*
> *Whether faithful or true—*
> *Say, what's the Gospel according to you?*

In one LaGrange school, a poster of the Lord's Prayer hung at the front of the room, while at a nearby school a large bulletin board, covered with cut-out pictures of sunrises and lit buildings and hand-drawn pictures of lanterns, flashlights, and cars with headlights blazing, proclaimed, "Jesus is the LIGHT of the world."

Unlike the Old Order Amish schools of the Holmes County, Ohio, area, which reach diverse populations, the schools in Centreville, Michigan, and Elkhart-LaGrange, Indiana, serve populations that are, for the most part, homogeneous. One woman, a member of the Centreville church-community who had taught several years in Indiana, pointed out that, while at least one of the Centreville schools did have some Beachy Amish pupils, and children from both sides of a recent schism still attended school together, the schools in Indiana served one large Old Order Amish community. "I don't think they've ever had a split," she said.[8] An Indiana teacher noted, "At this point in time our 100+ Amish churches all fellowship together here in Indiana." This homogeneity permits schools to reflect church practice and church teachings, a policy actively followed. "School is an extension of the church. And we hope it will be an extension in the home as they [today's students] marry and raise a family," asserted the state chairman of the Indiana committee for Old Order schools.

The Old Order Amish schools in Centreville and Elkhart-LaGrange are Christian schools devoted to reinforcing the lessons of the Bible. One teacher asserted, "The purpose of our schools is to teach the basic subjects, then teach them about Jesus Christ, getting along with your fellow man, lead them towards joining church later, accepting Jesus, and then inheriting eternal life." He added, "That's what we're after." As another teacher put it, "We believe the Bible is the inspired Word of God. It is the only Source of true knowledge. We feel the need of acknowledging the Creator in the schooling of our children." Asserted a Centreville woman teaching in Indiana, "I believe our main goal in having our own schools is to be able to implant more Christian morals into our children, to keep them away from (or being exposed to) the many things which aren't good for body and soul." "I feel religion is very important," noted another Centreville teacher. "To me, the salvation of the soul is primary and academic achievements secondary. It's not that I think lessons are unimportant! . . . But I try to put Christ first in my life—not just at home, but also in my career." Another teacher emphasized the school's role in ensuring that children get a necessary spiritual grounding:

Do we read the Bible and have devotions? Yes. Why? If we expect future generations of our people to be Christians, they must be taught Bible stories and principles. If the fathers leave for the factory at 4:30 a.m., before children arise, when will they get the Bible story? I know they should take time in the evening, many do. Mom should read a story or read the Bible. Yet, way too many times it is left to teachers. It is important that each day begin with Prayer and Devotions. They need to form convictions early in life.

Christian Education with Public School Standards

Old Order private schools keep children away from the evils of the world and reinforce church teachings, but the education they provide must also prepare children to earn a living outside of their church-communities. The curriculum of the Elkhart-LaGrange and Centreville schools reflects the need to prepare children to compete with their publicly educated counterparts.

As set forward in the 2002 *Indiana Regulations*, reading is one of the most important subjects for Old Order schools, and teachers are encouraged to hold reading classes (including phonics in first and second grades) at least four times a week throughout the year. Mathematics is acknowledged to be the subject that Amish children will use most extensively as adults, and teachers are encouraged to teach it four times a week as well. In addition, teachers are encouraged to teach English (including composition) twice a week, writing or penmanship once a week, spelling and geography or history twice weekly (geography one semester and history the next), health and safety twice a week for one semester, and German once a week (*Indiana Regulations* 2002, 10). In a schedule typical of those in Centreville and Elkhart-LaGrange, one school allotted even more time for mathematics, scheduling it during the first period, Monday through Friday. Other schools have incorporated art and Bible verse memorization (see Appendix D). As do schools in Holmes County, these schools use the *Bible Theme Memory Course*, a program designed, according to author Mrs. Norman Kauffman, because "God wants us to memorize Bible verses!" A member of the state board said, "It's good to have Bible verses to learn from memory. A very big asset to get them indoctrinated into their hearts."

The morning schedule for these schools is also standardized. School begins, usually at 8:15 or 8:30, when the teacher rings the bell. The teacher starts the day's lessons by reading a Bible story and asking the children about events in the passage. "Listen," warned one teacher. "You don't know who I'll ask." In one school, for example, after reading the story of Saul and the Ammonites (1 Samuel 8–10), the teacher asked the children "Who did Saul make the head of the army? How did Saul disobey God? Who told Samuel Saul had disobeyed God?" In another school, the morning Bible reading was the same story the eighth graders were studying in German, and the teacher related it to the sermon they had heard in church several Sundays earlier.

Following the Bible reading, all the children stand by their desks and say the Lord's Prayer in either German or English. Afterward, the children sing several songs in English.

Texts to Teach Skills and Values

The texts used in the schools in this region, like the daily schedules, vary little and are similar to those used in other Old Order schools. All use the *Pathway Readers* and the accompanying workbooks and vocabulary books, the Schoolaid *Climbing to Good English* series, the Spunky arithmetic books for first and second grade, *Practical Spelling* (a spelling workbook published locally by Miller School Books in Topeka, Indiana), and the *Pentime* series for penmanship and writing.

The schools vary somewhat in the arithmetic books they use for the third through eighth grades, in part because many of the schools, like those in the Holmes County area, are in the process of changing from the Strayer-Upton texts. In this Indiana-Michigan border region, most schools are adopting the locally produced *Study Time* series one grade at a time as Study Time readies new books. These books, as one teacher put it, are "published by our own people and [are] based on things in our everyday lives."

Unlike the Strayer-Upton texts, the *Study Time* series is clearly Old Order and most definitely Christian. Study Time texts do not overtly teach religion. They do, however, set the study of arithmetic in an Old Order context, intertwining stories of American and Anabaptist history and Old Order culture with the study of numbers. For example, a lesson on subtraction in the grade three textbook asks children a series of questions about events at the Lark Valley School:

> Joe Masts brought a box with 45 popcorn balls for the pupils of Lark Valley School. After the box was passed around, there were four balls left. *How many popcorn balls were taken?*

> The third graders were guessing how old Teacher Dave is. Martha said she thinks he is 35 years old. Levi guessed 42 and Abie guessed 45. Susan said, "I don't think he is that old. I think he is 30." *Teacher Dave said, "My age is the same as four tens and two ones."* Who is right?

In Unit 5 of the seventh grade text, students are told, "Michael Schneider, an Anabaptist, wrote 8 Ausbund hymns while imprisoned in 1535. Later, he wrote 37% more Ausbund hymns." Based on this information, they are asked to find out how many hymns Schneider wrote later and to calculate the total number of hymns Schneider wrote. In a later exercise, students are told, "In 1895, an Amish community was started in Yamhill County, Oregon, growing to 14 families by 1913. Then the bishop, the minister, the deacon, and 4 other families moved to California, followed by 7 more families." Students are asked to calculate the rate of decrease in the Yamhill settlement.

Some schools continue to use the Strayer-Upton texts while slowly phasing in the *Study Time* series; others have simply abandoned them because, as one teacher put it, "The Strayer-Uptons are too hard." A Centreville teacher, noting that "they [*Study Time*] don't have the eighth grade [text] done," reported that she "just uses the sixth [*Study Time*] book now" for the upper grades. Another teacher reported using the *Study Time* books for third and fourth grades and adopting the A Beka mathematics series. "I like A Beka," she said, "they're easier to use and more explanatory." Yet another had turned to out-dated texts from the public schools.

There is also some variation in the texts for geography and history in use in the Centreville and Elkhart-LaGrange schools. Some teachers use Gordonville reprints of texts written for use in public schools. For example, several schools use the Silver Burdett and Ginn Company texts *Old World Lands* and *Our Big World*, first published in 1968, although they may use them for different grades. One school, for example, uses *Old World Lands* for grades six, seven, and eight, while a neighboring school uses the text only for seventh and eighth graders, relying on *Our Country*, a 1965 Laidlaw text reprinted by Gordonville for fifth and sixth grade and *Our Big World* for grades three and four.

The majority of schools, however, are using the A Beka texts, which purport to be "unashamedly Christian and traditional" and to "look at the subject from God's point of view."[9] In one school, for example, although the third grade uses the Gordonville *Starter Geography*, the fourth grade uses A Beka *The History of Our U.S.*, a text that, according to the publisher, "builds character through a study of American heroes, including Pilgrims, patriots, inventors, scientists, teachers, scholars, businessmen, laborers, medical men and women, missionaries, hymn writers, and gospel preachers." The fifth and sixth grades use A Beka's *Old World History and Geography in Christian Perspective*, which provides "a good introduction to worldwide missions and missionary heroes and contrasts Communism and Americanism," while the seventh and eighth grades use A Beka's *New World History and Geography*, which claims to present "the history and geography of North and South America from a Christian perspective."[10]

The emphasis on evangelism and mission in these texts marks an awareness of and outward orientation to the world that is absent in the Swartzentruber and other less progressive schools and is problematic in the Holmes County area schools, which serve a mix of Amish church-communities, some less progressive than others. The widespread use of these texts in the Centreville and Elkhart-LaGrange schools is not surprising, however, for many these communities support outreach programs, often through such agencies as Christian Aid Ministries. One teacher argues that texts that "promote Christian principles" are "EXACTLY what we're looking for. The more scripture the better. We want to plant the Christian Faith in our children when they're young so it sticks for life."

Yet, even as these communities turn outward toward the non–Old Order world in business and Christian outreach, they consciously emphasize German in their schools. Noted one teacher, "We want to have German all year long; I think it's more useful than geography." German reinforces a line between Old Order and non–Old Order that is often blurred in other areas of daily life in these communities, and teachers realize its importance to the survival of the church-community. "We teach German two days a week, usually Tuesday and Friday," noted one teacher. "I feel it's important since that's what we use in church services, so we need to be able to understand what we read." Another asserted: "German is one of the top five reasons that we have our own schools. [. . .] I have German about twice a week. German is almost like the Pennsylvania Dutch we speak, and yet there's a big difference. In our Amish church services, the scripture is read in German and the sermons are a mixture of German, Pennsylvania Dutch, and English in that order. Mostly German. Our songbook, the *Ausbund*, is also German, so German is a big issue in our schools, churches, and homes."

Most schools use a combination of Pathway's *Let's Learn German*, Schoolaid's *German Phonics*, Pathway's *Let's Read German*, and Schoolaid's *Wir Lesen und Sprechen Deutsch*, but there is considerable variation. In one school, for example, *Let's Learn German* is used in third and fourth grades, and *German Phonics* is used in grades six through eight, supplemented with reading from the German Bible. Another school uses *Let's Learn German* in third grade, *German Phonics* in fourth grade, and *Let's Read German* in grades five through eight, supplemented by the workbook *German Exercises* (a Schoolaid text) and readings from the German New Testament. Yet another uses *Let's Read German* for the lower grades, and *Wir Lesen und Sprechen Deutsch* for the upper grades. All of these texts, like those used by the Swartzentruber Amish and in the schools of smaller, more isolated communities such as Ashland, present German in *fraktur* font, but as well, the German in the exercises is presented in standard font, which the Swartzentruber Amish refer to as "German written in English." Unlike the texts used in Swartzentruber schools, these texts also incorporate English to give instructions and translations of vocabulary words.

There are a number of supplemental texts as well. For example, each school has at least one set of encyclopedias and a number of dictionaries for the children to use. Children also have available a number of works for pleasure reading. The library in one school, for example, included a number of titles, not only from Pathway Publishers but also from Scholastic Books and Moody Press, and a variety of popular series, including the *Hardy Boys* and *Cherry Ames* series as well as works by Mark Twain. For the younger children, there was also a large assortment of *Berenstain Bears* books. Another school offered students a similar selection from Pathway, Scholastic Books, and Moody Press as well as classics such as the *Bobbsey Twins* books. Other schools also make use of the services of the local bookmobile.

Teachers play an influential role in choosing the texts for their schools, and therefore think seriously about the books they are using. One teacher, for example, in her first year at a new school, found that the *Helping With English* series she was now using was much easier than the *Climbing to Good English Series* she had taught from at her previous teaching position. "But I notice it in my students," she complained. "They don't have the proper English, and there's not as much writing." "In our school," noted one teacher, "the board would go with what the teacher thinks works best under certain circumstances." Another teacher noted that "if a teacher would rather not teach a certain book, she will present her desire for another book to the board members. They and the parents will then decide if they want to make the change." Yet another described the process of changing texts, noting that "if we feel there should be a change, we'd approach the board with our idea. We are in the process of switching *Helping With English* over to *Climbing to Good English*. We felt the former books were too easy and didn't take any lesson into much depth. After counseling with the school board, we decided to just work up one grade each year, like last year third grade got it and now this year fourth will; that way it's not such an abrupt change."

"As for having a say in which books we use," noted one teacher, "the board at this school feel the teacher knows more about the books than they do and usually agree if a change is suggested, although the final okay or 'go ahead' comes from them."

Training Future Church Members

Pedagogy reinforces both discipline and interaction as members of the larger community. As in the schools in Holmes and Lancaster Counties, teachers rarely just supply answers to pupils who have questions. Instead, as teachers guide their charges to arrive at solutions, a child who asks a question is likely to be answered with another question. One teacher, responding to a first grader who had asked the meaning of the word "sew," asked, "When you get a hole in your clothes, what does Mom do?" Another teacher, going over spelling rules, had the children take turns reading the rules and then supplying words that illustrated them. "Diagraphs," she asked, "Do we divide diagraphs? Larry, you read the last part. What do you think?" After going through all the rules and eliciting examples from the children, the teacher then set them to work, saying, "Okay, let's see if you can get the rest on your own." Prior to beginning a reading lesson, teachers question pupils about events in the story, and many question each student about the passage he or she has just read.

Not even first graders are spared from having to think things through for themselves. In a phonics class, for example, the teacher repeatedly asked the children to make judgments about their vocabulary words: "Frog and log. Do those sound the same?" Another teacher announced to her first-graders "We're going to do something different today." Asking one child to read the sentence at the top of a chart, she then announced that they would put words into columns according to whether the vowel sound was long or short. "Is 'Dave' a long vowel or short vowel?" she asked, and directed the children to fill in the chart. As each child read a sentence, she asked him or her, "Where do you write it?" Another teacher, reading a story to her first grade class, repeatedly stopped to ask questions about what was happening or to ask children about words. "How is 'mouse' like 'house'? What makes them different?"

In all of these subjects there is an emphasis on acquiring skills to use. Arithmetic exercises, for example, present students with problems that deal with real-life situations. As one teacher put it, pointing out that the Study Time texts used in his school had been written by a member of his community, "The story problems are based on farming, shops, greenhouses, etc. that the Amish children are familiar with." In their English work, children not only gain fluency in spoken English but also learn to write proper business letters and other reports. Teachers generally assign topics, and students write and then revise for a final draft.

In some schools, children are encouraged to write to elderly members of their church-communities, with the teachers even assigning the students pen pals, a practice that both helps the students improve their English and binds them more firmly to their communities.[11] "It makes a real tie for the children," noted one former teacher, whose students had had pen pals, "and they don't even realize what it does for the old folks."

This pragmatic approach is also evident in the teaching of German. For example, teachers emphasize translation work, and children are expected to be able to understand what they read and to use that knowledge. Unlike children in Swartzentruber schools or schools in Ashland and Fredericktown, children in Centreville and Elkhart-LaGrange are tested on their productive use of German through vocabulary tests and translation exercises.

Teachers also place considerable emphasis on the children's being able to work alone. Expressing satisfaction with the change her school had made from the Strayer-Upton arithmetic books to the Study Time texts, one teacher noted, "With Strayer-Upton, they [the children] couldn't begin on their own. Now they can begin on their own and have correct answers. They like that."

Accuracy and presentation are also important. A child who mumbles when he reads aloud must generally read the passage again. Children are encouraged to use dictionaries, and they often use a compass or protractor as their arithmetic work demands. Teachers also emphasize correct grammar. Several older girls in one school, preparing a bulletin board with the motto, "As dead leaves ruin a lawn, so bad habits ruin a life," had labeled paper leaves with various bad habits, including "carelessness," "pride," and "poor grammar"; a rake was labeled "diligence."

Many, though not all first graders begin school knowing English. When a first grader doesn't know English, according to one teacher, it makes it "a little tough for them and their teacher! We would explain it in Dutch [Pennsylvania German] too, to make sure they comprehend it." Another teacher noted, "We like if our first graders can speak English when they start school, but it's not always the case." As in other communities, "The more older siblings they have to teach them makes a difference."

School reinforces the role of older children in helping the first graders

Scholars bend over their work. As in all Old Order schools, these Indiana Amish children are expected to do much of their work on their own. (Photograph by Doris Kauffmann)

learn. In one school, for example, each first grader worked with an older student on flashcards to reinforce "word starters," a phonics approach to teaching reading. If first graders cannot understand what the teacher is telling them in English, the teacher will use Pennsylvania German to help them, but she will not use it at all with the older students. As one teacher noted, "We use English on the playground too. I only speak German when I need to."

Teachers as Authorities and Examples

Although teachers generally use the inclusive first person plural in making assignments, they are clearly in charge. Often much older than their charges, many with a number of years of teaching experience, they are also often removed from the immediate community of the schoolhouse. Those who board, for example, usually return to their home communities over the weekend and so are unlikely to attend church with their students. As a result, they are more likely to monitor play on the playground than to join in. One teacher, for example, observing that her students had started to play in same-sex groups only a couple of weeks earlier, noted that she was watching to see what would happen and would "make them play nice if there's a problem."

In these schools, teachers act as authority figures to direct play and ensure that children act as "good sports." Teachers are also expected to ensure that schools are orderly and disciplined. "Sorry to say," noted one teacher, "we've had problems with teasing. [. . .] We prefer talking with the pupil about the misbehavior, but if that fails to bring the needed results, the punishment will be more severe. Writing lines, missing recesses, putting the head onto the desk help them to think it over. We do resort to the paddle if need be and depending on the offense. Not the most exciting job, but it brings amazing results. In my six years I've spanked only once (something I thought I'd never do) and I hope I won't have to again." Another teacher explicitly outlined the teacher's role, noting that "the best solution for teasing or mocking is for us teachers to be out on the playground helping the children play and stopping bad attitudes and remarks [. . .] be[ing] a good example for them with God's help."

At the same time, teachers often provide students with experiences beyond those afforded by the traditional Old Order lifestyle. Field trips, for example, take Amish students into the world, giving them ample opportunity to put into practice the things they are learning. Not only do they often visit other Amish schools, but also, as several teachers noted, teacher and pupils "might visit ARC, a handicapped school, and Das Deutsch Kase Haus to watch the process of making cheese." Menno-Hof in Shipshewana, Indiana, an informational display about different Anabaptist groups, is also a favored stop, and some LaGrange area schoolchildren were surprised to see a picture of their school in the Menno-Hof slide show. One Centreville teacher commented that her sister, a teacher in the Nappanee area, had arranged for an elephant and a lion cub to be brought to her school; the Centreville teacher took her entire school down to Nappanee to visit and see the animals.

Even when activities are confined to the schoolhouse, they may introduce children to new ways of playing or interacting. Two teachers, for example, constructed a life-sized version of the board game *Candy Land* in the school basement. As one described it,

The children were overwhelmed and delighted when we informed them what was happening. We put their names on slips and picked out eight at a time. [We] played six different games, then took those six winners and played a game to find the "Grand Winner." There was candy at the different spots of the game that the children were free to help themselves [to] and the grand winner received a big Hershey bar. (It was one of our first grade boys.) Everyone really enjoyed it!

After we were done, we shared it [the game] with my sister's school too.

Teachers and Parents Working Together

Parents visit school regularly, and most schools have a small program that they present to visitors in which the children introduce themselves by family and then, as a group, sing several songs. Charts on the wall record visits, and all guests are asked to sign the visitors' book. At one small Centreville school with only twenty students, there were seventeen entries in the guest book by early October, six of them recording group visits. Past entries recorded visitors from Nebraska, Chicago, New York City, and Wyoming.

"It always brightens my day to visit school," noted one woman on her way to observe the school to which her children had gone and which some of her grandchildren now attended. Her sister-in-law, who was accompanying her, agreed, lamenting that she hadn't "gotten to ours yet." "Parents often visit during school hours," said one teacher who boarded at the school, "and we [teachers] are invited to their houses for the evening meal. They'll send in notes every so often, and we have monthly conferences. [...] I really appreciate the effort they put in to show they care and think of us." Another teacher commented, "We do have parents visit school frequently [though] not too often. Once a month two mothers bring hot lunch, which is a great treat. And we have parent-teachers meeting once a month." Still another noted, "Most parents visit at least once a year for maybe a half day. Some come more than once." "Since Christmas," he added, "we've had hot lunch brought in by parents every other Friday. They take turns. Three sets of parents at a time. I enjoy those meals." A Centreville teacher noted that the parents were very good about supplying them with everything they need. "We have towels here they take home and wash," she added.

Commenting on the help and cooperation he and his fellow teacher received from parents, one teacher asserted, "Ours get an A+ for being supportive and for visiting. Fathers visit when it is convenient, mothers take time off. Every two weeks someone brings in a hot meal for everyone." This teacher told how once he had commented at a PTA meeting that parents seldom came in large groups and then added, "Next Friday who came visiting? Cheers! More than twenty Mothers and Fathers! Fathers played softball till we were thoroughly rained out. Mothers brought finger foods. Is that an outstanding show of support or what? I still smile when I think of it."

In addition to informal visits, parents must support teachers who are boarding at the school. Groceries, for example, are generally part of the teacher's pay. One teacher, now retired, noted that her salary had included room and groceries, while her daughter, a teacher at a nearby school, had received a higher salary but had had to supply her own food. The teachers at another school reported that the families there take turns supplying provisions, each supplying food for two weeks at a time, and all the teachers need to do if they need something is send a list home with the appropriate student.

Expected to become involved in all aspects of school life, parents are counted on to support the teachers in other ways, as well. The *Indiana Regulations* state that parents should cooperate with the teacher and school board for the good of the child. It is the parents' responsibility, according to the *Indiana Regulations* (2002, 7), to inquire regularly about their child's progress, to dress children according to the rules of the church-community, and to work together with board members, teachers, and ministers to ensure that church standards are maintained in the school.

Parents, both fathers and mothers, are expected to attend the monthly PTA meetings, and most schools have posted charts for each family to track the parents' attendance. One former teacher noted that at PTA meetings every board member, parent, and teacher must "say their piece." She added that children never attended these meetings or the board meeting, which involved only board members and the teachers. Instead, perhaps fearing what their teachers might tell their parents, "they just stayed home and prayed." Another teacher, describing the board meetings and PTA that occurred every six weeks, commented that

At PTA, the board and teachers have a 30-minute closed-door meeting first to see if we have any major problems. Then the parents file in and pay their tuition. Next we sing a song and then have prayer. The president then tells everybody how things have been and are going to be if everybody agrees. Then we go around the rows of parents and everybody says if they're agreed. They are also welcome to give comments or suggestions. Now us teachers split up into our rooms, and all the parents of the children we have have a personal chat to see how their children are doing. Basically to keep the communication lines OPEN. This meeting lasts from 6:30 to 9:00 p.m.

Another teacher described a similar practice for his school, noting that "board members come at 6:00 p.m. and meet for half an hour before the parents come. Parents vote on any issues if it's necessary. Usually only men vote. Women can but they don't want to. After the meeting, parents talk to the teachers, check out their children's work and desks, talk, and play games."

A Centreville teacher said, "We usually have PTA meetings once a month and all the parents usually come. We sing together and then the board presents whatever needs to be discussed. We usually have a snack of sorts afterwards, while the parents all take a turn talking to the teachers—to see how the children are doing."

According to one teacher, "The interest a parent puts in will often be reflected by the students. If it is important for students to have an interest in school, it is no less important for parents to take an active interest." While teachers reinforce the teachings of home and church, parents are also expected to reinforce the teacher's work by standing by the teacher in disciplinary issues and in working with the teacher on difficult issues such as whether to promote a slow learner or to put a child into special education.

Teachers appreciate parental support. One teacher, for example, recounting how she had had to "whip" an eighth grade boy, said, "The parents backed me up. The father of the boy I whipped said 'I think he had it coming.'" Parents are also involved in decisions to hold their children back at the end of the term. "Most parents don't like the idea of keeping back their child, but I've done it and now they've come back and said how glad

they are that they consented to it. [. . .] And there are also the parents who
will refuse, so we try to work out something."

In Indiana, parents have a more formal role to play. Every other year
teachers in Indiana give the Iowa Tests of Basic Skills, on which 75 percent of the students in Indiana private schools score above the national
average. Over a three-day period, students are given eleven of the Iowa
tests: vocabulary, reading, spelling, capitalization, punctuation, word
usage, visual material, reference material, mathematical concepts, mathematical story problems, and mathematical computation.[12] "It's given just
for our own benefit," said a member of the state school board, "just to see
what we score." Yet, argued the state chairman of Indiana Amish schools,
"if parents help, we can make progress. Slips [about the testing] go home
to parents, encouraging them to 'play school.' Most parents join in. Thirty-
five schools were tested two years ago, and fifty-one were tested last year.
Only four [schools] didn't join in." An article on testing published in the
Old Order Amish journal *School Echoes* stated, "Each individual student's
test results are returned to the school for the benefit of the teacher and
parents. It is recommended that the teacher discuss each student's results with the student's parents. The parents are then given the student's
scores and they may choose to discuss it with their child if and when they
so decide."[13]

School Administration

The use of the Iowa tests demonstrates not only the way parents, teachers,
and community school administrators work together, but also the feeling
of many that having private schools is a privilege that could be revoked or
curtailed by state supervision if school standards start to slip. There is the
sense that schools and school officials must live up to the bargain struck
when community leaders signed the agreement with state officials. An article in *School Echoes* 2001, 19) explained:

It is true that the sub-committee has a tendency to strongly encourage the
schools to administer the tests. Why?
     First, we feel it is our duty as representatives of our Amish schools to
have records available in our schools to show that our students are learning in an acceptable level. Second, it can show the teacher (and parents)

where individual students, class, or school is weak at, and where more attention might have to be focused on.

To sum it up, it gives the school boards and state board an idea if our schools are accomplishing what is required in academic education. We feel these results would be recognized by the State Department of Public Instruction if the time ever comes that they feel it necessary to check us out.

Could this happen? We think it could happen very shortly that people in the state level might consider it important to come knocking on our doors.

Talking about the decision by the state board of the Amish schools to institute testing, the state chairman explained, "We needed something to measure ourselves. We weren't in it [testing] to see which school had the best score but to see if we could better ourselves." Noted a fellow member of the state school board, "There's no one breathing down the schools' neck to see what they're doing. As long as we educate our children and are productive members of society, they'll let us alone. If we become a burden, they'll get us." The schools' performance on the Iowa tests helps to keep the state at bay by demonstrating that the Old Order Amish schools work.

Primary responsibility for ensuring that schools function smoothly lies with the teachers and local school boards. As one teacher put it, "Our school board takes care of fixing up things or ordering materials for the coming year. (We teachers and board get together for the book order towards the end of the term.)" Board terms vary from district to district; in some schools members serve three years, and in others members serve six year terms, often rotating to different positions every two years: treasurer, secretary, president. The board meets every month or every six weeks, generally meeting with the teacher before parents arrive for the larger PTA gathering.

In Michigan and Indiana, local boards purchase materials, collect tuition payments, and maintain the buildings. Members, all male, are elected from among the families whose children attend the school. Ministers may serve, although, as one teacher noted, "usually we'd try to release them from that duty, so they'd have more time for the ministry. They would still attend PTAs. In our school the Bishop would attend, and his input is appreciated."

Although funding varies, schools are generally supported by tuition fees from parents,[14] which are on a sliding scale. For the first child in school the parent pays full tuition, for the second one-half the cost, one-fourth for subsequent children, and the fifth attends free of charge. Many schools have fundraising events, such as bake sales or auctions, to supplement income from tuition.[15] Commenting on school finances, a retired teacher from Centreville, who taught in both Centreville and Elkhart-LaGrange schools, noted, "One of the school board is the treasurer who goes and collects the money. Usually people bring their money when they have a school meeting and give it to the treasurer. This is once a month. Towards the end of the year, they sell lunches at an auction or a bake sale and that goes to the school. [. . .] Some places it's how many pupils each family has and some places it's however much a family can pay. [. . .] [It] depends on the school district whether families that don't have children pay. [. . .]When they start their school and build it, they decide how they're going to do it."

After five years on the board, the chair noted, "We have found that if the board is agreed on something and open with parents, usually anything reasonable is OK. But if the board is secretive about something, there will be trouble. Openness and communication is very important. Although prayer and God's guidance is most important."

The State Executive Committee of the Amish Parochial Schools regulates the conduct of the local boards. The *Indiana Regulations* mandates, for example, that "The school board shall work together as a unit and visit the school on a regular basis" (2002, 4). Most issues are settled at the local level, but as the chairman of one local board noted, "If there are problems that the local board can't handle, the state board will investigate and try to come up with a solution." The role of the State Executive Committee is farther reaching, for it mediates between the local boards and the state in a variety of ways. The Executive Committee helps to channel funds for new school buildings, which must be built according to plans approved by the Indiana Department of Public Instruction, the Administrative Building Council, and the State Fire Marshall's Office. The Executive Committee also establishes the school calendar, ensuring that each of the local schools meets for 167 days between August 15 and May 15, and gathers attendance information from the local school boards. Finally, the State Executive Committee furnishes each school with uniform report cards and recommends textbooks for all subject areas (*Articles of Agreement*, 1–3). In the words of the chairman, the committee "tries to come up with guidelines for all communities to get some uniformity."

Local boards hire teachers, but in its agreement with the State of Indiana, the State Executive Committee mandates teacher qualifications. Since the Old Order school has become, in the words of the chairman of the State Executive Committee, "an extension of the church," teaching has grown in importance as a profession, thereby motivating a reassessment of who is qualified to teach. The *Articles of Agreement* describe the ideal teacher as someone who

> must possess a good Christian character [. . .] be capable of getting along with children and be able to reason with their parents. The instructor must be willing to work with the school authorities, as the teacher is an important factor directing the child's future life. The teacher may be hired as a probationary teacher or substitute teacher for two school years and if the teacher proves to be satisfactory, they will receive a license from the local parochial school board and countersigned by the Chairman of the Executive Committee. (1967; 1984, 3–4)

The *Indiana Regulations* (2002, 13) affirm that "experience in teaching is not a fundamental, but a genuine interest in children and in teaching is. Enthusiasm is a power for success in any endeavor. Teaching is no exception." A teacher who is also a parent commented, "If I was choosing a teacher I would look for honesty, one that does not use bad language, good morals, a Christian, and maybe a little experience."

These qualifications do not rule out a non–Old Order teacher. According to Article G of the *Articles of Agreement*, local boards should, if possible, employ a teacher of the Amish faith, but they are not obliged to do so. In clear contrast to most Old Order communities, but in keeping with the emphasis on "Christian" rather than "Old Order Amish," the schools of Elkhart-LaGrange have employed non-Amish teachers.[16] Commenting on one such teacher, a member of a local school board noted that "parents were happy with him and he was well respected. An English [non–Old Order] person with good Christian Character should have no problem teaching in an Amish school." Another teacher noted, "Yes, we've had a few [non-Amish teachers]. It has seemed to work out, since they've taught quite a few years."

However, most teachers are Old Order Amish, and many teach several years; some have even made a profession out of teaching. Teaching positions are rarely advertised. Rather, the local board will come directly to the home of a prospective teacher, speaking to her parents if she is under twenty-one years old or directly to her if she is no longer a minor. If someone is interested in teaching, she will quietly tell someone else who will mention it to the school board.

While the overwhelming majority of teachers are female, there are a number of male teachers as well, although as Joseph Stoll, one of the founders of the Pathway Publishing Company and an editor of the *Blackboard Bulletin*, pointed out, "not as many as twenty years ago when the ratio of men teachers was higher." Stoll argued that "the role of the school is extremely important. Home, church, school—all work together, and if any one is weak, all are weak." For this reason, he added, "I wish we could have more men teachers, not because women teachers aren't capable, but because it indicates more community support."

Teaching and Changing Social Roles

As noted earlier, teaching in Old Order communities has always been a gendered occupation, attractive to single women as one of the few occupations open to them, but unattractive to men, who can earn much more at other trades. Teaching has offered independence to single women. Marriage and motherhood are the preferred lifestyle of Old Order women, however, so teaching has often been an occupation of the young and inexperienced.

Research suggests that the more the Old Order community engages with the surrounding society and is dependent upon it economically and spiritually, the less likely women in the community are to share in community decision making (Johnson-Weiner 2001b). In short, as long as the barriers between the church and the world remain intact, with men and women interacting daily on the farm, the male and female domains are complementary and interconnected, and men and women remain partners. As church-communities redefine the separation of the church from the world to permit members to engage in wage labor outside the church-community, the relationship between men and women in daily life changes, for men and women are generally given unequal access to such work.

Whereas even married men with families may work as wage laborers, the woman is expected to remain home after she marries and certainly after childbirth (Rogers 1978). As a result, the only women able to engage in teaching are single, and as such, are the least powerful in a church that incorporates a divine hierarchy, placing God over man and man over woman into its social and religious structure. Women leave teaching when they marry, which means that only those who have *failed* to reach this state will make teaching a career.

This emphasis on the divine hierarchy has led some to question the suitability of women for the classroom. For example, in a letter to the *Blackboard Bulletin*, one man argued that hiring women to teach violated God's divine order. "In thinking of the great responsibility teaching carries," he argued,

> we think of the three most important parts of the Christian community— the home, the church, and the school [. . .] In the home it is God's order and will for the man to be the head and to lead. [. . .] and also in the church we recognize God's will to lead through ministers, deacons, etc. [. . .]
> When I think of the seriousness of teaching and training children, why would we want to choose a 'weaker vessel' to teach and to be an example to our children?[17]

In responding, the editors of the *Blackboard Bulletin* noted that there might be a danger in asking women to "lead" by teaching school. "But," the editors continue, "a teacher in school does not have authority over other men and women, but only over the pupils she teaches. She herself is under the authority of the school board, and she has been hired by the board to be a teacher and example for the children in the school."[18] In other words, women are suitable for teachers because those they are teaching are below them in the hierarchy. In the structure of school administration, as in the hierarchy of the church-community itself, the female teacher is at a low level, just above the children.

The schools' perceived importance to the community, coupled with the greater interaction between the church-community and the dominant society, has had an impact on teachers' salaries. Teachers in Centreville and Elkhart-LaGrange earn more than their counterparts elsewhere, although salaries vary with the economy of particular regions. Where the dominant occupation of families in the school district is farming, salaries will be somewhat lower; in districts in which wage labor in non–Old Order enterprises is the norm, there is more money to pay teachers, and salaries must be higher to attract teachers. Teachers in more rural Centreville, for example, find employment more easily and earn more by traveling to Indiana. A teacher from Centreville in her fourth year of teaching earned $50.00 per day. According to a member of a local Indiana school board, the average salary in Elkhart-LaGrange is $55.00 per day, and boards "try to give a raise every year."

The institution of higher wages for men reveals that these communities are making a concerted effort to attract men to the teaching profession, further evidence of a reassessment of the place of the school in the community and the role of the teacher. Simply put, men make considerably more. A male teacher in his first year starts at approximately $70.00 per day, and male teachers in their second year reported earning $85.00 per day. A married man with a family in his first year as a teacher earned $125.00 per day. Non-Amish male teachers also make more than female Amish teachers, although not as much as their male Amish counterparts. One non-Amish man who had taught in Amish schools for thirteen years was, in his last term, earning $90.00 a day with three-weeks paid vacation.[19] An Amish woman who retired in the late 1990s after nearly two decades of teaching earned $40.00 a day plus room and board in her last term.

Teachers and Teacher Training

Unlike their less progressive counterparts, teachers in the Elkhart-LaGrange and Centreville settlements are expected to prepare themselves to teach. Perhaps the most controversial part of the agreement between the Old Order Amish and the State of Indiana governing the establishment of Old Order Amish private schools was the requirement that "the teacher will have passed the eighth grade satisfactorily and will make a passing score on a General Educational Development [GED] High School Equivalency Test or on a standardized 12th grade achievement test furnished, administered, and graded by the State Department of Public Instruction" (Articles of Agreement 1967, 3). In 1968, 53 Amish teachers took the test and received passing scores.

This classroom in Indiana has a non-Amish teacher assisted by an Amish helper.
(Photograph by Doris Kauffmann)

"How much right of control do public school officials have in the operation of our parochial schools?" asked a 1968 editorial in the *Blackboard Bulletin*, which asserted that the clause covering the qualifications of teachers in Amish schools in Indiana "may contain the germ of future trouble." The editorial went on to argue that the GED examination was inappropriate for Old Order schools because it graded the teacher instead of the pupils, and "it is not so important how much the teacher knows, as it is how much she is successfully transmitting to the pupils. We know of college-educated teachers who were outstanding flops when it came to teaching children anything. And we know of teachers with an eighth grade education who have the talent to bring their classes to life and to really inspire their children in the paths of learning." If the tests were done "on a purely advisory level to upgrade our schools," the editorial concluded, "they might be helpful. But if no teacher is to be allowed to teach without having passed the tests, the situation may indeed cause concern" (*Blackboard Bulletin* 1968, 132).

"Nobody pays any attention to that anymore. The GED was never mentioned [when they hired me]," asserted a woman who had taught in both Elkhart-LaGrange area and in Centreville. Still, as the chairman of the Executive Committee noted, "some teachers are volunteering to do the GED." "If the state board asks," noted a local school board member, "then we'll require the GED. But the state doesn't ask. For a while the state did the testing, but there were no problems, so the state backed off."

As in other communities, teachers attend regular meetings to reinforce skills and to exchange ideas with others. The annual Indiana school meeting, planned by the district that hosts it, is a two-day affair that covers nine topics and draws teachers from Michigan and other states. Indiana Old Order Mennonite teachers, whose schools "stand under the umbrella of the Old Order Amish agreement," also attend. Michigan teachers help to host an annual meeting that draws teachers from Ohio, Wisconsin, Virginia, and New York, as well as from Ontario and Michigan. At the Annual Michigan-Ontario Amish School Meeting, held in Aylmer, Ontario, in August 1999, for example, topics included "The Challenge of Giving Children Equal Love," "Leading the Learning Disabled," "Developing a Healthy Self-Image," and "Books: Handle with Care." There were 167 teachers in attendance, nearly half of whom had never taught or had only taught one year. Nine teachers had fifteen to nineteen years experience, and eight had taught more than twenty years. Michigan sent 43 teachers and Indiana sent 13.

Regular teachers' meetings at six-week intervals provide additional instruction. In 1994 the Old Order schools in Elkhart-LaGrange were divided into two districts for these meetings, and by 2002 the schools had been grouped into six districts. As described by the chairman of the Executive Committee, the meetings generally offer a class by a chosen teacher on a particular topic or a talk by a minister or committee member. The meetings are attended by board members, parents from the school hosting the event, and all the teachers in the district. A teacher describing the meetings noted that

At a meeting we always sing the song that is also sung every Sunday, 770 in our *Ausbund* books.[20] The bishop whose district the school is in will briefly welcome everyone and lead in prayer. Roll call follows. [. . .] Usually they have two topics. Men or teachers from Amish communities, not always the home community, are selected by the host school to orate on a specific subject. These vary too. Respect, Communication, Pros and Cons of parochial, Public versus Parochial, oh my, anything pertaining to school is bound to get hit sooner or later. Usually they include a class where a teacher, let's take Math for instance, takes a Math class and gives tips on making it interesting, using procedures he has found faster or maybe easier, and then he might address any questions that remain from the teachers. Before closing they have a questions-answers session where any questions a teacher may have are addressed via a small box with a slot in the top that is sent around for you to slip your question in. Anyone present may submit questions. Can you imagine how interesting [. . .] not only the questions, but the diversity of answers may become?

The closing consists of comments by district committee men and the State Chairman and finally a parting song. Afterwards everyone gets a small bag of popcorn and a soda while he chats and makes his way to the exit. I did miss that a new song or an old German song is usually taught to the teachers between topics.

In addition to the teachers' meetings, monthly teachers' suppers held throughout the term provide teachers an opportunity to socialize with their peers, share experiences, learn new songs and games to teach their students, and find support. Generally, teachers from six to eight schools come together, and the suppers rotate from school to school. Parents of children attending school are expected to furnish the meal when it is their school's turn to host the meeting, and the teachers at that school plan it. As one teacher described these get-togethers, "we take turns to furnish the evening meal at our school. Then we'd visit (not always about school related subjects either!) and perhaps play a game. It's the teachers' night out. These evenings are a highlight for me to get out and let loose of the responsibilities for a bit."

Vocational and Special Education

When the first Old Order private schools were established in Indiana, vocational education was part of the 1967 agreement with the state. As stated in the *Articles of Agreement*, pupils who graduated from eighth grade had to enroll in a vocational course until they are 16 years old. Under the plan, they had to be in school at least one day a week for five hours, during which time they were to study history, general business, basic mathematics, English, and spelling. They were also to work at least four hours a day outside of school on an individual project, for which they were not to routinely count chores or other household duties. Instead, choosing from ten general areas—livestock and poultry, fruits and vegetables, grains, tools and equipment, building construction and maintenance, farm finances and management, carpentry, landscaping, and horticulture, homemaking, and gardening—students were to formulate a description of the project, discuss its purpose and the procedures by which it would be carried out, and keep track of the time involved and the material and financial resources required to complete it (cf. *Articles of Agreement* 1967, 4–7).

The *Indiana Regulations* (2002) has altered the plan somewhat. Noting that, thanks to the Supreme Court's decision in *Wisconsin v. Yoder,* Amish children were released from any further required formal schooling after they turned 15, the *Indiana Regulations* excused from vocational education all 15-year-olds who had completed eighth grade, as well as all those who would turn 15 within sixty days after the start of school in the fall. Furthermore, the classroom requirement was lowered from five hours to three hours. Finally, students no longer had to submit a project. The *Indiana Regulations* stipulate only that

> the rest of the school week shall be used in a gainful occupation under the supervision of the parents. A daily record shall be kept by the pupil to report [the] nature and progress of work being done. This should be entered in detail into a composition book showing good penmanship, proper grammar, correct spelling and punctuation marks. Let it be a complete project report on worthwhile work done at home.

According to the *Indiana Amish Directory,* "Since most children pass the eighth grade by the time they become fifteen years of age, the vocational school that had been organized before, with few exceptions, has been discontinued" (J. E. Miller 1995, 13).[21]

The *Indiana Amish Directory* asserts further that, with the demise of vocational education, "More attention is being given, at present, to help slow learners with Special Education, so they will be able to help themselves better in later life" (1995, 13). According to the *Indiana Regulations,* schools offer special education when the local school board, parents, and teacher all agree that it is necessary; there is no systematic procedure for evaluating students with special needs. The *Indiana Regulations* stipulate only that the special education classroom should be located apart from the other classrooms, that special education children should attend school eight years, and that they should play with others at recess. In terms of curriculum, schools are advised to use "whatever works best" under the circumstances, and teachers are told not to give homework because "children need to rest and relax." Children in special education are permitted to work at their own pace, and they are passed each year regardless of the work accomplished. As noted in the *Indiana Regulations*, "Since Special Ed. children are in some ways different from other children, guidelines will be somewhat flexible. [...] We should always keep in mind our goal is to help the Special Ed. child reach its potential as closely as possible" (2002, 12). Ultimately, the *Indiana Regulations* conclude, "The program is a hand up to those who struggle, a light for those who seem to lose hope. It enables us to especially benefit those not able to progress with their group. 'Inasmuch as ye have done it unto one of the least of these [...] ye have done it unto me.' Matthew 25:40."

Competing with Public Schools

Describing the decision to start the first Old Order private school, a member of the Centreville community made it clear that it was not easy and hardly unanimous.

> The week before we were to start, opposition was the highest, with some of the parents now opposing that were in favor, and one of the board members getting discouraged came and asked what should we do. My answer to him was, if you are looking for discouragement you came to the wrong place and as far as I am concerned school will open, the Lord willing, on September 2 as planned. So on September 2, Spring Creek Private School had its first day of school with 21 students enrolled and Elsie Miller as teacher with all 8 grades and the parents of the children say each passing day brings a satisfaction they cannot put in words for which we thank the Lord for it. But the opposition is getting stronger, so we need your prayers and the Lord's help.[22]

Even after over a quarter of a century of Amish parochial school education, many on both sides of the Michigan-Indiana border, wary of Amish schools, continue to send their children to public schools. Indeed, just outside of Centreville in Nottawa, the majority of Amish children attend public schools.

Asked why Amish parents continue to send their children to public schools, especially since the public school term is 185 days while the private school term is only 167 days, a member of the Indiana Executive Committee replied, "Amish are stubborn. And back in 1967 public schools were not all that bad. Local schools were 95 percent Amish and the teachers were paid by the state. The teachers were teaching sound doctrine—no evolution or computers." He went on to note that a local principal had sent home a girl who was wearing trousers. "As long as things were like that, we didn't need our own schools. As public schools changed and became more worldly, more sent their kids to parochial schools."

On the other hand, one Centreville Amish woman argues that if she were raising children, she would send them to public schools, because "if they grow up Amish, go to the Amish church, go to the Amish school, and only see other Amish, they won't know anything about the world."

A number of factors contribute to Amish attendance in public schools. In Centreville, as one teacher noted, one family sent their children to public school because they worried about them taking the buggy across the busy road to get to the Amish one. A teacher who himself had gone to public school "partly because it was closer than an Amish school," noted that Amish schools used to have more problems with teasing and bullying. "That's one reason some Amish still go to public schools, because of things that happened 15–25 years ago. Mocking used to be a big problem back then."

Conflict within the community also motivates attendance at public schools. Noting that several families in one area had withdrawn their children from the Amish school and sent them to public school, a retired teacher commented, "There's been trouble there. At one time there was so much trouble it caused friction in the church [. . .] the teachers couldn't hack it together. The youngest wanted to tell the oldest what to do." When the trouble was resolved, she added, the children came back to the Amish school.

The teachers all agree that when children do transfer from a public school to an Amish one, they find the move difficult. A Centreville teacher said, "School was never hard for me. It was a change to come here [from public school as a student to the school at which she now teaches]. We had science, but we didn't have the vocabulary and geography, and their [public school] arithmetic is much easier. The blue Strayer-Upton is eighth grade in the Amish school but is twelfth grade in the public school." A retired teacher commented that "kids coming in from public school always started with much lower averages." Another noted that the impact of a growing number of students coming to the Amish schools from the public ones was greater than might be imagined. "Twenty-five per cent of our students are new. With children coming in from the public school, our singing took a nose dive."

The Centreville and Elkhart-LaGrange communities are determined to keep their schools performing at this high level to ensure their survival. Without an agreement with the state such as that enjoyed by Indiana Amish private schools, Michigan schools are in a more precarious position, in large part because Michigan law requires all teachers, in public as well as non-public schools, to be certified. Under a plan reached with the Amish in Camden, Michigan, which lies due east of Centreville, county school superintendents act as "curriculum supervisors" for the Amish schools, "make periodic visits to the school, make written reports to the State Department of Public Instruction concerning the school, and provide consultative services to the 'teacher aid' serving the children" (Fisher 1996, 127; Huntington 2001).

Yet the Amish in Michigan have no guarantee that the state will continue to allow them to operate private schools, and as Huntington (2001) notes, it periodically threatens to close them. Nevertheless, in a 1995 letter addressed to "Dear Friends," one Amishman described the visit of the Deputy State Superintendent of Public Instruction, Teresa Staten, to the local Amish school, which had taken place "a year ago." According to the letter, the author inquired of Ms. Staten after the visit whether she could foresee a time when the state would require the Amish private schools to have certified teachers.

This seemed to put her in deep thought for a few seconds, then she said, "No." I said, "How can you say that when the State says yes?" With a real serious look on her face she answered, "With what I have seen here today you are fulfilling the spirit of the law without the law. We in public school cannot do that with the law." I was stunned but asked, "Why can't you?" She answered quickly: "We don't have the building blocks you have which are, family, church and school. The records I have seen here today verifies [sic] strong family support. Strong families are built on dedicated church membership which in turn makes better schools."[23]

For Amish educators, maintaining strong schools is the key to keeping them. The *Indiana Regulations* asserts, "We have won the trust and confidence of the Indiana State Department of Public Instruction. We enjoy tolerance from local officials. We currently sense no opposition from the outside." Still, there's a warning:

> Are we thinking the courts will always rule in our favor? If another Amish school case ever comes up, for negligence or incompetence, the ruling could go against us. We could lose all we had struggled for and gained in the past. We hope all of us as patrons of our parochial schools will appreciate the privileges that have been given us. Let's accept our responsibilities to the fullest, not only because of a concern for government intervention, but also to the honor and glory of God and to benefit the next generation. "Except the Lord build the house, thy labor in vain that build it." Psalms 127:1. (*Indiana Regulations* 2002, 2–3)

Unlike the Swartzentruber Amish, who, isolated from non–Old Order society, refuse to evaluate their schools by any standard but the values of their own church-communities, the Amish in Centreville and Elkhart-LaGrange have attempted to build an educational system that, by meeting external standards, will prepare their children to compete in the world yet keep them safe from it by reinforcing Christian beliefs. The Iowa Tests and the voluntary GED, as well as careful record keeping and planning, all work to legitimize the schools in the eyes of the state and thus to strengthen Old Order education in Centreville and Elkhart-LaGrange.

Old Order Mennonite Schools in Lancaster County

*The goal of the Old Order [. . .] parochial schools is to prepare for
usefulness by preparing for eternity.*
—*Pennsylvania Standards*

The Old Order School Movement in Lancaster

The Holmes County area boasts the largest Old Order Amish settlement in the world, yet when people think of the Old Order Amish, they most often think of Lancaster County, which Klimuska (1998, 42) has called "the homeland of the Amish church." Since the first Mennonite settlers began to arrive in Pennsylvania in 1710, and the Amish not long after in 1737, the Lancaster area has been home to Anabaptist settlement, and today the Amish and Mennonite communities remain intertwined in Lancaster County.

With roughly 6,100 adult baptized members, the Old Order Mennonites are far outnumbered by the nearly 11,000 baptized Amish adults in the Lancaster area (Kraybill 2001) and are not nearly as well known to the general public. Yet although few tourists distinguish the Old Order Mennonites from the Old Order Amish, there are obvious differences between the two. For example, whereas the Old Order Amish continue to worship in each other's homes, Old Order Mennonites worship in meetinghouses.[1]

In addition, some Old Order Mennonite groups have sanctioned the use of electricity and telephones in members' homes.

Moreover, in some respects, the Old Order Mennonites are a more varied population than their Old Order Amish cousins. While the majority of the 150+ Old Order Amish congregations (see Kraybill 2001, 15) of the Lancaster Old Order Amish settlement fellowship with each other, that is, they have similar *Ordnungs*, the Old Order Mennonites comprise several distinct groups or conferences, including the Groffdale Conference, or Wenger Mennonites; the Weaverland Conference, or Horning Mennonites; the Stauffer, or Pike Mennonites; and the various churches of the Reidenbach Mennonites, known as the "35ers." While individual churches within a conference are similar and share *Ordnungs*, the conferences themselves are different from each other. For example, the Wenger, Stauffer, and Reidenbach Mennonites are "team Mennonites," meaning that they continue to rely on the "team" of horse and buggy for transportation, whereas the Horning Mennonites have cars.[2]

Despite their different lifestyles, Lancaster County's Old Order church-communities have often found themselves allies in struggles with non–Old Order society, particularly in their efforts to educate their children for Old Order life. In 1834, for example, when the passage of the School Law provided for state-funded elementary or common school education of all young people in the state of Pennsylvania and for supervision by locally elected officials, the majority of districts in Pennsylvania welcomed it; but there was considerable opposition, particularly "from supporters of German church schools, mainly Mennonites," and others who contended that "the law would remove their children from instruction in their own faith" (Fletcher 1950; rpt. in Lapp 1991, 66).

One hundred years later, plans to consolidate one-room schools, extend the school year from eight to nine months, and raise the age of compulsory education from 14 to 15 for farm youths again brought the Old Order churches into conflict with the state. With the Old Order Amish taking the lead, the Old Orders began to establish their own schools.[3] At first the Amish and Mennonites were united under Amish leadership, but in 1968, with the school committee becoming too large to be workable, the Old Order Mennonites established the Committee for the Mennonite Parochial Schools of Pennsylvania, which continues to work within the structure established by their Amish counterparts.

Today there are more than 150 private schools run by the Old Order Amish and Mennonites in Lancaster County.[4] The formal organization of Old Order parochial schools into Amish and Mennonite districts was undertaken in part "to stimulate the unity among the Parochial school boards to adhere to the elementary standards, which are not to exceed the eighth grade."[5] It has resulted in a cooperative effort between the Old Order Amish and Old Order Mennonite communities. Schools are Amish if they were built by Amish, and Mennonite if built by Mennonites. Where both Mennonites and Amish are involved in setting up a new school, the school will "belong" to the group in the majority.

Children attend the schools nearest their homes, so the classroom population reflects the settlement patterns of the immediate area. Where the population is predominantly Amish, the schools have a mostly Amish student population, and where the population is predominantly Mennonite, the students are mostly Mennonite. One teacher noted that at her Mennonite school "there are eleven Amish children, one Horning boy, and the other eighteen are from our [Wenger] church."

The makeup of the school board also reflects the population using the school, and both Amish and Mennonites will serve on the same board. Amish teachers may be hired for Mennonite schools.[6] As one Old Order Mennonite teacher, whose students represent Wenger, Reidenbach, the Mid-Atlantic Conference, and Hope Mennonites, put it, "Our school is interdenominational and it doesn't seem to cause a problem."[7]

The "Interdenominational" Schools of the Old Order Mennonites

Walbert (2002) argues that "in the long run, the greatest division created by the controversy in Lancaster County was the further isolation of the Amish from their fellow Lancaster Countians." He points out that "after the establishment of parochial schools [. . .] Amish children received the same rural education as before, walking to schools without electricity or central heat, learning the three Rs and traditional values, and leaving school at age fourteen to work on the farm. [. . .] Their religious beliefs had always made the Amish separate from the world, but now it was not just nonresistance and brotherhood that made the Amish different. It was their insistence on remaining rural" (Walbert 2002, 57).

Increasingly, however, Old Order Amish and Mennonite children in the Lancaster area are not growing up to lead rural lives. As suburban sprawl engulfs the region, growing numbers of Old Order church members earn their livelihood, not by plowing, but in carpentry and construction, manufacturing, and retail trade. Although some work with fellow Old Order employees in non–Old Order–owned businesses, the Lancaster Old Orders, unlike their counterparts in the Elkhart-LaGrange settlement in Indiana, or the Centreville, Michigan, settlement, have largely resisted entry into the non–Old Order labor market. Many, for example, are self-employed in home-based cottage industries or work for Old Order employers. Nevertheless, they labor in a global market, catering to neighbors and tourists within the county and shipping their products to a clientele around the world (Kraybill 2001, ch. 10).

Like parents in other Old Order communities, Lancaster Old Order parents hope that private schools will prepare children to earn a living and become committed members of their Old Order church-community, "to give their children," as Fisher and Stahl (1997, 4) put it, "the instruction they need to earn an honest living and to lead a Christian life." In Lancaster, however, preparing children to earn a living means preparing them to compete economically in non-farming occupations in an increasingly technological marketplace. They have to learn how to live in a diverse society, surrounded by many examples of what it means to be Old Order.

In these interdenominational schools, Old Order children daily encounter others from homes in which the church standards may be quite different from their own. Amish children from homes lacking electricity may play with Horning Mennonite children whose parents drive cars. While, as one teacher put it, "children from different churches live separated lives unless they're neighbors," in their exposure to other denominations in the Old Order school, Old Order children learn to draw the line, not simply between their church and others, but between Old Order churches and the world.

As a result, like the Old Order Amish schools in Holmes County, Ohio, which also accommodate children from different church-communities in the same school, the Lancaster Old Order Mennonite schools emphasize Old Order values read broadly, not those of a particular church-community. For example, *Schoolteachers' Signposts*, a handbook for teachers, asserts: "Respect for the community, the home, and the child is a prime responsibility for the teacher. If the community in which you are teaching is different from your own, make a serious and determined effort to accept their customs and understand their views. [...] Each family is entitled to being itself, to doing things their way, and it's your and my Christian duty to love and respect them as they are—their convictions, their standards, their weaknesses and strengths (1985, 25)."

A retired teacher active in teacher training said, "We want children to have enough education to make wise decisions in this world and the next." Another teacher, asked what she thought her church-community expected of private schools, responded, "The goal of all parochial schools is to teach our children more than just lessons. ... I think it's also necessary to teach them to be a Christian. We stress the Golden Rule: Do unto others as you would have them do unto you."

Lancaster County Old Order Mennonite schools foster an environment in which children play together regardless of the particular practices of their family. Parents from different churches serve together on school boards, and teachers instruct their pupils as Old Order *Christian* teachers, rather than as Wenger, Horning, or Amish ones.

Teachers and Students

In a number of ways, the Old Order Mennonite parochial schools in Lancaster County resemble their Holmes County Old Order Amish counterparts. As in Holmes County, there is considerable variation in schoolhouse architecture, for many schools were once one-room public schoolhouses built at different times. The Hill and Valley School near Fivepointville, for example, dates to the nineteenth century. It has hardwood floors and a gas furnace and was wired for electricity in the 1960s, but it lacks indoor plumbing.[8] A five-gallon thermos by the door provides drinking water for the children, and there are two outhouses at the edge of the schoolyard.

At Maple Hill, another Mennonite school, an additional classroom has been added to the original once public, one-room schoolhouse, and the hallway between the classrooms has become a cloakroom. Again, there is electricity but no indoor plumbing, and each classroom has a thermos for water and a rack for the pupils' drinking glasses. Even more recently built schools vary in how they are heated and whether they are wired for electricity or have indoor plumbing. For example, the Long Ridge School, built by Old Order Mennonites in 1971, is heated by a woodstove in the cellar and has gas lights, while the newer Eastside School has electric lights, an oil furnace, and indoor plumbing. Pleasant Valley, a fairly new Mennonite school with a majority Amish student population has electricity, and all the children, including the Amish ones, heat their lunches in the microwave on the back counter. As in most of the schools that have electricity, the teacher has a small photocopying machine.[9]

While the schoolhouses tend to be rather plain on the outside, they are generally anything but plain on the inside. Often plants hang in the windows or sit on the teacher's desk. Charts, mostly homemade, remind students of the parts of speech, the different arithmetic operations, and spelling rules. Children's artwork is everywhere.

Inside the Old Order Mennonite schools in Lancaster, order and discipline are tempered by a willingness to be flexible. In contrast to Swartzentruber teachers, and teachers in the less progressive, more homogeneous communities such as Ashland and Somerset, teachers in the Lancaster Old Order Mennonite schools play with the arrangement of desks in their classrooms. Although always in straight rows rather than the circles sometimes favored by public school teachers, the rows sometimes go off on a diagonal, and the teacher's desk may be behind the students' desks rather than at the front of the room.

Moving the teacher's desk from its traditional position and changing the arrangement of the students' desks downplays the overt authority of the teacher and suggests a more interactive relationship between student and teacher. As an experienced teacher pointed out in an address to beginning teachers, the teacher is "the boss, the authority, but it's better to talk to them [the students] as a helper."[10] While talking to them as helpers, teachers are expected, nonetheless, to guide students to maturity as members of the community and to do so firmly. "Consider this," urges a handout given to new teachers at the annual meeting for beginning teachers in Old Order Mennonite schools, "as a teacher you will be the leader of a group of God's precious children. Your example will be a strong influence in their lives, either good or bad. Your duty is to be a schoolteacher and friend, not a parent, guardian, or buddy." As a retired teacher warned at the same meeting, "What you expect of students will come out of them 99 percent of the time."

Unlike Amish students in less progressive schools who never question

Electricity and a photocopying machine make life easier for
the teacher in this Old Order Mennonite school.

authority, students in Lancaster schools are more likely to challenge teachers about assignments and about classroom expectations. In one classroom,
for example, the opportunity to earn extra credit by doing additional arithmetic problems led to much discussion between pupils and teacher about
whether students had to do the required problems first or whether they
could do all the problems in the order in which they appeared in the book.
In another school, a child wondered about a missing grade and claimed
that he had had an A. The teacher allowed that a mistake could have been

made and told the child he had "better hand it in. I must not have written it down."

In short, the relationship between teacher and student in these schools is less clear-cut than it is in Swartzentruber schools or in the schools of less progressive communities. The teacher is the authority figure, but rather than rule by fiat, she soft-pedals that authority. She has responsibility for running an orderly school, but she engages the help of her students to do so. An Old Order Amish teacher teaching in an Old Order Mennonite school with both Amish and Mennonite students explained that Old Order Mennonite schools are different from those of the Amish because "the Amish encourage respect much more than the Mennonites." This teacher noted a clear tension in the private schools between "education" and "respect," arguing that "the Amish don't encourage education like the Mennonites do." She added, "I think that [respect] is more important in eternity."[11]

Part of the reason teachers in the Lancaster area Old Order Mennonite schools relate differently to their students may be the number of students in the class and the number of families served by the school. In the majority of schools, there is only one teacher, although she often has the help of a teacher's aid several days each week. School size varies but averages between 20 and 30 children. One teacher, on learning that Swartzentruber Amish schools in upstate New York are often of similar size but generally serve only three to five families, commented with surprise, "That would mean each family must have 7–8 children going at the same time." Her school, she noted, had 23 pupils from 13 families. "Five families," she pointed out, "had only one student to each. This happens because it's either the last/youngest or the first/oldest child going from that family. When I was in eighth grade, seven from our family attended, which is very uncommon in our community." Another school, which had 17 pupils, had ten sets of parents, while its nearest neighbor drew 30 pupils from twelve families.

The large number of families, coupled with the fact that not all the families are from the same church-community, means that teachers in the Lancaster Old Order Mennonite schools, unlike their counterparts in the Swartzentruber schools or the Old Order Amish schools in Ohio, Indiana, or Michigan, cannot cast themselves in a parent-like role. They are authority figures and must watch out for their charges, but because they are not reinforcing particular church teachings and likely do not see their students outside of school in the way that teachers in smaller or more homogeneous communities do, they remain more distant from them. One teacher, noting that "we expect the parochial schools to be a place where students learn to work and play with other students [and] respect authority other than just their parents," casts herself as that "other authority," and asserts her desire to be "the teacher my students need."

In the classroom, the tensions between education and respect or obedience and between being an authority figure and being a helper play out in different ways. "One of the most difficult things I find about teaching," says one teacher, "is trying to get unenthusiastic pupils enthusiastic. You kind of feel exasperated, and your well-organized plan dwindles to disappointment." As the leader and guide in the classroom, a teacher bears great responsibility for the child's success or failure as well as for the school's. Whereas Swartzentruber teachers, parents, and students alike all appear to accept that school can and will be boring and that one must plow on, nevertheless, to finish the material, teachers in the Lancaster Mennonite private schools accept responsibility for making the work interesting and for helping students to become engaged in their studies. "Some may not be eager," acknowledged the retired teacher, but "if they're bored, maybe it's you. Teachers might be boring sometimes. You need to boss your brain."

Teachers use the physical space to keep their students alert. In sharp contrast to other Old Order schools, the Lancaster Old Order Mennonite schools do not have a table or bench at the front of the room at which children sit when their grade is called for a class. Instead, there is often a tall table around which students must stand. For reading classes, many teachers dispense with the table altogether; children line up in front of the room facing their classmates, and as they take turns reading, it is as if they are addressing the other grades. Teachers may even stand at the back of the room while their students line up in the front. One teacher reports that she usually had the children stand to take their classes, or then just stay at their seats because "that was the way I was used to in school. [. . .] I also get my pupils to stand while I explain classes though not always. I guess it's mostly when I'm explaining something new. I like that because I'm right at the blackboard where I can set up step by step, and I usually find it more successful to keep their minds with the class while they are undergoing explanation. If I explain while they are seated, it's much harder to know if they are fully with the class."

Whether the students stand around the table or stay at their desks is up to the teacher. As one noted, "I don't always conduct my classes in the same way. Sometimes they stay sitting, or then they stand around the table, then yet sometimes [. . .] standing up front. Most often the lower grades stand around the table mainly because they can concentrate better being all together plus the blackboard is right for us to do our drill [. . .] also I think it's good for them to stretch their muscles." Similarly, another teacher asserted, "I think it [having the pupils stand in class] benefits them to have a change of position, although I have had them sitting around a table already. Doing it different ways keeps it more interesting." Teachers also change position, and many will walk up and down the rows to watch the students working at their desks.

Teachers encourage their students to do their best in a variety of ways, most importantly, perhaps, by emphasizing individual responsibility. In sharp contrast to the practice in Swartzentruber and less progressive Old Order Amish communities, where the children are generally addressed by grade alone even if there is just one child in the grade (e.g., "Fourth grade, open your book"), Lancaster teachers frequently address children individually and by name, forcing them to speak for themselves. While "fourth grade" may be used to call the children to the front or to gain their attention as a group, "Johnny" or "Deborah" will be used to draw a child back to his or her task and to acknowledge a raised hand. "Ivan," said one teacher to a child as she stopped by his desk and looked at his workbook, "Why are there blank lines here?" Moreover, teachers are quick to praise individual students for such little things as completing a difficult problem successfully. One teacher complemented a student for reading aloud with expression. Another, working with her first graders on flashcards, turned the exercise into a race, saying, "Let's see who can get the most." At the end, rather than praise the winner, she commented on how well the other child had done in coming in only one card behind.

As in the Elkhart-LaGrange and Centreville schools, as well as in the schools of the less progressive settlements such as Ashland and Fredericktown, charts are posted recording 100s received on weekly tests in spelling, reading, and arithmetic. Yet sometimes there are additional incentives to do well. In one school, for example, the teacher offered students a penny for every five extra arithmetic problems they did beyond those required for the assignment. "So if you do them all," she encouraged, "you'll get an extra five cents." Students at this school regularly earn two cents for every 100 percent they earn on tests, and they might receive one cent if they only miss one or two on a hard assignment. The teachers call it the "Penny System." Children are allowed to spend what they earn in school at a small "store" in one of the classrooms, which the teachers open "when there's time, generally at the end of the week." The store offers a mix of things, including candy, books, plastic and stuffed animals, and a variety of erasers. "It gives the scores a boost," one of the teachers reported, "and the children really like it." That the older children learned to save their pennies so that they could purchase nicer, more expensive items was viewed as another lesson learned. Another teacher noted that one school where she had taught also awarded the children pennies for good scores, and that at the end of the term, they had held an auction in which the children could spend their earnings. A parent had served as auctioneer.

There is negative incentive as well. Teachers routinely note on the blackboard the names of students who have not completed assignments or must redo assignments with too many errors. Those who do not finish their work must stay in at recess or even take the assignment home to complete.

Teachers' instructions to their students reinforce not only the school lessons but also appropriate behavior and good work habits. Assigning arithmetic problems, one teacher reminded her students to raise their hands if they had questions and to follow all of the steps. "It will get harder [as the term goes on]," she warned, but she stressed how working out the easier problems would help with the more difficult ones later. Another teacher reminded her students to be careful with assignments. "Have you checked your work?" she asked them. "Are you sure? Some of us make mistakes when we go too fast."

Teachers often answer questions with questions, for as a retired teacher involved in training new teachers for the parochial schools argued, "We should teach children to help themselves. Never give your students a direct answer. You [the teacher] are not a walking encyclopedia. You should encourage children to think for themselves." For example, one teacher responded to a child's question by asking, "What are you going to do? What does it say?" Asking him what to do at each step, she led him to complete the problem and then, stopping to look at the rest of his work, told him simply that he'd made a mistake in the previous problem and left him

The walls of Old Order Mennonite schools in Lancaster County
are well decorated with inspirational posters.

to correct it. Another teacher turned helping a child into a group effort.
When the child was unsure of a vocabulary word, the teacher asked his
peers, "Can anyone help him?" and a number of children from different
grades raised their hands.

As in the schools of Elkhart-LaGrange and Centreville, posters and
wall displays encourage discipline and cooperation. In one school the bulletin board posed the question, "What Makes a Happy S-C-H-O-O-L?"
The letters for "school" were arranged vertically, and each began a word
that helped to answer the question: Study, Co-operation, Honesty, Obedience, Order, Love. At another school, the teacher had drawn a large light-
house with rays of light emanating from it, each labeled with a quality
prized by the community: responsibility, compassion, honesty, self-disci-
pline, fairness, trustworthiness, citizenship, integrity, perseverance, and
respect. The title of the display was "Good Character Shines Through."
Mottos hung in other schools encouraged productive work and humility:
"A man never plowed a field by turning it over in his mind"; "If you stop
to think, don't forget to start again."

Nor do lessons end when recess begins. Teachers structure play, deciding what the game will be, assigning teams, and ensuring that the rules are clear. One teacher said, for example, "Children will be children and, if left to themselves, they may invent their own inappropriate play, so I try to always have the children involved in decent constructive activities at recess." Another reported lecturing her students for poor sportsmanship. "I just decided it's time for another lecture on: are they really playing for fun or why must they act as if it's a life or death matter." Teachers reinforce notions of community by reminding older children to include younger ones and encouraging them to play together. That play is an extension of school is evident in charts on good sportsmanship that hang in many classrooms.

Finally, as in other Old Order schools, children in the Lancaster Old Order Mennonite schools are responsible for the daily upkeep of their school. Teachers assign chores on a rotating basis, and charts in each school keep track of who has what task. Children are expected to keep their desks clean, help each other, and do their jobs without complaint, just as they are expected to do at home and will be expected to do as adults.

Scheduling the Day

The average daily schedule in Lancaster Old Order Mennonite schools is much like that in the Holmes County area and in Elkhart-LaGrange and Centreville schools. Most schools begin at 8:30, with a fifteen-minute morning recess at 10:00. Lunch is at 11:30, and the children have an hour to eat and play before returning to the classroom at 12:30. There is another fifteen-minute recess at 2:00, and school is dismissed at 3:30. This schedule effectively divides the school day into four periods. Teachers try to have what they believe are the most difficult courses in the morning, so for many the typical school day begins with arithmetic, taught all five days (Fisher and Stahl 1997).

Nevertheless, how a teacher fits different subjects into the schedule may vary considerably. At the Old Order Mennonite Meeting for Beginning Teachers, held in August for all teachers who have taught fewer than two years, one long-time teacher presented a "suggested frequency list" for scheduling subjects. Penmanship, she suggested, should be taught four times a week, arithmetic daily, and English daily for grades two to four and three times a week for grades five through eight. Reading should be taught twice daily as needed for second graders, four times a week for third graders, and three times a week for grades four to eight. The remaining subjects—social studies, health, German, and spelling—should, she suggested, be taught twice a week, and she added time for students to work on memorizing Bible verses (see Appendix D).

Ultimately, according to *Schoolteachers' Signposts*, "Planning a schedule is a matter of fitting your subjects into your class periods." Advising teachers to prepare a rough draft of their schedule ("Write lightly with pencil because you'll be erasing and rearranging."), *Signposts* encourages them to "start filling in the schedule with subjects you will have every day. Since minds are freshest in the morning, schedule harder subjects then. Every grade should have at least one subject in each class period. Some class periods will necessarily have more than one. It may take some juggling, fitting, and refitting until you're satisfied with it. And it will probably take some sacrificing. A teacher with eight grades is quite limited in time" (1985, 112). Most of all, an experienced teacher reminded the beginners, "Take time to smell the roses with your students, and try to remember to pray daily for your schools."

This last was probably good advice, for there is much more going on in the Lancaster Old Order schools than class schedules reveal. Reading, for example, includes oral reading, workbooks, and vocabulary exercises, while spelling includes the initial presentation of the week's list of words, practicing the words in sentences, practice quizzes, and the final weekly spelling test.

"It's important to prepare well for the day's schedule," said one teacher, who added that she liked to study all the lessons the evening before she was to teach them. "I go to school around 6:30 in the morning. [...] I like to go over all eight grades' arithmetic in the morning before the pupils come. The pupils start arriving between 7:45 and 8:00. It's such a joy to listen to their chatter—and their News that they want to share with me. 'Teacher, you know what? We got six puppies at home. And just last week my second grade girl bounded in the door. 'Teacher! We have a Baby!'"

When the teacher rings the bell to start school, children come in from the playground, stow their lunch pails on shelves, hang up their jackets, and go straight to their desks. Most of them have already greeted the teacher individually, but now the teacher says "Good morning" to the group as a whole, and they respond in unison. The teacher starts the day by reading

Singing is important in Old Order Mennonite schools. Gathering by age in the
front of the classroom, children sing for visitors.

from the Bible. After she finishes, the children stand to the right of their
desks and recite the Lord's Prayer in English. This is followed by singing,
for which, at most schools, children file by rows to the front of the classroom, where they line up by grades, with the oldest in the back.

In Swartzentruber Amish schools, the children sing only in German
and do not pray. In the schools of the more isolated, homogeneous Old
Order Amish church communities and in the Holmes County vicinity,
children say the Lord's Prayer only in German and singing is done in both
languages. In the Lancaster County Old Order Mennonite schools, by
contrast, children sing and recite the Lord's Prayer in English, and many
of the songs are those one might hear in Sunday schools in mainstream
Protestant churches. In one school, for example, the first song chosen was
"What a friend we have in Jesus," while at another school it was "Stand
up, stand up for Jesus." Some schools have put together their own song-

books, collections of mimeographed song lyrics, while others use collections such as *The Church and Sunday School Hymnal*.[12] Often there is part singing or singing in rounds.

"I feel singing is important," said one teacher. "I tell mine [my students] we are praising God." In a number of schools, there are even music classes. "It's usually a voluntary thing. Somebody in the neighborhood who knows music," noted a retired teacher, who added, "We like when a man does it. Boys listen when a man does it." Music teachers instruct children in how to read the shaped notes of the Old Order Mennonite songbooks,[13] teach children to recognize what key a piece of music is in and to find the pitch, and, perhaps most importantly, teach them new songs.

At one school, the teacher for the Friday afternoon music lesson was a young woman from the neighborhood who brought a toddler along. She began by taking the first graders to the front of the room to work on "Ten Little Indians," which they had begun the Friday before. After they sang the song together, the teacher encouraged each to sing it alone. Then she taught them a new shaped note and reviewed the ones they had previously learned. The second graders had a sheet of music showing the musical scale in shaped notes. Using a pitch pipe, the teacher started them off singing scales, while the children kept time. She then drilled them with flashcards; as she showed them the particular note, the children had to sing it.[14]

By the time the children are in eighth grade, they are able to recognize the different musical keys, harmonize, sight read, and lead singing. They also have a large repertoire of songs that they know by heart. Finally, they are prepared, once they are old enough to join the "young folks,"[15] to take part in the Old Order Mennonite singing schools, held Saturday evenings in the schoolhouses during the summer, where they learn the German songs and where boys learn to lead the singing in church.[16]

Not all schools have formal music lessons. "My students don't have a music teacher," noted one teacher somewhat sadly, after visiting a neighboring school and hearing the children sing. "I can't compare them [to those she'd heard]. They [the other school] had everything—tenor, bass, alto, soprano." Perhaps because of worries that musical training will elevate some singers over others in the church-community and reinforce harmonizing in song, which is not acceptable in church singing, not everyone supports music classes in the schools. Thus, although they might receive gifts and even some payment "under the table," music teachers volunteer their time and lessons are kept informal. As one teacher pointed out, "It's harder for folks to object if it's just someone coming in to help them sing."

While learning to sing reinforces a musical tradition in the German-speaking Old Order churches, singing and praying in English reflect the realities of these neighborhood schools, which also draw children from church-communities that have shifted to English.[17] "We sing German in church," acknowledged one teacher, but "we have English in school because of some of my English-speaking pupils are of another denomination." Still, she noted, speaking English benefited all of her pupils. "English is very much encouraged in our schools [...] they [parents, the board] encourage English. It's embarrassing if the children get to the point where they talk to city folk in broken English. Also it's harder to do business."

As in the Elkhart-LaGrange and Centreville Old Order Amish schools, the majority of those who begin first grade in Lancaster County Old Order Mennonite schools speak some English, and those with older siblings are often fluent. As one teacher put it, "There's usually at least one that doesn't speak English. That's a first child." Another teacher noted, "For the first grade, I'll say something first in English, but I'll use German later if necessary." She also acknowledged using German to explain difficult vocabulary or asking children to supply the German equivalent to an English vocabulary word to ensure that they have understood it. For the most part, however, "I'll use German to show that I mean it and am serious. I punish in German," she reported.

The Curriculum

In sharp contrast to schools in Swartzentruber Amish communities, in which German provides security and belonging and is often spoken in school even during lessons, Old Order Mennonite schools are English-dominant. "This is an English country," an experienced teacher announced to beginning teachers at the Old Order Mennonite teachers' meetings, explaining how to respond to parents who might resist the emphasis on English. There is, in fact, just as likely to be resistance to German. One teacher told of a family in her school from an English-speaking church-community that objected having their children taught German; the parents wished the children to do more Bible study in its place. "Finally, they left," said the teacher. "The other family from their church accepted the German." In another school, a Horning student who "couldn't seem to grasp the German very well" was excused from studying it; one of the teachers noted that, "as he won't be using it at home or church, they decided to give him science instead."

Since not all Old Order groups in the Lancaster area use German, interaction between different Old Order communities requires groups to negotiate language use. For example, as one Old Order Mennonite teacher noted, the Old Order Amish school meetings are often held in German, but the Mennonite meetings, which generally include Horning Mennonites, are usually held in English. Horning Mennonite teachers in Old Order schools may not be native speakers of German and so may be teaching German as a second language.

In the Lancaster Old Order Mennonite schools, which draw children from both German- and English-speaking church-communities, German language instruction isolates school from church in a way it does not in the schools of the Swartzentruber and more conservative Amish groups. In Swartzentruber schools and schools in smaller, more conservative communities such as Ashland and Somerset, teachers do little grammar instruction and do not emphasize pronunciation differences between the German dialect the children speak at home and the "Bible German" they read in school. Swartzentruber teachers teach the *fraktur* script and German spelling so that their pupils will be able to read the Bible and the *Ausbund* or church hymnal and so will be able to participate fully in church events. Moreover, since they are using Bible stories and the New Testament for their texts, there is little or no discussion of the material. In short, in more conservative schools, German is the language of the church, taught only so that children can participate fully in the church.

In contrast, German may not be taught in every Old Order Mennonite school, nor is it taught as something that the children will need to be good church members. Divorcing written German from the Scriptures, Schoolaid's *German Phonics / Deutsche Lautlehre*, the introductory German text in most third grade classrooms in the Lancaster Old Order Mennonite schools, uses pictures of children playing, clocks, cowboys, and kittens to teach German sounds and the *fraktur* script. In addition to phonics, children learn basic grammar, draw pictures to fit short stories, and do word games. As a follow-up text to *German Phonics*, many schools use Pathway's

Let's Read German, which introduces New Testament vocabulary in stories set in Amish communities. Implicitly suggesting that standard written German might have a nonscriptural use, the Pathway editors argue in
the foreword to *Let's Read German* that "learning any language is more than
merely learning to read it," and the text emphasizes the productive use of
German in exercises that require students to answer questions and write
paragraphs.

Schoolaid's *Wir lesen Geschichten aus der heiligen Schrift*, used by many
fifth and sixth graders, and *Wir lesen und sprechen Deutsch*, used by seventh
and eighth graders, go even further in separating standard written German from the domain of Scripture. These texts present stories and dia-
logues about nature, history, human relationships, and church history. In
sharp contrast to Swartzentruber schools and schools in more conservative
communities, which use German instruction to reinforce identification
with a particular church-community, the Lancaster Old Order Mennonite schools do not link German instruction to particular church practices.
Signposts suggests that German will be helpful to the child because "by
studying another language the pupil learns many valuable lessons. [. . .]
To be able to pick up literature of another language and actually read and
understand it, is an enviable accomplishment" (1985, 96).

Reinforcing the role of German in the Amish and team Mennonite
communities, which use German in church services, but not imposing a
particular religious viewpoint on children from English-speaking Mennonite churches, German instruction helps to prepare children for this diversity. As one teacher noted, "With the mixture of church denominations in
our schools, children learn to respect others [and] to respect that different
churches have different rules and that's how it is."

An "extra subject," German is part of an expanded curriculum that encompasses far more than the reading, writing, spelling, arithmetic, and
Bible German of the most conservative Old Order Amish schools. Old
Order Mennonite educators and parents feel responsible for ensuring that
the private schools provide an education comparable to that provided by
the public schools. As one mother explained, "We appreciate the parochial school setup. We try as hard as we can to get as close to a high school
curriculum as possible. This shows we're willing to work with the authorities. We strive to push what we can in eight years." As another put it,
"We're fortunate that the public has let us go this far." The notion that the

state has granted a privilege that must not be abused is evident even on the school report cards, which remind parents that "in return for the privilege of being granted our Parochial schools," they should help to ensure that schools have a record "that will be respected *by the state as well as having a feeling of satisfaction and sincerity for our own group.*"

While there is some variation in the textbooks used in the Lancaster Old Order Mennonite schools, for the most part the texts are standardized, a combination of old public school texts and new publications by Old Order and more mainstream Christian presses. All use the *Pathway Readers* and the workbooks that accompany them, for example, and most use *Learning to Spell*, a 1951 Ginn and Company text. One teacher suggested that the texts used in the schools revealed a difference between Amish and Mennonite schools. "The Amish," she said, "like to stick to their traditions. They don't feel it necessary to change for more up-to-date books."[18]

Not surprisingly, given that Schoolaid, a publishing house run by a retired Old Order Wenger Mennonite teacher, is located in Lancaster County, most schools use Schoolaid texts, including the Schoolaid language series, *Climbing to Good English*. Designed to give the teacher in the one-room school greater flexibility in scheduling English lessons, these texts emphasize productive English skills. By the time they are in the eighth grade, children are easily diagramming English sentences and writing long compositions and letters. Unlike Swartzentruber Amish teachers, who identify writing with penmanship, teachers in the Lancaster Old Order Mennonite schools are anxious that children learn to write grammatical sentences and well-formed paragraphs. As one experienced teacher noted, "improper grammar is like groundy potatoes." This particular teacher emphasizes writing even in the early grades, requiring second graders to make sentences at least six words long with their spelling words and averaging their composition scores in with the scores on other English exercises.

Teachers supplement formal lessons in a variety of ways that encourage their students to use English productively and fluently. Many teachers have their students keep diaries, and the teachers read and correct these. Most read to their classes, often a chapter a day during scheduled story time, and they ask their students questions about the previous day's reading before they begin. One teacher tries to introduce a new vocabulary word each day and does a word review after the chores are done and before the school lets out.

In addition to the Schoolaid English series, most schools also use the Schoolaid health series, including *Healthy Happy Habits*, which introduces health in third grade in most schools; *The Good Growth Guide* for fourth graders; *The Body's Building Blocks* for fifth and sixth graders; and *Mankind Marvelously Made*, a text for seventh and eighth graders. While third graders study safety habits and sportsmanship, healthy eating, cleanliness, and good manners, seventh and eighth graders study the different systems of the human body, nutrition, food preparation and storage, safety and first aid, and mental health.

This is not science education, for there is no emphasis on data collection and hypothesis testing. Rather, health education is designed to provide children with practical information about themselves as human beings; to reinforce community standards of cleanliness and hygiene; to understand practical aspects of food gathering, storage, and preparation in Old Order homes; and to reinforce social standards of behavior, including community notions of good sportsmanship and fair play. As the editors note, "The facts and knowledge presented [...] are meant to give an elementary and practical foundation for healthy living, touching upon the physical, mental, emotional, and social aspects of our lives." While science teaching in the public schools seems to threaten religious belief, health is taught in Old Order schools to reaffirm the teachings of the church-communities. Ultimately, the editors assert, "the study [...] leaves us in awe of our infinitely great God who has created both the microscopic world and the great universe of stars and space. These orderly and unchangeable laws of nature working together so perfectly reveal a glimpse of the omnipotent nature of the Creator."

The arithmetic texts used in the Old Order Mennonite schools vary. Most schools have replaced the Gordonville workbooks with the Schoolaid Spunky books for first and second grades; and in grades three through eight, the Strayer-Upton texts have, for the most part, given way to either the *Study Time Arithmetic Series* produced by an Old Order Amish publisher in Topeka, Indiana, or the Rod and Staff *Mathematics for Christian Living Series*.

Like the *Climbing to Good English Series*, the Spunky texts have been designed specifically for one-room schools, and thus provide a number of opportunities for the teacher to mix group work with individual practice. The "To the Teacher" note at the beginning of the Teacher's Manual for books 1[1] and 1[2] acknowledges that "a teacher with eight grades will not have the time needed for as much individual, one-to-one teaching as most of the available textbooks require. He will not even have as much time to spend per class, let alone per individual. Therefore he needs materials that take a minimum of teacher time." The text goes on to provide teachers with tips for establishing a class routine and making teaching aids, and some hints of what to expect in the first few weeks of school.

The Spunky texts give children practice in counting, making change, and telling time, and provide them a solid grounding in addition, subtraction, multiplication, and division. As would be expected in books written for Old Order schools, there are no pictures of children, and examples are drawn from elements of the rural Old Order. Addition problems, for example, require children to add up the number of rabbits a child has raised or to figure out how many tomato plants a farmer has left after a heavy frost. Moreover, unlike examples given in the Gordonville workbooks, which are reprints of the 1933 texts by Clifford Upton, money-based problems in the Spunky books give prices for objects that reflect modern reality.[19]

In third grade, however, whether schools have adopted Study Time or Rod and Staff texts, exercises subtly begin to infuse the study of arithmetic with religion. As does the teaching of health, the teaching of arithmetic provides students grounding in practical skills while emphasizing the orderliness of God's creation. For example, as noted in chapter 6, the Study Time series defines arithmetic as evidence of God's creation and brings Old Order history into the problems and examples.

The Rod and Staff *Mathematics for Christian Living Series* is far more overt than Study Time in the way it mixes religious teaching with the study of arithmetic. For example, the grade three text first presents the number system as evidence of "God's Order" and then introduces subtraction in a unit entitled, "God Gives and Takes Away." Children are introduced to the story of Joseph in exile in Egypt and, based on the ages given for the principle characters at various stages of the story, are asked to answer questions such as, "How many years was it from the time Joseph was sold into Egypt until he became ruler?"[20] Other problems are less biblical, but no less religiously oriented: "On his eighteenth birthday a young Christian resolved to pray to God at least 5 times daily for all 365 days of the year. He kept his resolve throughout his life. He died on his seventy-third birthday. What is the minimum number of times in his life that he spent in daily prayer after his resolution?"[21] Bible verses are printed throughout the text.

The use of Rod and Staff texts distinguishes the Lancaster schools from the schools of less progressive Old Order communities, in which arithmetic is only a matter of learning numerical operations. One teacher noted that her school was using the Strayer-Upton texts when she first began teaching because the board considered the Rod and Staff texts "too religious." Only when the board heard that the texts had been revised, did it agree to try them. While A. S. Kinsinger noted that Old Order schools try "to teach religion all day long in our curriculum (lesson) and on the play ground" and suggests that this might be done in arithmetic by teaching accuracy, he observed that religion should be mentioned "seldom, just enough to bring the whole subject to a point, now and then" (Kinsinger 1997, 152; see also Fisher and Stahl 1997, 4; Hostetler and Huntington 1992, 72–73). The Rod and Staff series uses religion to provide a context for the study of arithmetic.[22]

While the arithmetic texts bring religion and history into the study of numbers, social studies texts take children in Old Order Mennonite schools, Amish and Mennonite alike, out into the world, albeit through outdated (though reprinted) public school texts or texts written from an Old Order point of view by Old Order authors. Most schools use a mix of texts to teach social studies to children from third to eighth grade. One school, for example, used a 1962 text from the Follett Publishing Company, *Working Together*, for third graders, and another Follett text, the 1962 *Exploring Regions Near and Far* for fourth grades. For grades five and six, the children had the A Beka *Old World History and Geography*, and for grades seven and eight, they had A Beka *New World History and Geography*. At another school, the teacher has put social studies lessons into a four-year cycle involving fifth to eighth graders. As she described it, in the first year of the cycle all the children study the United States, while in the second they focus on Latin American and Canada. In the third year, the children study Europe, and in the fourth, they focus on Asia and Africa. All children complete the cycle, although they do not all cover the geographic regions in the same order.

At another school, different grades do different regions. While the fourth graders use the 1947 Ginn and Company text *Visits in Other Lands*, fifth graders use the 1960 Ginn and Company *Your People and Mine*. The sixth through seventh grade use the 1982 Silver Burdett and Company *The United States and Its Neighbors*, and eighth graders read the 1968 Silver Burdett and Company *Old World Lands*, a text the Gordonville Print Shop School Supply Room describes as "much cheaper and kept in print for our one-room schools." In a neighboring school with a predominantly Amish population, third graders use the Gordonville *Starter Geography*, fourth graders use a 1968 text from the General Learning Corporation, since reprinted by Gordonville, entitled *Our Big World Geography*, and fifth graders use Laidlaw's 1965 *Great Names in American History*. Seventh and eighth graders use *Old World Lands*.

Clearly, despite the variety of texts used, children in Old Order Mennonite schools are all introduced to the diversity of the world around them. That they acquire information that is often outdated and inaccurate in many respects is both offset and reinforced by the willingness of teachers to draw on a variety of other resources. In social studies, as in other subjects, teachers routinely engage in exercises that supplement the book work. In one school, for example, a visitor who had been to Africa on a church-sponsored visit came in to talk with the children about his experiences and left behind a photo album of pictures taken during his journey. Following his visit to the school, and supplementing their own geography readings, the fourth graders made small versions of "Negrito huts" out of straw. Other children, studying pioneer days, made their own "hornbooks" out of paper. Another teacher provided her pupils with old geography texts and *National Geographic* magazines and had them prepare "journals" of their trips to distant regions. They had to find pictures representing the clothes they would need in the region's climate, the food they would eat, famous sites they would visit, the crops they would see growing, and various industries they would encounter.

By exposing children to outdated pictures, descriptions and evaluations of life in other lands, these exercises may reinforce a U.S.-centric view of the world, one that takes for granted the superiority of the culture and economy of North America in general and their own community in particular. Nevertheless, they also make children aware that there is a world outside Lancaster County in which things may be done differently, and they give children some experience in that world. Moreover, asking children to imagine a journey to a different land in the context of a school exercise may encourage some to make the journey in real life. Imagining what clothes one might have to bring to a different climate suggests that clothing could be adaptable and could vary from church standards. In other words, in an Old Order context, children are exposed to the possibilities of life outside of their communities and challenged to understand it against a backdrop of Old Order values. As they enter the workforce, or even the mission field, these children will be prepared to encounter difference while upholding the rules of the church.

Indeed, together the textbooks, workbooks, and supplementary exercises prepare children to work in the non–Old Order world and to interact with those outside the church-community. In providing them arithmetic skills while teaching that these illustrate God's order, in introducing them to the larger world while emphasizing its limitations, in teaching them to read while guiding them only toward the literature their communities find appropriate, schools educate children who will be adept at meeting difference and whose beliefs will not be challenged by it.

Teachers and School Administration

Texts subtly reinforce church teachings, yet for many teachers and parents, an important goal of education is to encourage independent thought. A motto on one schoolroom wall, for example, says, "An answer found by yourself is worth twenty told you by your teacher." A mother, hearing of a teacher who had simply told her students the answer to questions they could not get, exclaimed, "But how will they learn to think?" The tension between encouraging children to think for themselves and reinforcing a particular context through which children can evaluate the world outside their church community and thus reaffirm the discipline of their church-community informs the Lancaster Old Order Mennonite schools.

Ultimately, notes *Signposts*, "A teacher needs determination and willpower to help a child develop his God-given talents and channel them constructively" (1985, 26). Teachers in the Lancaster schools are given responsibility far different from that borne by their Swartzentruber counterparts, for they must resolve the personal conflict between doing what they desire and doing what will benefit the community. As *Signposts* asserts, "the decision to teach is not one to be made lightly." Prospective teachers are encouraged to be sure that there is not some other work for which they might be better suited, to be sure that they believe in the goals of the private schools, and to be realistic about the sacrifices of teaching: "If you feel your time is wasted on dirty, ill-mannered, unambitious children, you really are no teacher at heart. But if this reading has triggered within you a slumbering desire, an eager reply, you should respond in a positive way. [. . .] Listen to your inner impulses" (1985, 28).

Having been asked to teach by a school board and having chosen to accept, teachers in Old Order Mennonite schools are expected to take advantage of opportunities to train for the experience. According to the *Pennsylvania Standards*, "the Parochial school board will recognize that when a new or young teacher is accepted on the job, the first three (3) years she will teach as a substitute or on trial. [. . .] When the teacher has taught for three years as such and proved her ability to teach to the satisfaction of her local board, they shall immediately after her third year grant her a diploma showing her capability of teaching a [sic] Amish or Mennonite Parochial school from grades 1 to 8 in English and German."[23]

Although the *Pennsylvania Standards* recognizes further that "a teacher for a[n] Old Order one-room Amish or Mennonite Parochial school is considered a self-employed church worker, being able to teach by the talents and qualities that she has acquired and are God given" (1969, 18), most new teachers attend the meetings for beginning teachers held every year in early August. These meetings are, in fact, an outgrowth of the regular teachers' meetings that have been going on since the 1960s. At first organized informally, the teachers' meetings are now managed by an elected committee of three teachers, each of whom must have at least three years of experience. One teacher noted that "as of yet we haven't re-elected anyone who has already served," although, she acknowledged, "it was about time to."

In 1994, recognizing the need to provide new teachers with training and support, a small group of the more-experienced Old Order Mennonite teachers invited all teachers in the community with six years or more teaching experience to come together to plan a special series of meetings for beginning teachers, those with less than three years experience in the classroom. Today these meetings for beginning teachers last four days and draw beginning teachers from Old Order Mennonite church-communities across Pennsylvania, New York, and Ohio. In describing the meetings, one of the organizers notes that the topics they have chosen to cover are "areas a teacher won't need to hear as much after several years in the classroom." Asked why the meetings were limited to only four days, she responded, "We are not a people who think a person should spend his prime years age 6–20 only in cultivating academics—or in going to school. Rather we feel an 8th grade education is sufficient. I think the leaders fear we may be approaching school for grown ups—or a higher education. Where would we stop? How many days would we need? It is better to put a potential teacher into the classroom to learn hands on as a helper."

In August 2002, roughly 150 new teachers and teachers' aids were at the meetings, which took place at the Riverside School. Of this number, approximately one-sixth were Old Order Amish; three were men. Divided into four groups on the basis of the mix of grades they would be teaching in the fall—first to fourth grades, fourth to eighth grades, a mixture of lower and upper grades, and all eight grades—the teachers followed a schedule similar to that of the Old Order schools; in fact, many referred to the meetings as "school." Starting at 8:00 a.m. the teachers gathered to sing three hymns (in English), listen to a Scripture reading, and recite the Lord's Prayer. They then attended four classes, each lasting 45 minutes, with a fifteen-minute break between classes. Lunch was between the third and fourth classes, and the day's session ended at 1 p.m.

By the end of the week, the teachers had received intensive lessons in the teaching of reading, English, arithmetic, and phonics, and had been told what kinds of records to keep and how to plan their daily schedules. In addition, they had had the opportunity to purchase home-made valentines and bookmarks and stickers, exchange home-made charts and posters, purchase books, and even peruse advertisements for teachers wanted in smaller, newer settlements.

The week following the Old Order Mennonite meetings for beginning teachers, many of the Old Order Amish teachers also attended the meeting for teachers in Old Order Amish schools, a one-day session that, according to one teacher, was "*very* interesting," although she noted that the emphasis was far more on discipline than on methodology. According to one of the organizers of the Old Order Mennonite beginning teachers' meetings, the Old Order Amish have tried for several years to organize meetings of their own for beginning teachers but have been stymied in their efforts by church leaders. "They don't want any other group to gain control," she asserted, "especially not women." Limiting the Old Order Amish teach-ers' meetings to a single day and not focusing on "how to teach" seems to head off complaints, similar to those that limit the length of the Old Or-der Mennonite beginning teachers' meetings, that the meetings provide "higher education." As an Old Order Amish teacher acknowledged, "The Amish just do not stress education like the Mennonites do."

Most Old Order Mennonite teachers, both beginning and experi-enced, also attend the two-day "all teachers" meeting, generally held the week after the meetings for beginning teachers.[24] As one of the organizers of the beginning teachers' meetings noted, these two days focus mostly on "topics touching every area of school life as follows: penmanship, music, discipline, routines, management, and various helpful talks meant for en-couragement as well as instruction."

Teachers are encouraged to invite the members of their school's board to attend the morning session of the second day, which is called the Teach-ers and Directors' Day, and many school board members do come, some accompanied by their wives. The chairs of the different Old Order Men-nonite regional districts address the teachers, offering encouragement. In-dicating both a greater professionalism on behalf of the teachers and an acknowledgement that the relationship between the board and a long-time teacher might become adversarial, a number of this second day's presentations feature board members and teachers giving their respective views on topics such as discipline, the celebration of secular holidays (e.g., Halloween, Valentine's Day), and visitors to the school. As one regional director put it at the August 2003 meetings, "For a board to be able to help, it needs to be told what the problems are. Teachers should respect the board as people of authority, but it's really not authority, it's responsi-bility. Many board members don't know much about teaching. If a board makes a recommendation that the teacher doesn't like, the teacher should express an opinion, not just ignore it." The director went on to suggest that board members should occasionally substitute so that they can understand teaching better. "I consider it [substitute teaching] a privilege," he added, "because I was only asked to do it once. They haven't asked me again." An-other board member recommended that teachers "tell your boards about things. I'd rather deal with problems when they're small." He went on to note that boards should support the teachers. "If we're too busy to support our teachers, she might be too busy to teach our school. Teachers should be paid good and be paid fairly so that they're satisfied with their wages. At monthly meetings, teachers should have a chance to talk."

The meetings for beginning teachers are funded by the teachers themselves, who are asked to give a donation to cover the costs of using the school building and supplies. Any money left over is divided between the teachers who organized and presented topics. At the Directors' Day meeting, there is a "kitty" to which all attending can contribute to cover expenses. The importance of these large meetings, which draw attendance from across the Lancaster settlement and beyond, to the Old Order Mennonite parochial school system is evident in the construction of Riverside School outside of Ephrata. Riverside, built in 1968 and remodeled in 1982 to include two classrooms on the ground floor and one in the basement, indoor plumbing, and electricity, is larger than most of the Old Order Mennonite schools so that it can also serve as the venue for these gatherings. The wall between the two main floor classrooms can be pushed back to create one large meeting room.

Teachers continue to meet throughout the year. One unstated purpose of the meetings for beginning teachers appears to be to provide them with the opportunity to construct a support network, to draw on the ideas and experiences not only of those instructing the meetings but of others attending. Regional teachers' meetings, organized by the teachers' committee and held approximately every six weeks at different schools during the school year, continue to provide opportunities for teachers to meet and exchange ideas and experiences and to discuss topics of relevance to them all, including discipline and working with children with special needs.[25] Each meeting has a theme, one teacher pointed out. "In September, meetings are about things not covered during the August meetings, like health and social studies." This meeting, she added, was a big time for questions. "In October, the meetings might be about first grade or reaching goals or discipline and in November it might be about how to have a Christmas program."

"There are meetings throughout the term," according to a new teacher. Describing the first she had attended, she noted that there were 67 teachers present:

After singing we had three topics, the first one was Are you back into routine?

2nd Health, 3rd Getting Along.

At each meeting we have a song we sing and also do a review if any one wants to. After that they have a question and answer session. They pass a box around and anyone can put in a question they want answered. They give it to teachers who have been teaching a while already and they try and answer the question. If they don't know they can ask if anyone else has an idea of what to do for the problem. At times it will be questions on where to get a certain kind of book or if any school has any they can borrow. After that they usually have a time called Memorable Moments where teachers, usually two at each meeting, will tell or read about memorable things that happened at their school. And we were served supper on the porch at school. Spaghetti and Banana Splits.

The second meeting of the term, she added, was similar. "There were 71 teachers there (this includes two helpers). Our first topic was 'What did grade 1 learn?' Our second topic was 'Organizing a Christmas Program.' Our third topic was 'Discipline!' We had our song before our third topic." Again there was a time for questions and Memorable Moments.

Perhaps it is because of this support network and the regular opportunities to explore new aspects of teaching that many Lancaster Old Order Mennonite teachers make teaching a career. Indeed, according to estimates by the *Blackboard Bulletin*, Lancaster County may have the greatest percentage of "older single women who have been teaching for long periods of time."[26] Teaching as a career is also possible because the pay for teachers in Lancaster County is somewhat higher than it is for teachers in the smaller, less progressive settlements, although less than teachers earn in the Elkhart-LaGrange and Centreville settlements. Most of those teaching in one-room schoolhouses earn between $20 and $50 a day; those teaching in two-room schools earn more. One teacher with over two decades of teaching experience earned $43.00 a day, a sum she guessed was "high to average." But, she noted, she did not pay Social Security or Workman's Compensation. "I'm considered self-employed," she said, while acknowledging that in fact, "I'm working for the board."

Most often a school board, composed of three fathers elected to be directors, administers a single school; in some cases, a larger board of five members may administer more than one school. One teacher, whose board also governs two neighboring schools, noted that the board met once a month, but the meetings rotated among the three schools. "Parents," she added, "usually come only when the meetings is at their children's school." The directors of all the schools meet once or twice each year and "vote from this pool for head directors called Committee men."

The school boards are responsible for making sure that schools fulfill their obligations to the state, and the committee of representatives from each district, the "committee men," ensures that all act according to the agreed standards. As one retired Mennonite teacher described it,

> In late summer, the fourth Wednesday in July to be exact, there is an annual Directors' Meeting for the directors of all Old Order Mennonite schools under the Lancaster County Amish plan. Our main committee for all these schools organizes this meeting, and all teachers are invited. The purpose of the meeting is to inform all individual school boards of school laws, duties, and anything pertaining to running our schools, including recommendations of textbooks, etc. This meeting is also held at Riverside school (where the summer teachers' meetings are held), but a week or two before the teachers' meetings. Nearly all schools are represented here because this is where school directors get their instructions.

As would be expected in a system of schools that serves families from different church-communities, this hierarchical system of school governance is separate from church organization. As one teacher noted, "Ministers are welcomed to attend board meetings, but because of their church duties, they don't need to serve on the board." Another teacher noted, "Ministers attend parent-teacher board meetings, but do not serve on the board nor get involved in school problems." "Parents from different denominations," she added, "serve together on the board. Our committeemen stress that we keep school, school and church, church and not mix the two."

Schools are funded by the parents of the children attending. Noted one teacher, "The school parents all pay the same amount to send their children no matter how many students they have." According to another, "The board adds up its expenses, teachers' salaries, fuel, supplies, and divides it evenly among the patrons (school families sending children) every six weeks. That is also when they give me my salary." This teacher noted that elderly couples, those who no longer have children of school age, do not attend meetings or contribute financially to the schools, although some did make donations. Another teacher noted that "the elderly couples help financially by paying head taxes, that is, if they wish to." There may also be additional fundraisers, such as yard sales or auctions. Finally, some Old Order Mennonite schools may receive funds from outside sources. According to one long-time teacher, "a multi-millionaire designated some of his estate to be donated to the parochial schools in Lancaster County. [. . .] This [. . .] helps us out."

For special needs, financial support may be solicited on a church-wide basis. One teacher noted that "during the last, say maybe 10 years, our schools are learning to help children with learning disabilities, and they take much time." A number of schools have tutors working one-on-one with children with learning disabilities. Tutors meet with the children one to two hours a day on the average, and tutoring continues through the summer with parental involvement. The school boards are responsible for funding tutoring services, and these costs are factored into the schools' expenses. For children who are unable to participate in regular schools, there are two special education schools in Lancaster County.[27] In these schools, the student-teacher ratio averages three to one. A retired teacher active in teacher training and curriculum development noted that the Old Order Mennonite schools were now using the Stevenson Learning Skills Program and were even at the point of evaluating children. To fund these schools, the different church-communities take up freewill offerings. As the retired teacher noted, "There has never been a lack of funds for that."

As special needs education has grown in importance in the Lancaster Old Order Mennonite schools, so too has support for tutors and teachers. As one teacher noted, identifying children with special needs has had an impact on her school. "This was the first term our school set up a LD (learning difference) organization. They have meetings about once in two months for parents with such children and tutors. We are glad for all the young girls who take time to help these special children. [. . .] I would have found my ADHD pupil a frustrating challenge without his tutor and my helper." When possible, however, children with special needs remain in the regular classroom. As *Signposts* points out in the chapter on "Special Classroom Issues," "The child must learn to accept himself and his drawbacks, and he will be helped in doing this by others who accept him yet sympathize with him in being patient and tolerant. Such things must be

A curtain creates private space where a tutor can give a
"special child" extra help with lessons.

accepted in the same way as the shape of a person's nose or the color of his
hair" (1985, 148).

Community Involvement with the Schools

Children with special needs must learn to accept their limitations. So too
must the other children, who are expected to help each other and show
patience and good sportsmanship to those who are less able. Interestingly,
"the fast learner" rates his own section in *Signposts* in the "Special Classroom Issues" chapter. Implicit is the expectation that all will simply do
their best, and it is the teacher's task to provide the encouragement and
opportunity for them to do so.

Parents are expected to provide teachers the support and encouragement teachers need so that they, too, can do their best. "I often meet my
students' parents," said one teacher. "They come visiting several times a
year. A highlight to us is when they bring hot lunch to school. We have
board meetings once a month. A few mothers with small children might

not attend, but the majority do. What I appreciate about my parents is if I'm having a problem with their child and I discuss it with them and then they drop in soon after to see how he's doing." Yet another teacher noted, "Having the parents involved does make my job easier. We stress good communication with teacher and parents."

Parent support comes in different forms. In one school, for example, one Amish teacher had a number of weddings to attend throughout the fall "wedding season." Aware that the teacher would probably be very tired the next day, the mother of one of the Amish students would take the teacher's lunch pail home with her the day before the wedding, and the student would bring it to school the day after, saving the teacher the chore of getting up earlier to pack her lunch pail. Students at another school arrived one day in early fall to find a giant pumpkin outside the door. "Welcome to our school" had been carved into the pumpkin's shell before it was fully grown so that the words grew into the skin of the pumpkin and stood out sharply.

Parents visit schools regularly, and schools emphasize the importance of visitors. Each school has a wall display celebrating visitors. On the back wall of one school, for example, was a large black construction paper kettle overflowing with popcorn; above it was the slogan "We Love When Visitors Pop In." The next year the slogan was "Visitors Keep Us On Track," the words encircled by a paper train. One room of a two-room school featured a cutout silhouette of a young girl, her dress blowing forward gently as if in a breeze, in a heart-shaped frame of smaller cutout hearts. The slogan above the display read, "Visitors Gladden our Hearts." The other room showed a large black frying pan overflowing with "sunny-side-up eggs" and the slogan "Visitors are Egg-zactly What We Need." The visitors' display at a third school pictured a "Precious Moments"–like cutout of a small boy in a wooden bathtub surrounded by bubbles, with the slogan "Visitors Add Bubbles and Joy to Our Day!"

Unlike the spiral notebooks of the Old Order Amish communities, which contain only the signatures of visitors, the date of their visits and their comments, the guest books offered to visitors in Lancaster Old Order Mennonite schools tend to be elaborate affairs, large binders or scrapbooks with decorated covers that give visitors detailed information about the students in the school, including their parents' names, their hobbies, favorite chores, and wishes for the future. The first page of one book featured a construction-paper bear holding balloons, each with a letter that together spelled "w-e-l-c-o-m-e." Page two listed all the students by name with their father's name in parentheses. The third page was a letter of welcome, which told visitors about the school and invited them to become involved in the daily activities. The fourth page gave the daily schedule of subjects, the fifth featured a paragraph on submission, and the sixth allowed visitors to "Meet the Teacher," listing her parents, her birthday, her favorite subjects, likes and dislikes, and the names and ages of her siblings. This was followed by pages the children had completed giving similar information, and pictures colored by the children. Only at the end was there room for visitors to sign. Another guest book offered an essay on "Summer Vacation," written by the teacher's helper, and a list of all of those who had taught at the school as well as an explanation of the school's name. In addition, there was a page listing the families of all those with children in the school. Again, the children had colored pages about themselves to tell the visitors their date of birth, favorite chore, and least favorite food. By the beginning of November, this guest book had recorded visitors on 17 different school days, and on 11 occasions the visitors had come in groups.

At the All Teachers' Meeting in August 2003, in a presentation on visitors entitled "A Knock on the Door," one experienced teacher acknowledged being nervous when visitors came to her school. At the same time, however, she talked about being impressed by schools that made visitors a top priority. "Get visitors involved," she advised, and suggested having parents listen to the younger children read or quiz students on their spelling words. She went on to present ideas for visitors' charts and welcome books.

Yet, perhaps because the teacher and the families of children attending school are not all from the same church-community, families do not know each other as well and are not as familiar with the teacher, who is often older and more experienced and has a support network of other teachers on which to draw. As a result, parent-teacher relationships appear to be more formal. Parents attend the monthly board meetings, and these are times when they may talk with the teacher about their children's progress. The children also put on programs for their parents at holiday time and at the end of the school term. One teacher summed up her relationship with the parents at her school when she said, "We had parent-teachers meeting once a month where we discussed problems and events. Also, the parents usually come to visit now and then. I was so thankful that the parents were all willing to do their part and caused no trouble. We had very good support in everything."

At the Meetings for Beginning Teachers, one experienced teacher emphasized the need for teachers to keep parents in touch with the school. Unlike Swartzentruber parents, who are little concerned with their children's school, and parents in Old Order Amish communities who are *expected* to take an active interest in what is going on at the schoolhouse, parents of children attending the Old Order Mennonite schools in Lancaster County—Amish and Mennonite alike—are interested but often uninvolved. *Signposts* suggests a number of reasons why parents might not reply to a teacher's letter requesting a meeting: "Sometimes parents don't respond because their minds are swamped with other matters which take priority. Some are embarrassed, some hesitate for fear of finding their child at fault, and some simply don't know how to respond" (1985, 65). All of these suggest that the teacher must negotiate a relationship with parents that will allow both to cross a divide between the boundaries of home and church-community and those of the school.

"The parents and the teacher are working together to reach a goal. That makes them partners," *Signposts* asserts (1985, 65). Explicitly denying teachers the parent-like role teachers in communities such as Somerset, Ohio, or the Ashland area assume, *Signposts* advises teachers, "If you can make the parents feel you're in this together for the good of the child, the results will be good. But again, don't go to the extreme of calling pupils 'our children' when talking with parents. Parents will consciously or subconsciously resent this and it will put a barrier between you" (1985, 66).

When there are difficulties between teacher and parents, most likely over discipline and other issues involving the children, the teacher's recourse is the school board, which serves as go-between and arbiter. One teacher, who had just completed a difficult term, said, "I never thought it would be I who would need to face such difficulties, but no it [difficulties with parents] is not unusual in our schools, because I know my parents were not as harsh or cruel as [parents I have heard about from other teachers]. I feel I have not lived through this in vain. Actually I often pity them or feel more compassionate and realize they need my prayers."

In schools that are separate from the church-communities whose members help to support them, the Lancaster teachers play a more professional role than their counterparts in Swartzentruber schools, in the smaller communities such as Fredericktown and Ashland, and in the large, homogeneous settlements of Elkhart-LaGrange and Centreville. They are responsible for record keeping and for reporting enrollments and absences to the board, and each term's records and grade books must remain with the school for three years. Teachers must also keep a list of needed school supplies, not simply so that they do not run out, but so that the school board can plan ahead. They must keep track of things they wish to see discussed at the monthly "patrons'" meeting, including problems, daily events, and things of special interest to the parents. Finally, teachers must be responsible for continually improving themselves and for playing a role in the support and training of other teachers.

Old Order Schools and the Future

In a 1938 commentary on the decision of the Pennsylvania legislature to allow Old Order parents to continue to send their children to the one-room schoolhouse in East Lampeter in Lancaster County, the New York Times noted, "When the Amish youngsters climbed out of their sleighs in the early morning hours they had to bring in coal from the shed to light the school stove, fetch water and do other chores." Suggesting that this was perhaps the best way to educate children, the article concluded, "Forty years later they will be the big industrialists and labor leaders and give orders to the graduates from our chromium-plated central schools."[28]

While today's Old Order youngsters will likely not become big industrialists of the kind the New York Times writer had in mind, they will probably live a far more industrial—and economically privileged—lifestyle than did their grandparents who graduated from the East Lampeter school. Swartzentruber Amish have reacted to progress and technological change in non—Old Order society by seeking further isolation, limiting the range of subjects taught, and giving a greater role to German in the school. In Lancaster County, however, the goal of Old Order education is to help instill Old Order religious values in children while preparing them for a changing life in which manufacturing more than farming will be their lot. "To prepare [children] for usefulness, by preparing [them] for eternity" (Pennsylvania Standards, 2) has meant expanding the curriculum, trying new textbooks, and creating a more professional teaching staff by offering teachers greater support and training.

Being neighborhood schools rather than church schools, the Lancaster County Old Order schools emphasize a Christian approach to education rather than one defined narrowly by the practices of a particular church. At times this causes conflict. One teacher acknowledged that she felt herself to be "more conservative" than the families of most of her students and suggested that education in Old Order schools was changing because families were changing. "Students are much less farming-based now and more affluent," she asserted. "Children use paper tissues now, rather than cloth hankies." And whereas in previous years her pupils had had heavy plastic cups that they labeled with their names and kept all year on hooks by the water jug, mothers had recently decided that this was unsanitary. Now every two weeks the disposable plastic cups on the hooks are discarded and new ones put in their place.

The move away from farming and the increasing affluence of Lancaster County's Old Order population may, in the future, have an even greater impact on Old Order schools. Currently the system of vocational education agreed upon in 1955 is still in place for children who are not yet 15 when they finish eighth grade. Children attend the neighborhood private school for three hours a week and keep a journal of their daily activities. Yet, as a retired teacher pointed out, the vocational classes were really designed for farming families who needed their children's help on the farm. As families move away from farming and there is less work for children at home, vocational classes may no longer meet the needs of particular church-communities. A number of Horning Mennonite families, for example, now send their children to one of the Weaverland Mennonite Schools, which do not operate under the Old Order plan. The Weaverland schools are larger and go up to grade nine or ten.

Moreover, the Weaverland schools no longer offer German, and they place a greater emphasis on Bible study than do schools that are attended by children from different Old Order church-communities. While some credit the emphasis on German language teaching with helping to improve the fluency of Wenger Mennonite ministers and to reinforce the role of German in the Wenger Mennonite churches, others fear that, with the directors' and teachers' meetings in English, English will become increasingly dominant in Old Order education.

The Lancaster Old Order Mennonite schools prepare children for life both in their church-communities and in the non–Old Order world in which many of them will earn their living. Part of that preparation is exposing them to others whose lifestyle may differ, to technology that they may not have in their homes, and to the world outside the limits of their home and county. The other part is teaching them the discipline that will keep them close to home and church. In all things, there is tension between encouraging independent thinking and inculcating conformity to values. In Lancaster, perhaps much more than in less progressive communities, one-room schools remain as they were when they were public, meeting objective standards for success, concerned with providing excellent teachers, and training children for a broader life, all under neighborhood control.

Publish or Perish

This work [publishing] is not a normal occupation for Amish people.
—Old Order Amish printer

The Gordonville Print Shop: Realizing the Need

Key in protecting children in private schools from the influence of the non–Old Order world is controlling the information they receive. Despite variations from church-community to church-community, children in Old Order schools generally acquire many of the same skills as their public school peers, and many acquire similar knowledge. But they learn through texts that, in different ways, reinforce the values of the church-community and its separation from the dominant society.

Developing to meet the growing needs of Old Order private schools, Old Order publishers, like the schools they serve, offer varying responses to the forces of consolidation and modernity that threaten to assimilate the Old Order church-communities. Like the schools that use their respective products, the three primary suppliers of texts to Old Order Schools—the Pathway Publishing Company, founded by Old Order Amish in Aylmer, Ontario; the Gordonville Printing Company, founded by Old Order Amish in Lancaster County, Pennsylvania; and the Schoolaid Publishing Company, founded by Old Order Mennonites also in Lancaster County—as well as Study Time, a new press recently founded by Old Order Amish in Indiana, and A Beka and Rod and Staff, non–Old Order Christian presses, reflect different community-based notions of what it means to be Old Order, how the Old Order must interact with the dominant society, and, most importantly, what values are to be reinforced through the schools. As such, these publishers act as powerful agents to reinforce the values that keep the group intact and the world out.

As noted earlier, the first Old Order schools were an effort to maintain the status quo, to continue unchanged that which the dominant society was bent on changing. When possible, Old Order communities took over the old one-room public schoolhouses, and in some cases, even continued with public school teachers. Moreover, they continued to use the same texts as the neighboring public schools, often relying on cast-offs. John Martin, a retired Old Order Mennonite schoolteacher still active in Old Order publishing, says, "They [public schools] would want to change them [for revised or updated texts] and we could buy them cheap."[1] The difficulty was that "as the number of [parochial] schools multiplied, they [the books] ran out." Moreover, Martin notes, although "at first they were the same books we'd been using, after [the public schools started revising them] we weren't so satisfied, and we thought we should have our own."

The Old Order Book Society of Pennsylvania was formed in 1948 to discuss, among other topics, the standardization of books to be used by the Old Order schools of Pennsylvania (Fisher and Stahl 1997). In 1958 Andy S. Kinsinger, secretary for the Old Order schools in Leacock Township, was elected chair. Kinsinger had had the responsibility for furnishing the books, castoffs from the public schools, for the Leacock schools, and having purchased the Gordonville Print Shop in 1956, he found publishing texts specifically for Old Order schools to be the next logical step. As his daughter, Susan Kinsinger, writes, suitable books "were getting harder and harder to get. [. . .] Having the printing press gave us cause to start printing schoolbooks, workbooks etc. and mostly reproducing old books which were no longer available but well liked by the Amish schools" (A. S. Kinsinger 1997, 244). In 1958 Gordonville acquired the rights to reprint a number of editions no longer in use by the public schools and, according to the current owners of the Gordonville Print Shop, started in the 1960s or 70s to supply parochial schools with books.[2] As Alta Hoover, a textbook publisher and retired teacher, put it, "Kinsinger began his business at a time when the public schools started to change [the textbooks]. They met and decided what to use and have stayed with it."

A horse waits patiently in front of the Gordonville Print Shop in Lancaster County.

Under the direction of the Old Order Book Society, the Gordonville print shop, described by Susan Kinsinger as "a small business but using lots of paper," continues to supply Old Order Amish schools in the most conservative Amish communities with texts that were standard in public schools in years past, including the 1919 *Essentials of English Spelling* and the 1934 *Strayer-Upton Practical Arithmetic Series*, and that the Old Order Book Society approved for the schools in 1959. "We knew these were good texts because school boards had approved them, so why change?" argues the Gordonville printer. "We print what the schools ask for." In Andy Kinsinger's words, "The School Supply Room [of the Gordonville Print Shop] took over printing and supplying practically all the school books for the Parochial school, but the Old Order Book Society still has authority to keep tab on what books are being used" (1997, 164).[3]

The Gordonville Print Shop prospered, and according to Susan Kinsinger (1988, 245), employed "6 or more people" by the late 1980s and offered "a full line of books and supplies . . . used by the Amish and Mennonite schools." She also noted that the print shop had "several offset presses, collator, cutter, paper punch, folder and numerous equipment found in a print shop" but had removed the letter press and hand type "to make room for more up-to-date equipment." Conforming to the rules of the Lancaster Old Order Amish church-community, there is no electricity in either the print shop or the sales room; the printing presses are driven hydraulically and powered by a diesel engine located outside the shop (Loyd 1975).

In supplying Old Order schools with archaic texts, Gordonville and similar print shops, including Raber's Bookstore in Baltic, Ohio, which offers reprints of the 1879 *McGuffey's Readers*, reinforce a boundary between the "unchanging" Old Order Amish communities that still use these books and the dominant society that has discarded them. Children using these texts will not learn much about the world outside their church-communities, for the illustrations and examples used often present a world that no longer exists. The *Strayer-Upton Arithmetics Series*, for example, presents children with story problems that feature biplanes carrying "express, mail, and passengers between large cities" and grocery stores with clerks who write out sales receipts by hand. Numerous woodcut illustrations in the *McGuffey's Readers* offer Old Order children images of little boys in knee-length trousers, short coats, and ruffled shirts, little girls wearing numerous petticoats and ruffled bonnets, women in floor-length skirts, and men in bowler hats.

In these texts, little boys help an old widow take her basket of apples to the town to sell or help other children whose fathers are too poor to send them to school to learn to read and write, families ride in fine carriages, and convicts wear striped clothing and break rocks with large hammers. The spelling lists in the 1919 *Essentials of English Spelling* include such little used vocabulary words as "adz," "magneto," and "chifforobe." In the *McGuffey's Eclectic Primer*, used by first-graders, children walk to the schoolhouse with their books and slates, knowing they must arrive before the bell rings. In the world of the Strayer-Upton series, one can still buy a house for $6,000.

For the Swartzentruber Amish, perhaps the only group to still use the *McGuffey's Readers*, and isolated homogeneous and more conservative communities such as those in Somerset, Fredericktown, and Ashland, Ohio, which continue to use the *Dick and Jane* series (popular in the 1950s and 1960s), these archaic texts are ideal. They offer children a non-Amish world that vanished decades ago and so do not expose them to the dangers

LESSON XXXVI.

Mĭss   wạnts   wọuld   tĕllş

rụle

kēep

ḡŏŏd

thăt

ēach

ụ

The girls and boys all love Miss May; she is so kind to them.

Miss May tells them there is a rule that she wants them to keep. It is, "Do to each one as you would like each one to do to you."

McGuffey's Eclectic Primer. Rev. ed. 1881; 1906.
Available from Raber's Book Store, Baltic, Ohio, p. 41.

The *McGuffey's Readers* and other archaic texts
present a world that vanished long ago.

of modern society. Moreover, the books are valued for their straightforward approach to practical knowledge. For example, in the Preface, the authors of *Essentials of Spelling* present the text as "an attempt to teach only the essential words of the written vocabularies of children and adults" and advocate the presentation of fewer words and increased drilling.[4] Similarly, the *Strayer-Upton Practical Arithmetics Series*, with page after page of story problems and arithmetic worksheets, "aims to give the child the ability to compute easily and accurately and to interpret and solve the quantitative situations which he will meet in everyday life" (Preface, Book 3, p. iii).

In conservative schools there is little discussion of the material. Spelling words are often not presented in context, and on the rare occasions when teacher and students do discuss stories, they talk, not about the non-Amish characters, but rather about what Amish people might do in similar situations. Again, the values learned are those of the church-community. As Keim (1975: 14) notes, "The Amish view education as a way to encourage the child to follow instructions, respect authority, and master basic information. They are skeptical of education which stresses engagement, critical thinking, or asking questions. They favor rote learning. The community can survive only if authority and tradition are respected and upheld."

The more conservative Old Order communities that use the Gordonville texts tend to expect little from the school except that their children learn to read, write, and do arithmetic (Huntington 1994; Johnson-Weiner 1998). Moreover, they expect that their children will simply do the lessons and not talk about them, just as they must do the work they have at home without discussion. Divorced from both the non-Amish world children see around them and the Old Order world in which the children live, Gordonville texts support a pedagogy that encourages rote learning, a mastery of basic information, and respect for authority, while at the same time downplaying engagement with the material, critical thinking, and question asking (Keim 1975).

Further subordinating the teachings of the school to those of the home and church, the Gordonville texts are moralistic and God-fearing, but religiously neutral. Early on, the Book Society debated the role of religion in schools, agreeing finally that "religion is nothing to play with and should not be used in text books in the elementary grades" (Kinsinger 1997, 246). Today, in the most conservative Old Order schools, there is no discussion of biblical topics or even prayer before the noontime meal. The teacher must help children learn to work together and to do their best, thereby reinforcing the lessons of church and home, but she must not usurp the place of the parents and ministers in providing religious instruction.

Finally, reprinted generation after generation, the Gordonville texts reinforce a sense of continuity in the community, the notion that important values are unchanging. Facilitating the use of the same texts generation after generation, the Gordonville Print Shop makes it possible for the textbooks, like other symbols of Old Order life, including distinctive dress, horse and buggy transportation, and the one-room schoolhouse, to serve as a physical bond uniting parent to child, older sibling to younger (Johnson-Weiner 1997).

Yet, while the Gordonville printers, committed to continuing unchanged the practices of their church-communities, kept the old public one-room school houses as their educational model and wondered "how to keep the same texts [... when ...] publishers kept putting out new texts and new additions,"[5] others were beginning to redefine Old Order education as education in a *Christian* context. In Old Order schools, one Amishman wrote, "we have the privilege of teaching the regular branches, and at the same time we can interweave the doctrine of God, Christ, and the Church in all our studies, even in arithmetic" (*Challenge* 1959, 69). Envisioning the private school as being as important as the home in preparing children for Old Order life, they began to question the suitability for Old Order schools of any texts written for a secular, non–Old Order world.

The Pathway Publishing Corporation: Amish Books for Amish Schools

In the early 1950s, while the Old Order Book Society was beginning to discuss standardizing Old Order schools in Pennsylvania, a group of Old Order Amish teachers in Ontario, Ohio, and Indiana began a circle letter to offer all participants the opportunity to seek help, share tips, and keep in touch with the others.[6] In 1957 the letter became *The Blackboard Bulletin*, a monthly teachers' journal that had, as a primary goal, the development of Old Order schools that would ensure the spiritual survival of the church-community.

The *Blackboard Bulletin* aggressively promoted the Amish school movement in editorials and articles. In "Why Do We Have Our Own Schools?" Ervin N. Hershberger wrote in April 1958,

Perhaps one of our first reasons for establishing our own schools is to keep our children out of the present-day public schools. [...] Most of us are at least partly aware of the inroads which immorality and corruption in various forms have made in our public schools of today, such as abbre-

viated gym suits, dancing lessons, distorted teachings on sex, a Christ-
less man-centered curriculum, etc. Space will not permit a discussion of
these other than the passing caution against them, and more especially
to remind us of the urgency of replacing such characteristics with Christian purity, virtue, and a Bible-centered, Christ-exalting program in our
own schools; lest we only develop an Amish version of the same evils. To
safeguard against evil is always a justifiable motive. This scores one good
motive to withdraw from a system which has gone beyond our control,
particularly in highly consolidated schools."[7]

Similarly, in a pamphlet entitled "Who Shall Educate Our Children?"
Blackboard Bulletin editor Joseph Stoll, asserted, "Teaching, commanding,
training, bringing them up, these are the duties of parents to their children. But we might ask ourselves a question. Are we training and teaching
our children, if we send them to state schools five days a week? Is not the
state training them?"[8]

Although Stoll argued later that the private school movement was already starting to spread and that rather than creating it, the *Blackboard Bulletin* "just got in on the beginning and it mushroomed,"[9] the *Blackboard Bulletin*
helped to redefine education for a number of Old Order church-communities,
encouraging a different, more interactive pedagogy and fostering a view of
the school as central to community life (Delval 1986). While teachers in the
more conservative communities—usually underage, unmarried girls, in many
cases only a year or two out of school—generally teach only one or two
years, the teachers who subscribe to the *Blackboard Bulletin* often teach
several years, some even making teaching a career; and the journal has
become an expanded circle letter, a collection of submissions "news, articles, reports, announcements, poems, stories, editorials" from and for not
only teachers but also parents and schoolchildren.[10] "Massive and active
involvement of the readers indeed suggests that the *Blackboard Bulletin*,
and consequently to a broader extent education, are a concern for all,"
notes Delval (1986, 75).

Gordonville does not work directly with teachers other than to fill their
book orders. "You can't train [a teacher] to give a good basic education,"
says the Gordonville printer. The *Blackboard Bulletin*, however, takes for
granted that teaching can always be improved. As Joseph Stoll wrote in
the first issue of the *Blackboard Bulletin*,

We do want to put out a paper that is interesting; one that is informative; one that has clean and wholesome material; one that is inspiring; and last but not least, one that is simple and informal, yes, a publication that will appeal to the readers, one in which they feel they have a part, a share, an interest. [. . .] In issues to come, we'll try to discuss discipline, teaching methods, parent-teacher relationships, subject matter, and a host of related school problems. [. . .] We have a wide open field to work in, and if we all work together we can put out a paper that will be indispensable to the teacher who is still learning from day to day. (And what teacher isn't?)

In the summer of 1963, *Blackboard Bulletin* editor Joseph Stoll was threshing oats with David Wagler, who had just started Pathway Bookstore to supply the Old Order Amish in Aylmer, Ontario, with appropriate reading material. As Stoll remembers, David Wagler had started a bookstore a year earlier, mail order, and was getting requests for out-of-print books. "[We] came up with the idea for reprinting them themselves and maybe some of our own. [I] decided [I] could turn the *Blackboard Bulletin* over to the new printing company. There was some question about who would be the printer. We turned it over to Jacob Eicher (then a minister), who said, 'I can't write or sell books, but I can run machinery.' Of course he had a lot to learn too."

On March 9, 1964, Stoll, Wagler, and Eicher incorporated the Pathway Publishing Company as a nonprofit organization. The three had different hopes for the new publishing corporation. While Stoll was looking forward to sharing with others some of the responsibility for publishing the *Blackboard Bulletin*, which he had been editing, duplicating, and mailing from his home since 1957, "Wagler's primary interest was in reprinting old books no longer in print, plus also publish[ing] new titles. (He had a bookstore and had become aware of the demand for certain books.)" Eicher was willing to run the machinery.

Today, Pathway Publishers is chartered in Ontario as a nonprofit organization and in the United States as a public charity. Pathway has about 25 members, and it is run by a board of five directors, who are elected from the membership. The staff employees at Pathway are paid for their work, but the directors, who are not considered employees, are not.[11] The 2000 *Aylmer Amish Directory* notes that "there are about ten main workers em-

The Pathway Publishing Company in Aylmer, Ontario, is surrounded by cornfields.

ployed at Pathway, but hardly any of them actually work full time, with the editors doing most of their work at home. A number of girls also help out with assembling and addressing the magazines" (40).

Pathway is not solely a textbook publisher, but rather a publisher that includes in its book list texts for school use. Nevertheless, Pathway's involvement in textbook publishing began soon after its founding, when the editors began contemplating a series of readers for use in Old Order schools. Editor Joseph Stoll notes that he had "taught school and seen the need for a series that was heavy on morals and religious content." As he wrote to Andy S. Kinsinger, "I don't even know what books you are using there in Pennsylvania, but all the books I have ever seen (and this includes most of the old ones of 50 and 100 years ago) have war stories, political and patriotic stories, a good deal of nonsense."[12]

In the initial stages of preparing the *Pathway Readers*, the editors attempted, like the Gordonville printers, to select appropriate editions of out-of-date public school texts that could be reprinted. As Stoll wrote in 1966, "What we have in mind is to prepare a set of Christian readers, at least for the upper elementary grades, for our parochial schools. We would choose selections from these old readers and from other sources; in other words pick off the cream."[13]

Writing to the editor-in-chief of Ginn and Company, another Pathway editor noted that Pathway was especially interested in books published prior to 1950.[14] Yet, although the older texts appeared more acceptable simply because many of the selections were "moralistic," some found that "the kind of stories, fairy tales, etc. which they contain, we feel, have no place in a Christian School."[15] Joseph Stoll lamented that "even with these old books we find a good many war stories and political speeches, and articles with an objectionable slant on patriotism."

In the end, the Pathway editors decided to follow the example set by Uria R. Byler, one of the original circle letter participants, who in 1963 had written an eighth grade history text, *Our Better Country*, specifically for Old Order schools. As a writer to the Amish newspaper *The Budget* had noted at the time, "*Our Better Country* is the first book ever written by an Amishman as a textbook for Amish children. As you would expect of an Amish text on history, there is more of peace than war, more of love than hate, more of God in man than of the devil in him."[16] "I am convinced," Stoll asserted, "we are missing a golden opportunity if we don't do something like this . . . get up our own set of readers. We could add a touch of Anabaptist history, with selections from the Martyr's Mirror, etc. The possibilities are endless."[17]

The first of the *Pathway Readers*, a series designed specifically for Old Order schools, appeared in 1968, and there are now 13 textbooks and 16 workbooks. As editor David Luthy notes, "The workbooks were totally compiled by Amish people, most of whom are [Pathway] staff members."[18]

Unlike the archaic texts published by Gordonville, the *Pathway Readers* are removed from the modern world, not by age but by intent. Fewer than half of the selections in the readers for the upper grades, the first to be produced, are original. In these first readers, the editors combined stories and essays carefully selected from old readers with original selections adapted from Anabaptist writings or written especially for the readers. For *Our Heritage*, the eighth grade reader, the editors chose selections by a number of different authors, including William Cullen Bryant ("To a Waterfowl"), Walt Whitman ("Miracle"), Alfred Tennyson ("Prayer"), Henry Wadsworth Longfellow ("The Arrow and the Song"), John Greenleaf Whittier ("The Barefoot Boy"), and C. Carol Kauffman ("Regina's Visit to Zurich"). The reader begins with seven selections that focus on early Anabaptist history, including a reading on Dirk Willems, "Bonfire of Books," from *The Martyr's Mirror*, and "One Dark Night," a retelling of the Hochstetler Massacre, a defining event for the Old Order Amish.

In the seventh grade reader, *Seeking True Values*, there are selections from writers such as Samuel Pepys ("Great Plague of London"), Louisa M. Alcott ("A Song from the Suds"), John Bunyan ("Place of Deliverance"), John Greenleaf Whittier ("The Bible"), Johann Von Schiller ("Three Lessons"), and Francis of Assisi ("Channels of His Love"). Again, there is a section on Anabaptist history featuring a piece by Nicholas Stoltzfus on the Waldensians ("Trek Across the Mountains"), several selections from *The Martyr's Mirror*, a story about the Amish in Waldeck, Germany, in 1759, and a story about the Ephrata Cloister's printing of *The Martyr's Mirror*.

Yet a number of the selections were written expressly for these first readers in the series. Commenting on the upper-grade readers, one of the editors noted:

> We selected prose and poetry from a great variety of books, but we could not find enough to meet our "informal unwritten guidelines." So [...] we ended up writing 41% of the stories (prose) but none of the poetry. The four books contained more than 1,400 pages. Our goal was to create and publish a "values series" of reading textbooks with stories that teach lessons without being preachy and which deal with human values and virtues found among all Christians. We did not want to have a doctrinal slant. Since we are Old Order Amish, we naturally wrote our stories in horse and buggy settings but not with the idea that everyone must have a horse and buggy. Our stories do not promote our religion but are religious in the virtues they teach.[19]

While the upper-grade readers introduce children to the literature of the non–Old Order world, at least to that judged suitable, the lower-grade readers present original material that has, in Joseph Stoll's words, "heavy phonetic content." For these texts, the editors at Pathway used original material, stories that focus on elements of modern-day Old Order life. For example, *Days Go By*, the grade one primer, introduces children to Rachel,

Susan, Peter, and Levi, their pets and the farm. The majority of selections in *Building Our Lives*, the fourth grade reader, were written specifically for this text; unlike the upper-grade readers, which list the selections and authors in the table of contents, not all reprinted articles carry the author's name, although their original publication is acknowledged at the back of the text.

Although illustrated, the *Pathway Readers* contain no images of people; drawings portray the farms and other unchanging elements of Old Order life. Moreover, as a letter to Old Order congregations advertising the series points out, many stories "contain the atmosphere of farm life and the country one room schoolhouse. These stories will come alive to your children and the lessons will be meaningful, for Amish children will feel right at home with these stories. [. . .] And why not? They are for our schools!" Insisting that "every day of the year the world stares your children in the face in the stories they have in their readers," the editors argued further that parents concerned enough to withdraw their children from the world's schools should "go all the way" and remove the world from school.[20]

The Pathway Publishing Company serves a different kind of Old Order community than does the Gordonville Print Shop, one that has redefined the role of Old Order schools. Asked why more conservative communities often limit the use of *Pathway Readers*, particularly in the younger grades, and why more conservative teachers seldom read the *Blackboard Bulletin*, Joseph Stoll answers, "One thing that might come up—too much religion. They might be afraid of Pathway influence. There's the threat of more progressive influence."[21]

Pathway's approach alters the role of schools in the church-community, blurring the sharp distinction made in more conservative communities between "schooling" or "book learning," in which one acquires basic skills or information, and "education," which is the inculcation of values. In the most conservative Old Order communities, schools are seen as offering the much less valued book learning. True education, the most conservative Old Order parents believe, comes in shared labor and the enjoyment of fellowship at home, at church, and at chores (Huntington 1994; Johnson-Weiner 1998). Pathway texts, produced with the goal of interweaving religious doctrine in all studies, give the school a primary role in values education, not merely a supporting one.

This does not mean that the Pathway texts teach religion overtly. In a letter to Joseph Stoll about the Pathway Reader project, a reader from Ohio argued,

> As for me, I'm well agreed with the material selected, but do be cautious about the scriptural references etc. to be included. I recently talked with one of the men in an eastern state who also has a copy to read, and he said he's afraid it might not go in their locality. You know, I once made up a sheet of 20 Bible questions to administer with our regular 8th grade tests and there was so much opposition that I had to drop it. There is so much at stake; very much work, time, money etc, let's not have it all go down the drain. WE want the readers![22]

Many were inclined to agree with Andy S. Kinsinger, who, describing the discussions of religion in the schools, had noted, "We felt it was good to learn to read and spell and sing in German but not to get in Bible quizzes and that using books with the words Jesus and God in many of the lessons is not good. These words would have a special meaning to us and not to be used to play with or class room study as it is my opinion that the time will come when these words will not have any special meaning if used as a classroom book" (1997, 246). Nevertheless, in Pathway texts religion is pervasive in the emphasis on Old Order values, history, and Old Order life.

Schoolaid Publishing: Revising Old and Developing New

Today, Pathway continues to publish the *Blackboard Bulletin* as well as two other magazines, *Young Companion* and *Family Life*. It also publishes two texts for teachers, *Tips for Teachers* and Uria R. Byler's *School Bells Ringing*, as well as *Chalkdust: Selections from Blackboard Bulletin (1978–1985)* and a variety of other books. Nevertheless, although textbook publishing remains approximately 50 percent of the Pathway business, the editors at Pathway currently have no plans to revise the materials or to develop new school texts.[23] In this sense, they are like the Gordonville Printers: the books work, so there is no need for change. As Pathway editor Joseph Stoll put it, "If we ever revised them [the readers], maybe there would be some changes, but there are no plans for revision. If it's not broke, don't fix it."

In contrast, Alta Hoover, a founder and editor at the Schoolaid Publishing Company of East Earl, Pennsylvania, sees revision as a means of working with teachers and texts to improve both, a process of change and renewal necessary for strong education. Whereas the Pathway editors have no plans to offer a wider range of textbooks and urge would-be textbook writers to find an alternative publisher, Schoolaid continues to survey teachers about the texts and to produce new texts, most recently a health textbook, *Mankind Marvelously Made*, the production of which was motivated in part by desires expressed by Old Order Amish in Michigan for an appropriate textbook. Schoolaid also publishes the Spunky arithmetic books for first and second grades, *Climbing to Good English* (a graded English grammar series), and a variety of phonics workbooks and teacher aids modeled on similar texts used in public schools. The publishing house has also gone beyond textbooks and now produces a game to promote farm safety.

"I just grew into it [Schoolaid Publishing]," says Alta Hoover. "I started teaching school and making my own materials, and other teachers started borrowing." Hoover worked initially with Pathway on the phonics workbooks for grades one and two. As she put it, "Pathway started us out. I helped them with *Learning Through Sounds*. Then I wanted to go on." In 1983, reflecting her strong interest in phonics, Hoover prepared *German Phonics*, a beginning German workbook, which she first submitted to Pathway for publication. Pathway turned down the proposed text, which would have duplicated, in some respects, its *Let's Learn German* workbook, but the Pathway editors encouraged Hoover to work on her own. "Pathway didn't want to get too big," according to Hoover. "They thought it would be better to have more publishers."

"First German phonics and soon after German readers," notes John Martin, who helped produce the readers *Wir lesen Geschichten aus der heiligen Schrift* and *Wir lesen und sprechen Deutsch*. The readers were first published in 1984. In the same year, the name "Schoolaid" was adopted "and came to apply to the loose organization of five individuals: Alta Hoover, John Martin, Alice Shirk, Mabel Shirk, and Martin Fox."[24] By 1988, seeing the need for a more formal business structure, the group established Schoolaid formally as a nonprofit church-related school support organization.

Unlike either Gordonville or Pathway, Schoolaid is devoted to the publication of textbooks and teaching materials. The board of Schoolaid sees the organization's purpose as twofold:

Schoolaid's new warehouse in Lancaster County, Pennsylvania,
provides space for a growing business.

1. Primarily, Schoolaid is intended to be a supplier of printed materials, working as closely as possible with both teachers and school committee members in providing materials that are suitable, not only academically, but also in subject matter and emphasis. We believe that we need a Christian influence in textbooks, but without the depth of doctrinal content or other undesirable elements of some available Christian-oriented materials.
2. Schoolaid is also dedicated to helping teachers. Our teachers face the challenge of keeping children in as many as eight different grade levels gainfully occupied and learning. To help these teachers, Schoolaid works to provide inquiring teachers with the opportunity for self-improvement in education and also for personal correspondence, such as through the Teacher-Aid Series.

In preparing appropriate texts for Old Order schools, Schoolaid fills in and expands on areas not covered by Pathway and other publishers. It has not, for example, developed a reader series "because Pathway has them," and has decided not to take its arithmetic series beyond grades one and two, ceding the upper grades to Study Time. The German texts illustrate the cooperative nature of Schoolaid publishing. In the Introduction to *Wir lesen Geschichten aus der heiligen Schrift*, published by Schoolaid in 1984, the editors note that the book is the third in a series for learning German on an elementary level. While the first is Schoolaid's *German Phonics*, the second is Pathway's *Let's Read German*. Demonstrating Schoolaid's commitment to providing a "Christian influence" without "doctrinal content or other undesirable elements," the Introduction notes further: "We prayerfully introduce this book as a learning aid in Bible German; though not a teacher of Scripture, yet Biblically sound."[25]

Schoolaid tests its materials first in mimeograph form in Lancaster Old Order schools, and the textbook committee includes teachers and students. As Hoover put it, "To get out a good book, you should see it in use. You'd have to teach it to know. In *German Phonics*, we saw problems only when we used it. I've got plenty of teachers out there to tell me what to change." According to Hoover, it's most important that the material catch the child's interest. "If it holds the child's [attention], it will hold the teacher's, and it takes experienced teachers to get this." She adds, "We work in the things we think the child should learn and fool them into learning." In addition, the content must be acceptable to parents; there is, of course, no teaching of evolution. According to Hoover, editors must "write something to please [the parents] enough that the book goes over" and "enough on the child's level that he can identify with it but high enough to challenge [him]."

Ultimately, according to Hoover, the book is only as good as the teacher; and Schoolaid, unlike either Pathway or Gordonville, is proactive in training teachers, holding regular teachers' meetings to show them how to use the texts. In addition, Schoolaid publishes a Teacher's Aid Series, including *Schoolteachers' Signposts*, listed in the Schoolaid order form as the "teacher's handbook," as well as *Arithmetic for Reference and Review*, *Spelling and Word Study/Maps and Geographical Terms*, and *Understanding English*. These texts constitute a review course at the eighth grade level to help teachers, who might be several years removed from their student days, to review and prepare to teach. As the introduction to *Arithmetic for Reference and Review* points out, "To be able to teach anything, we must know the subject. The only way to know a subject is to study it and actually do the lessons. While you're teaching is not the time to start learning. Both you and your pupils will suffer if you depend on that. We are not recommending higher education, but we do recommend a solid eighth grade education."

Schoolaid is a product of a community that, while separate from the world, is actively involved with the dominant society through mission outreach and charity work, and its texts are designed to prepare students to participate.[26] Schoolaid English texts, for example, emphasize productive language skills, with a focus on writing, especially in the upper grades. Interestingly, while many in Old Order Amish communities see English as the language of the world—as Joseph Stoll wrote, the language associated "with the forces that have become dangerous because they make inroads into our churches and lure people from the faith" (1969, 208)—Unit 1 of the Schoolaid fifth grade reader begins with an introduction to "the Study of Our [emphasis mine] Language." "If we didn't study language [English]," the chapter begins, "We would be unable to read, write, or spell. That means we couldn't enjoy reading stories, books, or magazines. We couldn't read, let alone find important information of any kind. We wouldn't be able to make a shopping list or even go shopping without someone's help. We couldn't write letters or cards to our friends, nor read them if they wrote to us. What a miserable, dull life that would be!"

Schoolaid texts are not designed to keep children separate from the world, but to prepare them to interact with it in church-sanctioned ways. "Our goal," asserts Hoover, "is to contribute to the world while remaining strong church members." According to Hoover, Schoolaid texts provide practical knowledge for everyday living but with a Christian base. There is not too much religion, but it's there. "We're not teaching doctrine," says Hoover. "We believe in God, but we're not saying we're the only church, not like some."

Study Time: Breaking New Ground

Pathway editor Joseph Stoll notes that Pathway "has encouraged others to go ahead and publish their own stuff," and others besides Alta Hoover have done so, including Delbert Farmwald, a member of the Old Order Amish community in the Elkhart-LaGrange area, who founded Study Time in 1995.[27] The newest of Old Order publishers, Study Time now publishes an arithmetic series that was designed to begin where Schoolaid's Spunky series leaves off and is replacing the Strayer-Upton texts in a number of schools. The Study Time texts are helping to redefine the role of schools in Old Order communities and changing how children are educated to face the outside world.

A former teacher, Study Time editor Delbert Farmwald notes that he and his wife, Linda, became involved in producing the new arithmetic series because they observed widespread dissatisfaction among teachers with the other texts available. According to Farmwald, "All this brought about a situation where school board members found themselves being asked to switch math series to accommodate the teachers they hired. Some school boards complained of having to switch series several times in a 5– 10 year span because their new teacher(s) was unfamiliar with the books they had. This was, of course, costly, and seemingly unnecessary."[28]

Responding to teachers' needs, Study Time encourages a different view of teachers and teaching than that implicit in the continued use of archaic texts by more conservative communities. "Our aim has been to produce a series that teaches math effectively, interestingly, and realistically," says Farmwald. "We feel a math series should be student friendly as well as teacher friendly, knowing that our teachers are very busy people and any minute we can save for the teacher is valuable." In an extensive introduction for the teacher, entitled "Becoming Acquainted With Your Book," the editors explicitly encourage teachers to improvise or use their own ideas.

Moreover, like Schoolaid, Study Time emphasizes the importance of having children work for themselves to see solutions to problems. Echoing Schoolaid editor Alta Hoover, who argues the necessity of teaching children to "help themselves" and to "think for themselves" and advises teachers, "Never give your students a direct answer. You're not a walking encyclopedia," Farmwald asserts that the editors at Study Time "feel the average student should be able to do the majority of the lessons with a very minimal amount of teacher help. Almost anything that we figure out for ourself [sic] sticks better than if I have to rely on detailed step by step instructions from the teacher for everything I do." Confirming a pedagogical approach that reinforces individual self-reliance over rote learning and dependence on external authority, the note to the teacher at the beginning of the Teacher's Manual for Study Time Grade 3 Arithmetic asserts that the book is designed to encourage students to think for themselves: "Study

Time Arithmetic is arranged to use the natural curiosity of the children and the heightened interest in digging for one's own solutions to present the concepts more clearly to the young minds. Also, the problems, reviews and practice sections are designed to have the pupils pursue their studies more on their own and less on the teacher's time" (viii).

While teaching children the skills that will help them be successful adults, Study Time is also designed to prepare them for eternal life. The Study Time arithmetic series, for example, like the Schoolaid health texts, defines its subject matter as evidence of God's creation. "To us," assert the Study Time publishers in a note "To the School Board, Parent, or Teacher" printed on the inside of the front cover,

> it is obvious that numbers, facts, and their calculating procedures are so orderly, so accurate, and so consistently dependable that the Author of this entire system of concepts must have been infinitely greater and wiser and keener than the human mind. Who, other than God Himself, could have set a law into motion that never changes and always works out correctly each and every time when its concepts are learned and followed carefully? [...] So, a study of mathematical concepts is really a study of the orderly and unchangeable laws of nature—a study of nature itself. And when we respect them as such, this study reveals a glimpse of the omnipotent nature of the Creator of the universe.

In preparing the arithmetic series, the Study Time editors, like those at Pathway and Schoolaid, designed texts specifically for an Old Order audience. Asks Farmwald, "Why ask [children] to work with story problems about going to the circus or figuring bowling scores or batting averages of professional baseball players when we don't want our children involved in such activities in real life? Why not have math exercises about working in the kitchen or on the farm or in the shop? What Amish child can't relate to being asked to carry 40 jars of canned peaches to the basement, 2 at a time? Or to pick out enough buttons for his new shirt or dress while Mom is sewing the garment?"[29] Yet, while Pathway's stories shield children from the dominant society, the Study Time texts intertwine Amish life and Anabaptist heritage with world events, creating a text for Old Order children who will interact daily with the broader, non–Old Order world.

The few pictures in the texts present the world that children see, with backhoes and dump trucks as well as horses and baskets of corn, while the problems reinforce Old Order ways of dealing with that world. In the third grade text, for example, children beginning chapter 1 are welcomed with a picture of a note written on a spiral binder that reads:

Away from all the great outdoors
Our eager minds are turning.
To school and books and pens and to
The big wide world
of learning!

By the seventh grade, their arithmetic text will draw on American, European, and African history, and students will do circle graphs to show the ingredients of margarine and calculate the average number of patents issued per year from 1500 to 2000.

Although Study Time Publishers was organized "basically as a vehicle to bring about the math series," it now publishes a number of other titles, including E. Wengerds' geography textbook, *Glimpses of the Eastern Hemisphere.* Most interestingly, Study Time has also produced a four-book preschool activity set. In the progressive Amish communities that are the market for Study Time's texts, parents see the school as having a central role in training their children to be good church members. While Swartzentruber Amish parents delay sending their children to school as long as they can and do little reading or other activities to prepare them for their school lessons, parents in the most progressive Amish communities prepare their children to do well in school by beginning school-like activities in the home.

Different Texts, Different Goals

The different Old Order book publishers reach different audiences, and the acceptance of some texts but not others by different Old Order communities suggests much about how Old Order groups draw the line between what is acceptable and what is not. For example, while Schoolaid's seventh and eighth grade health text, *Mankind Marvelously Made,* is widely used in Old Order Amish schools in Ohio, Indiana, and Michigan, and in Old Order Mennonite schools in Lancaster, the Old Order Amish in Lancaster have rejected it because there are two Bible verses in the text.

The even more overt Christianity of other texts makes them unacceptable for many groups. For example, while Centreville and Elkhart-LaGrange schools, like the Old Order Mennonite schools in Lancaster County, have adopted Rod and Staff texts, others object to their overtly Christian grounding. Similarly, A Beka, with its "unashamedly Christian" approach, is deemed unacceptable by many more conservative communities.

In Lancaster, the Old Order Book Society discourages the A Beka texts because, although they are "Christian-based," they use Scripture in the lessons. In a 1987 meeting of the Old Order Steering Committee, for example, one member warned that

> Presently there is one book creeping into the Amish schools that are a major concern for the Amish schools and I would suggest the Directors check into this. The A Beka books seem to be coming in. PA does not have so many but some States do have more. Apparently they are interesting and good books to learn from but the subject matter need also be considered. [. . .] Some place much emphasis on Missionaries and their work and others, especially the English [texts] using so many words or sentences with (God or His Saints) [. . . that] one sentence may be made with Jesus the subject matter, the next maybe using clown as the subject matter and the next possibly monkey as the subject matter. In my mind it is placing all in the same class.[30]

At the same meeting, the chairman asserted that the saying, "God and His Saints are not to be used in textbooks" had been impressed into him by the old directors of years gone by.[31]

Mennonite historian Amos Hoover tells of a meeting at which Andy Kinsinger, founder of the Gordonville Print Shop, responded to someone who wondered why Gordonville kept reprinting old public school texts, which had a lot of fairy tales and other nonsense, instead of using new Christian curriculum. According to Hoover, Kinsinger responded that the Christian texts were, in fact, more dangerous. It would not take a young child long to understand that "a cow jumping over the moon" was not true, but tales of missionaries in foreign lands would lead to other lifestyle changes as the child learned to "spread the word." Soon there would be pressure for cars, devices of mass communication, and so on.

The use of A Beka and Rod and Staff in other schools demonstrates a different orientation to the world and the role of the Old Order community in it. As has been noted, the schools that have adopted these texts have begun to emphasize the Christian nature of their schools and to educate children for a life engaged in the world as members of the Old Order church.

Gordonville, Pathway, Schoolaid, Study Time—and even Rod and Staff and A Beka—all serve the needs of communities that consciously and deliberately separate themselves from the dominant society. Whether the approach to publishing is to hold to what was always done because what is good does not change, to develop new texts that will bring the church-community's own unchanging beliefs overtly into the schoolhouse, or to develop new texts and revise them continually to meet the ever-changing needs of students who must interact with an ever-changing world, these publishers reflect the assumptions, values, and beliefs of the communities whose schools they serve, and, in providing appropriate texts, reinforce these. Moreover, in their creation of a body of Old Order literature that highlights certain cultural practices while downplaying others, these publishers actively represent and reinforce very different Old Order identities.

CHAPTER 9

What's Education For?

So up to grade eight we are watched, but what after that?
Have we built something so our children can go from there?
—Old Order Mennonite teacher

Which World?

The 1939 *Report of Committee of Plain People* included a letter from a father in New York State who wrote, "The apostle Paul admonishes us to bring up our children 'in the nurture and admonition of the Lord' (Eph. 6:4). Therefore it is certainly our duty to guard them as much as possible against the corrupting and blighting influences of the world, whose prince is the devil. But the public school system is controlled by 'the world' and 'the world lieth in wickedness' (1 John 5:19)" (Shirk 1939, 67).

Thirty-three years later, in the "Opinion of the Court" in the 1972 case *Wisconsin v. Yoder et al.*, Chief Justice Warren Burger argued that "Old Order Amish communities today are characterized by a fundamental belief that salvation requires life in a church community separate and apart from the world and worldly influence. This concept of life aloof from the world and its values is central to their faith." Burger noted further that "a related feature of Old Order Amish communities is their devotion to a life in harmony with nature and the soil [. . .] Amish beliefs require members of the

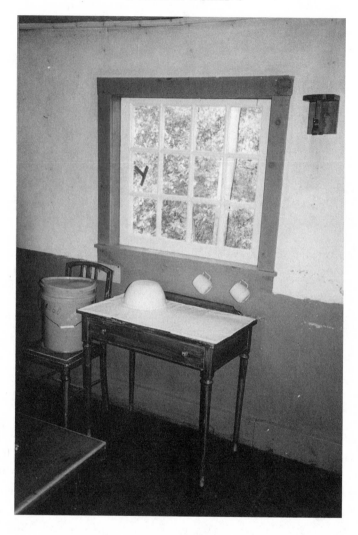

From primitive . . .

community to make their living by farming or closely related activities" (in Keim 1975, 152).

Today the diversity of Old Order life challenges any attempt to describe Amish or Mennonite church-communities so simply or so monolithically. While the Swartzentruber Amish, like the New York father quoted above, see the world as a corrupting influence and continue to shun even participation in farmers' markets, Old Order Amish in Indiana work side

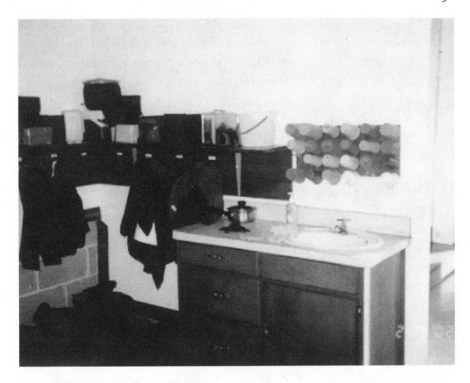

. . . to mainstream, Old Order schools are striking in their diversity.

by side with non-Amish laborers in factories that produce mobile homes. In isolated homogeneous settlements like the one in Somerset, Ohio, Old Order families live without indoor plumbing or ice boxes, while in the large Old Order Amish community of Holmes County, Ohio, families enjoy hot and cold running water, indoor bathrooms, and refrigerators. The most conservative groups pay little attention to the beliefs and actions of their non–Old Order neighbors and carefully regulate interaction with them, but the most progressive work in non–Old Order factories, wait on non–Old Order customers in shops and restaurants, and socialize with non–Old Order friends and neighbors.

The private schools of the Old Order Amish and the Old Order Mennonites reflect these differences and reinforce them. While some Old Order children attend schools that would make a visitor from the nineteenth century feel at home, others attend schools that would be familiar to any modern-day public school teacher. Old Order education is even more diverse than is evident in the private schools, for some Old Order children are schooled at home, and others, like their parents before them, attend public school with non–Old Order peers and are taught by non–Old Order teachers.

Many in Old Order church-communities would agree with Joseph Stoll (1975, 42), who has argued that "the public schools are not striving for the same goal Christian parents are. We are not interested in building missiles and jet aircraft. They are not interested in building Christians. We must go separate ways." As Hostetler and Huntington (1992, 109) put it, "By design, Amish schools are not suited for training artists, musicians, painters, and actors; nor for training science-oriented individuals who would pursue engineering, astronomy, paleontology, chemistry, or space technology; nor for training business executives, corporation managers, or occupations leading to government or military careers. The Amish school, by intent, does not function as an institution for upward mobility in the modern industrial complex."[1]

Others, however, declare Old Order private schools to be anathema to Christian life. As Mennonite historian Amos Hoover notes, "The Aaron Martin group in Snyder County, Pennsylvania, wouldn't tolerate parochial schools. The old way was to go to the public schools. If they had parochial schools and someone doesn't attend the way they should, the teacher would be obliged to notify the [state] authorities. You would have the threat of being involved with the law."[2]

In every way, Old Order schools and Old Order education demonstrate the values of the community and the differences between communities. In the most conservative communities, schools turn inward, using archaic texts to shield children from modern events, technological advances, and religious and cultural difference. German is used in social interaction to unite the groups linguistically; games reinforce cooperative group dynamics; and teachers, seldom much older than their students, exercise an authority that comes from age and family dynamics as much as from position. For conservative groups such as the Swartzentruber Amish, school socializes children within the community, providing them the opportunity to interact with peers outside the immediate family; it reinforces the teachings of home and church by remaining a subordinate institution, a place where songs are sung only when children are old enough to begin reading the German songbook, where the Bible is read in German but not discussed, where prayers are not said because there is no one with the authority to lead them, where children learn to do what they are told without questioning. There is no exploration of community beliefs or of the relationship between different church communities. Children do not study why they do things in particular ways, but they learn that there are particular ways in which things must be done. School teaches them that learning by doing is far more important than learning by the book; family tasks and community events that take place outside of the classroom take precedence over schoolwork, and working hard is more important than good scores. Parents do not involve themselves in school events; school boards do not meet; and teachers are young, female, and inexperienced, teaching because it is their turn.

At the other end of the spectrum, in the most progressive schools, children learn the skills they will need to interact with the world as members of an Old Order church-community. Their gaze is directed outward as they study geography, hone their English language skills, and read and hear stories of people and events removed from their Old Order community in time, place, and culture. Schools in these communities emphasize Anabaptist values broadly writ. Lessons reinforce the connections between communities, toleration for church differences, and the knowledge children must have of the world around them if they are to compete in the world while remaining separate from it. In these schools, children sing, hear the Bible read in English, pray, and memorize Bible verses.

At the 16th Annual Meeting of the Old Order Steering Committee, held October 27, 1982, a school director from Michigan reported that one local attorney had been pushing to have Amish children go through high school so the children could find their way in the world. In response, another director at the meeting asked, "Which world?" Which world? is the question that guides Old Order communities as they establish private schools that, from the most conservative to the most progressive, reflect and reinforce the values of the church-community. The variety of curricula and pedagogical practices in Old Order Amish and Mennonite schools reveals multiple Old Order realities.

Because of this diversity, Old Order private schools work, with one important caveat: the Elkhart-LaGrange schools work for the Old Order community in Elkhart-LaGrange, and the Swartzentruber schools in up-

state New York work for the Swartzentruber Amish. Neither community
would find the schools of the other acceptable for their children. Similarly,
the schools of the Ashland Amish community would not serve well the
needs of the Amish in Centreville, Michigan, or of the Old Order Mennonite community in Lancaster.

The Limitations of the "Old Order Model"

That Old Order education limits the options of Old Order children has
been one of the sharpest criticisms leveled at the decision in *Wisconsin v.
Yoder et al.* Dissenting in part from the Supreme Court's decision in the
case, Justice William Douglas wrote, "The Court's analysis assumes that
the only interests at stake in the case are those of the Amish parents on
the one hand, and those of the State on the other. The difficulty with this
approach is that, despite the Court's claim, the parents are seeking to vin-
dicate not only their own free exercise claims, but also those of their high-
school-age children. [. . .] The right of the Amish children to religious
freedom is not presented by the facts of the case." Douglas noted further
that "if the parents in this case are allowed a religious exemption, the inevitable effect is to impose the parents' notions of religious duty upon their
children" (in Keim 1975, 175–76).

Huntington (2001, 26) argues that "the conflict of values" between
Old Order communities and the state "is raised dramatically in the area of
education." Since the Old Orders believe that "parents are accountable to
God for their children who are a gift from Him," she asserts, "certain aspects of education are not negotiable." Seeking to prepare children to lead
Old Order lives, Old Order schools educate children for life in church-
communities that, to varying degrees, have erected strict boundaries between themselves and the dominant society.

Contemplating the role of education in a diverse and liberal society,
however, Reich (2002, 102) asserts that education must allow children
to achieve "minimalist autonomy" or the ability "to examine and evaluate their underlying commitments, values, desires, motivations, and beliefs." He argues further that "Children are owed as a matter of justice
the capacity to choose to lead lives—to adopt values and beliefs, pursue
an occupation, endorse new traditions—that are different from those of
their parents," suggesting that, to the extent that Old Order schools fail

to provide children the education they need to do so, they fail to educate them adequately (Reich 2002, 163; cf. Gutmann 1999). Similarly, Howe (1997, 73) writes that "Amish schooling fails to provide the intellectual skills and knowledge that enable persons to decide for themselves what kind of lives to lead. Worse, it may permanently block the possibility of acquiring them. It thus sacrifices the cherished ideal of autonomy [. . .] to the interests of the community."

Citing a number of Supreme Court rulings since 1972, Peters (2002, 175) notes that the "constitutional legacy" of *Wisconsin v. Yoder et al.* has not proven "especially durable." Nevertheless, pitting the right of a culture to survive against the individual right to choose one's future, *Wisconsin v. Yoder et al.* continues to challenge those who attempt to formulate educational theory.

Old Order schools do not attempt to prepare children to be knowledgeable citizens of the broader society, for the Old Orders assume an identity that rejects many of the responsibilities—and questions many of the rights and privileges—that mainstream Americans associate with citizenship. They do not run for public office, nor do they typically vote in elections. Committed to pacifism and nonresistance, they will not serve in the military. The Old Order appreciate the necessity of government and view rebellion as unchristian. For Old Order church-communities, citizenship in the national polity thus means passive obedience to laws, provided that these laws do not conflict with church doctrine. As this work demonstrates, however, no Old Order church-community isolates itself completely from the non–Old Order world. Consequently, suggesting either that "the child's development is somehow threatened by giving priority to the preservation of the minority culture" (Snauwaert 2001, 447) or that Old Order culture will be imperiled by the child's independent development oversimplifies Old Order reality.

In their ongoing negotiation with the dominant society, Old Order church-communities make conscious choices about their place in the world. To the extent that these shape curriculum, pedagogy, textbook choice, and teacher selection and training, children are introduced early to the struggle to define Old Order life. Moreover, Old Order children grow up surrounded by alternatives to their Old Order lifestyle.

Finally, in contrast to ethnically or racially defined groups, Old Order church-communities are constituted by the individual choice of each adult to join the church-community. As a result, ultimately, Old Order children must consciously make a choice few of their counterparts in the non–Old Order world ever contemplate—to stay in their respective communities and live the life of their parents or to leave.[3]

Implications for the Secular World

The decision of the U.S. Supreme Court in *Wisconsin v. Yoder et al.* was based on a particular notion of Old Order community, one that emphasized the agricultural basis of the Old Order world and focused on the Old Order desire to remain "a separate and peculiar people."[4] As this work demonstrates, however, the range of Old Order lifestyles is far different from the picture of isolated traditionalism presented to the U.S. Supreme Court. Today's Old Order parents and community leaders are struggling with questions of modernity, change, and identity, and, like their counterparts in the non–Old Order world, are realizing this struggle in the way they educate their children. In their early confrontations with secular authorities over school consolidation, longer school years, and the number of years of mandatory schooling, the Old Orders were united in their desire to hold to what they had. Now, however, Old Order church-communities are themselves changing private school education, some even on the verge of introducing the same innovations that the Supreme Court gave them the freedom to resist.

In contrast to their secular counterparts, however, the Old Orders have kept educational debates close to home and within the church-community. Swartzentruber parents do not look to the Amish church-communities in Fredericktown, Somerset, or Centreville as they build schools, hire teachers, or make textbook decisions. While school centralization has left many parents of public school children feeling powerless to influence the direction of their children's education, Old Order parents retain control over what and how their children learn. In this sense, perhaps, Old Order schools have something to teach their public school counterparts.

In the twentieth century, many viewed school consolidation, which shrank the number of school districts in the United States from 160,000 to 16,000 (Guthrie 1979), as a way to cope with a fast-changing world. Educators argued that larger, centralized schools were not only more cost-effective but also more educationally efficient. A larger school and broader

tax base meant that children could be exposed to a wider range of subjects; they would enjoy access to better, more expensive technology and
would benefit from classroom diversity. Teachers would be able to special-
ize, thus bringing more advanced methodology to the classroom (Howley
1989).

The Old Orders resisted, and their small, community-based private
schools contribute to a growing body of evidence that smaller schools
are often better and that community involvement contributes to school
success. Barker and Gump (1964), for example, found that students in
smaller schools had greater access to extracurricular activities and more
opportunity to exercise leadership. Arguing that large school size may be
contributing to lower test scores and school violence, Barker (1986) asserts, "The restructuring of schools to smaller entities may ameliorate some
of the problems facing today's educators." Other studies have found that
students in small schools seem to learn more (Lee and Smith 1995), have
a lower dropout rate (Pittman and Haughwout 1987), and behave better
(Stockard and Mayberry 1992). Barker (1986) notes that smaller schools
permit multi-grade teaching, a flexible curriculum, and learner-centered
instruction. Similarly, Roellke (1996, 4) suggests that although small
school size can't guarantee a good curriculum, "it does appear to facilitate
its development."

Perhaps more importantly, smaller size permits community involvement
in the schools. As a result of her work with the Central Park East schools
in Harlem, founded in an attempt to create educational institutions that
were both "child-centered" and "community-centered," Deborah Meier
(1995)has found that small schools offer safety and reinforce a sense of
responsibility on the part of students, teachers, and parents. Moreover,
she suggests, students are immersed in the community and thus connected
to the culture of their parents, reinforcing adult standards and values and
offering "a chance, not a guarantee, that children will glimpse possibilities that make them want to be grown-ups" (Meier 1995, 113). As Barker
(1986) argues, teachers in smaller schools interact more with their students and are more likely to know their students and their students' families. Thus, teachers have the knowledge to meet individual needs more
effectively. In addition, Barker suggests, "Because relationships between
teachers and administrators tend to be more personal and informal, there is
a greater tendency for cooperation among the staff. Also, teachers who live

and work in small communities are more likely to be viewed as respected and valued citizens by other community members" (1986, 2).

Maintaining parental and community involvement has been key in the evolution of the Old Order private schools, which, as Hostetler (1993) points out, are only part of the way in which children are prepared for adult life. In fitting the school into the fabric of community life, the Old Orders help to ensure that children learn social responsibility as well as reading and arithmetic.

In their small private schools, the Old Orders have maintained what mainstream educators offer as new. In 1981, for example, public school teachers "interested in exploring developmentally appropriate practices and devoting classroom time to what was considered social curriculum" (Delisio 2003, 3) developed the Responsive Classroom approach. According to the Northeast Foundation for Children, a private not-for-profit organization that is a chief advocate of the Responsive Classroom philosophy, the approach values the social and academic curricula equally, considers *how* children learn to be as important as *what* they learn, and argues that children need particular social skills—including responsibility, empathy, and self-control—if they are to succeed socially and academically. The approach is further informed by the belief that family participation and the involvement of the adult community are essential to children's education (cf. Northeast Foundation for Children 2004).

Delisio (2003, 1) notes that the Responsive Classroom approach attempts to integrate social and academic learning; by emphasizing discipline and personal responsibility, teachers find they have a more productive classroom. Teachers begin the school year by working with their students to develop classroom rules and to initiate a program of logical consequences for breaking those rules. In short, having made disciplinary expectations clear, teachers ultimately spend less time on discipline and more time on instruction.

Although *Education World* ("The Educator's Best Friend") describes "Responsive Classroom" as "a major shift with a big, big payoff for kids, teachers, and parents" (Delisio 2003, 4), it offers little new for most Old Order schools. In a 1962 submission to the *Blackboard Bulletin*, for example, M. A. Lee of Missouri encouraged all teachers to plant a "Garden of Character."

First, five rows of peas . . . Preparedness, Promptness, Perseverance, Politeness, and Prayer. Next, three rows of squash, . . . Squash criticism, Squash indifference, Squash gossip. Then five rows of lettuce, . . . Let us be faithful, Let us be unselfish, Let us be loyal, Le us love one another, Let us be thankful. No garden is complete without turnips, . . . Turn up for church and Turn up with a smile. (Challenge, 150)

From their inception, Old Order schools have enjoined parents and teachers to work to create schools in which children learn respect and personal responsibility. In a March 1962 letter to the *Blackboard Bulletin*, one parent wrote, "I think the most essential thing for the child to learn is obedience, and that should start in the home. If our children are obedient at home they are likely to be obedient in school, and later as members of the church." Discussing visits made to several Old Order schools, another parent wrote, "We saw instances of teachers and pupils, board members and parents, working together in a harmonious effort to obtain a good education, in a Christian environment. We also noticed a sharp contrast where this cooperation was not present. A schoolhouse with some books and a good teacher are the bare necessities of a school, but that combination alone is rarely able to reach the goals set for our parochial schools" (*Blackboard Bulletin*, May 1960). Further emphasizing that the smooth running of the school must be a community endeavor, another parent noted, "It takes more than just the financial end to make a school a success. [. . .] Our teachers have a great responsibility, and need our full support and encouragement" (*Blackboard Bulletin*, March 1960).

In offering small-scale, community-based instruction that emphasizes individual responsibility and discipline, Old Order schools reaffirm qualities secular educators are once again coming to appreciate. Like the small schools Barker and others have studied, Old Order schools are accountable to a clearly defined, community-based authority. Children know their teachers personally as community and family members, and instruction is individualized even though the curriculum is not. As in classrooms employing Responsive Classroom practices, Old Order children learn to take responsibility for their actions and to behave in a disciplined manner.

Brown (1991) argues that students can learn to understand themselves and construct "coherent, purposeful" adult lives only when there is a strong sense of community. The challenge, he notes further, "[is] to go beyond the mere technology of education, to build and sustain coherent, vital communities in and around their schools" (1991, 56). The Old Orders have met the challenge. In keeping their schools small, the Old Orders have made them more responsive to the needs of individual students and families and to the concerns of the group, building into Old Order education the accountability encouraged by the Responsive Classroom. Integrating education and community, Old Order schools offer the cultural coherence Meier, Brown, and others implicitly demand. Children learn in a secure environment from a teacher who knows them well and whose actions reinforce the lessons, values, and discipline important to becoming successful adults. Even when the teacher comes from a different church-community than her students, she understands the culture from which they come and the expectations parents have for their children's success. When there is a conflict between parents or between parents and teacher, they can work out their differences in face-to-face discussions in which all involved understand each other and identify with each other as neighbors, Christians, and Old Order church members.

The Challenges for Old Order Schools

Writing in "The Opinion of the Court" in *Wisconsin v. Yoder et al.*, Chief Justice Warren Burger noted:

> The record shows that the respondents' religious beliefs and attitude toward life, family, and home have remained constant—perhaps some would say static—in a period of unparalleled progress in human knowledge generally and great changes in education. The respondents freely concede, and indeed assert as an article of faith, that their religious beliefs and what we would today call "life style" has not altered in fundamentals for centuries. Their way of life in a church-oriented community, separated from the outside world and "worldly" influences, their attachment to nature and the soil, is a way inherently simple and uncomplicated. (in Keim 1975, 158)

As this work demonstrates, however, Old Order life is neither simple nor uncomplicated, and it is hardly static. Moreover, as Peters (2003, 155) notes, internal ideological change in Old Order church-communities can pose a greater threat to Amish church-communities than external forces.

Nevertheless, Old Order private schools, because they are community institutions, provide a context in which the community can negotiate its response to change. An Old Order teacher in Indiana said, "When all Amish were farmers [. . .] some parents put more emphasis on the farm knowledge than on the basic studies." "Now imagine," he added,

> [that]Farmer Brown's boy decides to go into construction. [. . .] The boy finds building an apartment house has more to do with math and a good reading ability than it does with fixing tractors and baling hay. He decides to put more emphasis on the basic studies for his own son in hopes it will make life easier for him.
>
> At this time a low percent of Amish young men enter agriculture as an occupation. [. . .] Instead they go to the factory and make from 15 to 45 dollars an hour. Many have their own businesses. Now you can easily see the change in view of education. The people's needs are changing. Along with more interests in studies, parents are showing perhaps more support to school now than they have in the past. [. . .] and that results in students with a better education when they graduate.

This teacher foresees the Old Order Amish schools in the Elkhart-LaGrange community changing in the future, although not necessarily for the better.

> Do I look for more grades being added? [. . .] Yes, eventually I look for more grades. I don't think we'll be a better community for it, but it will very likely happen. Already a factory has this policy: you must have a high school diploma to apply here . . . unless you are Amish! I don't think that is a very good plan. It is not fair and will result in bitter feelings toward Amish.

At the same time, by helping the community limit the access young people have to the world outside their Old Order community, Old Order private schools enable more conservative communities to resist change. As the Swartzentruber Amish in their isolated settlement in upstate New York have established their own schools, they have adopted texts more archaic than those many Swartzentruber parents used in Holmes County, Ohio, limited the subjects taught, and fostered a school environment in which German predominates.

Understood as a culturally shaped response to pressures from the dominant society, to changes within the plain community, and to the perceived threat of "drift," or religious and cultural assimilation, Old Order schools reveal, as Keesing (1992) asserts, how religious and ethnic minorities may actively engage the outside world to preserve the linguistic, cultural, and religious integrity of the group. In resisting school centralization and the loss of local control over education, the Old Orders have retained community control over what constitutes acceptable schooling.

The private school offers Old Order communities both a means of isolating themselves from the dominant society and a means of facilitating their interaction with it. When Old Order children attended public schools, it was made clear to them daily—in the dress and activities of their public school peers—what was worldly and so what their community wished to avoid. In the mixed schools of Holmes, Wayne, and Lancaster Counties, this is still true to some extent, for children are exposed constantly to the borders of their own church practice. Mixed schools tend to be more conservative in adopting new texts and new pedagogical practices and in providing for religious instruction because of the need to accommodate the most conservative elements. As is evident in the Crossroads School in Holmes County, Ohio, more progressive parents are willing to accept the limitations imposed by a teacher from a more conservative church-community. When more progressive parents insist on changes that less progressive ones cannot accept, someone will leave, as happened in Lancaster County when Horning Mennonite parents, thwarted in their attempt to replace German classes with Bible study, removed their children from the school.

A Wenger Mennonite educator asserts that "the best schools combine different churches. If I respect you, I will tolerate things from you I would not accept from my own group. If it's all your own people, then you quarrel with each other." Certainly educators in communities in which schools serve a homogeneous population face different obstacles than their peers in mixed schools. Attempts at innovation, for example, necessarily become identified with "higher" church groups. This is evident in the difficulties Old Order Amish educators in Ashland and in Lancaster County experienced when they attempted to institute meetings for beginning teachers.

In homogeneous settlements such as Norfolk, Somerset, Fredericktown, and Ashland, higher church groups serve as reminders of "drift," helping to check innovation even as these rural, isolated groups engage more with the dominant society. Restricted to limited economic interaction in the non–Old Order world, members of these communities make use of English and arithmetic skills learned in school while remaining firmly on the religious grounding supplied by church and home.

The large homogeneous settlement of the most progressive group, the Elkhart-LaGrange, Indiana, settlement, along with the church-community in Centreville, Michigan, with which it fellowships, faces a unique challenge, for there are no sizeable competing groups to serve as a check to change. Indeed, less progressive groups are generally seen as losing out on the true meaning of Christian faith as they devote themselves to particular rules of behavior instead of focusing on the spirit of the gospel. More importantly, the Elkhart-LaGrange community allows a wider range of engagement with the world, permitting members not only to work outside of the community in factories and other non–Old Order work sites, but also to interact with those outside of the church who are engaged in "spiritual" work or missionary outreach.[5] As one teacher noted, these changes worry some: "Most of the old timers with experience found that when people leave our faith to go do mission work, they drift more and more into the world and it might be a hindrance to your own salvation. Others are involved with Mexico and CAM [Christian Aid Ministries] [. . .] Personally, I like to reach out and help what I can from home base. [. . .] We have a lot of missionary work right here in our community if we just do it."

He noted further, "I'm not going to get a car or an airplane so I can help other countries that way. But for people who are doing that (English who were brought up that way), I support them."

Support for the activities of non-Amish Christians and willingness to work side by side with non-Amish at jobs outside the Old Order community challenge the Elkhart-LaGrange-Centreville Old Order Amish to remain separate, even as they redefine separation in their interaction with the world. Writing about a friend's co-teacher who was planning to go to Mexico "to help a community who took pride in being Christian," one teacher noted "they [the Mexico community] took it to extremes. All education was slowly lost [because] they classified it as heathen. Well, without education you can't read. If you can't read or add, just what can you do?"

In their study of Amish children, Hostetler and Huntington (1992, 94) concluded that "standardized test results indicate that the Amish parochial schools, now taught by teachers educated in Amish schools, are continuing to give their students an adequate academic education, even when judged by measures designed to test students in our modern, technological society. Amish parochial schools are preparing their students for successful, responsible adulthood within their own culture and within the larger society."

Some Old Order children do finish eight grades with an education similar to that achieved by public school peers in twelve years of study. Other Old Order children most certainly do not and are, in important ways, ill-equipped to deal with the non–Old Order world in any but the most basic social and economic intercourse. In contrast to their progressive counterparts, the Swartzentruber Amish have pared down formal education in private schools to the minimum necessary for survival. They have privileged the knowledge needed to live in a Swartzentruber Amish church-community and ensured that children will remain separate from the world and within their particular group. Regardless, they, like all Old Order children, are educated in a manner that supports and reflects particular beliefs about children, discipline, gender, and the place of the church-community in the world.

In a 1956 article, John A. Hostetler characterized the conflict between the Old Order Amish and public school authorities as "a conflict between two systems of values, the primitive religious way of life of the Amish and the general secular culture of America" (42). Actually, it is more complex. While the public schools grapple with the role of religion in secular education, the Old Order Amish and the Old Order Mennonites face the problem of teaching children to deal with the secular within the domain of the religiously grounded Old Order school. Fisher and Stahl end their work on the Amish school with a comment on the quality of Old Order education, noting, "If children do leave the Amish community, their skills and ethics are a solid base for making a living. In every community where Amish are settled, one can find want-ads in the local paper requesting

Amish women to help cook, bake, and clean. The skills of these hardworking people and their conscientious honesty are greatly sought after" (1997, 91). Ironically, if children leave the Old Order community, private school education has failed.

In every way, establishing a private school is an act of faith on the part of an Old Order community. Commenting on the success of Old Order private schools, a 1970 editorial in the *Blackboard Bulletin* noted,

> There is really no accurate way of measuring the value of our private schools, because we never know how the pupils would have turned out if they had attended public school. But we still have reason to think that [. . .] our schools do have something better to offer. A person has to be pretty pessimistic to say that our work is in vain. . . . The grim truth remains that a certain percent will cause us concern or stray away never to return. But that does not give us the right to give up. If we can influence only a few then our work will not have been in vain.

Ultimately, for the church to continue, Old Order education must prepare children to interact with the outside world to keep their communities intact. In reflecting and reinforcing the way each community interprets the nature of this interaction and what it means to be "in the world but not of it," schools help to define what it means to be Old Order now and in the future. They demonstrate both the connectedness of Old Order communities and their diversity.

APPENDIX A

Informants

This research is based on interviews and correspondence with 142 members of Old Order Amish and Mennonite communities in New York, Ohio, Pennsylvania, Michigan, Indiana, and Ontario. Of this number, 78 were teachers at the time of the interview. The others were church members in their respective communities and engaged in a variety of economic pursuits.

In addition, repeated visits were made to a total of 38 schools throughout these communities. All schools were visited at least twice at different times of the school year, and at least a third were visited repeatedly over a period of several years.

Hostetler and Huntington (1992) note that one of the criteria they used for selecting the schools in their study was that the teacher have taught for a minimum of three years. As pointed out in the text, the role of the teacher differs greatly from community to community, and it is unusual for teachers in the less progressive groups to teach more than one or two years. Klimuska (1995) quotes an Amishman in Lancaster County as saying, "The three biggest problems we have are taxes going up, the milk check going down, and teacher has a boyfriend." In larger Old Order communities with more than one school, the schools visited were chosen largely on the recommendation of community members as well as on the advice of local teachers and former teachers, who often chose to come along on school visits.

Table A.1. Informants

	Teachers	Nonteachers	Total
Female	71	38	109
Male	7	26	33
Total	78	64	142

Table A.2. Informants (Teachers), by Community

Community	Female	Male	Total
Swartzentruber	11	0	11
Norfolk, NY	4	0	4
Somerset, OH	2	0	2
Fredericktown, OH	2	0	.2
Ashland, OH	2	1	3
Holmes County, OH	6	2	8
Elkhart-LaGrange, IN	20	3	23
Centreville, MI	10	1	11
Lancaster County, PA	14	0	14
Total	71	7	78

Table A.3 Informants (Other), by Community

Community	Female	Male	Total
Swartzentruber (NY)	8	7	15
Norfolk, NY	3	0	3
Somerset, OH	5	1	6
Fredericktown, OH	1	1	2
Ashland, OH	3	3	6
Holmes County, OH	5	2	7
Elkhart-LaGrange, IN	2	4	6
Centreville, MI	3	1	4
Lancaster County, PA	5	5	10
Other	3	2	5
Total	38	26	64

Table A.4. Number of Schools Visited by Community

Community	Number of Schools Visited
Swartzentruber	8
Norfolk, NY	2
Somerset, OH	1
Fredericktown, OH	2
Ashland, OH	3
Holmes County, OH	3
Elkhart-LaGrange, IN	7
Centreville, MI	5
Lancaster County, PA	7
Total	38

Schools and Locations

The names of schools have been changed to protect the privacy of teachers, students, and parents.

Swartzentruber Schools

Line Road	Heuvelton, St. Lawrence County, New York
Lake Clear	Heuvelton, St. Lawrence County, New York
Kendrew Corner	Heuvelton, St. Lawrence County, New York
Ridgeview	Heuvelton, St. Lawrence County, New York
Woodland	Heuvelton, St. Lawrence County, New York
Little Brook	Heuvelton, St. Lawrence County, New York
River View	Holmes County, Ohio
Maple Tree	Rensselaer Falls, St. Lawrence County, New York

Small Amish Schools

Brook*	Norfolk, St. Lawrence County, New York
Brookview	Norfolk, St. Lawrence County, New York
Grove	Somerset, Ohio
Maple View	Fredericktown, Ohio
Oaktree	Fredericktown, Ohio
Brookside	Ashland, Ohio
Valley View	Ashland, Ohio
Mountain Top	Ashland, Ohio

Mainstream Amish Schools

Forest View	Holmes and Wayne Counties, Ohio
Crossroads	Holmes and Wayne Counties, Ohio
Millersburg	Holmes and Wayne Counties, Ohio

Progressive Amish Schools

Pine Tree	Centreville, Michigan
Creekview	Centreville, Michigan
Hill Top	Centreville, Michigan
Mountain Top	Centreville, Michigan
Grove	Centreville, Michigan
Creekside	Elkhart and LaGrange Counties, Indiana
Trail Run	Elkhart and LaGrange Counties, Indiana
Tree Top	Elkhart and LaGrange Counties, Indiana
North Ridge	Elkhart and LaGrange Counties, Indiana
Shady Valley	Elkhart and LaGrange Counties, Indiana
East	Elkhart and LaGrange Counties, Indiana
Brook	Elkhart and LaGrange Counties, Indiana

Old Order Mennonite Schools

Hill and Valley	Lancaster County, Pennsylvania
Pleasant Valley	Lancaster County, Pennsylvania
Eastside	Lancaster County, Pennsylvania
Little Stream	Lancaster County, Pennsylvania
Maple Hill	Lancaster County, Pennsylvania
Riverside	Lancaster County, Pennsylvania
Long Ridge	Lancaster County, Pennsylvania

* Brook School was the first school built by the Norfolk Old Order Amish church-community. It was a two-room schoolhouse and, initially, served a church-community with two church districts. For a variety of reasons, a number of families in this church-community have moved elsewhere, and the center of population has shifted far from the Brook School. For several years school was held in the cellar of an unfinished house. In fall 2004, the church-community built a smaller one-room school, the Brookview School. Because of the differences between the two (e.g., the difference in size, location, church-community during time of operation, and number of teachers), I have listed them separately.

Hectograph Recipe

Recipe for a Hectograph (from a Swartzentruber Amish teacher)

1 pint pure glycerin
2 boxes gelatin (8 envelopes)
2 cups water

Heat glycerin to boiling point over low flame. Moisten gelatin with cold water. Be sure it's thoroughly soaked. When glycerin boils, add gelatin slowly, stirring until dissolved.

Allow the hectograph filler to set for 24 hours before using. This filler works just as good as a filler bought in store.

Use hectograph carbon paper!

(Caution!) Glycerin does not boil like water but more like lard. It becomes very hot if left boiling and will boil up when the gelatin mixture is added.

Have Good Luck!

Additional instructions from a Swartzentruber Amish teacher

In printing with the hectograph, lay the original face down on the gelatin surface and wet it. Slowly peel the original off the surface of the hectograph, taking care not to smudge the lines. Then lay a blank sheet of paper on the hectograph, smooth it out carefully, and slowly lift it up. The original design will have been transferred to the paper.

One can make up to 100 copies of a single sheet. Before reusing the hectograph, let it sit for three days. To make a number of different copies in a short time period, re-heat the hectograph between each different design and page you wish to copy. The hectograph will not last as long (maybe only a year) if you heat it often.

Representative School Schedules

Table D.1. Swartzentruber Schools

	Monday	Tuesday	Wednesday	Thursday	Friday
1st period	Reading	Reading	Reading	Reading	Reading
2nd period	Arithmetic	Arithmetic	Arithmetic	Arithmetic	Arithmetic
3rd period	English (Phonics)	English (Phonics)	English (Phonics)	English (Phonics)	German 3, 4, 5, 6, 7, 8 (Phonics) 1, 2
4th period	Spelling	Spelling	Spelling	Spelling	Spelling

Table D.2. Brookview School (Norfolk, New York)

	Monday	Tuesday	Wednesday	Thursday	Friday
1st period	Arithmetic	Arithmetic	Arithmetic	Arithmetic	Arithmetic
2nd period	Upper grades: vocabulary Lower grades: reading	Upper grades: reading Lower grades: reading workbook	Upper grades: vocabulary Lower grades: reading	Upper grades: vocabulary Lower grades: reading	German reading
3rd period	Spelling	Geography	English	Penmanship	Art
4th period	English	Oral spelling	Spelling (2nd page)	Written spelling	Cleaning the school

Table D.3. Grove School (Centreville, Michigan)

	Monday	Tuesday	Wednesday	Thursday	Friday
1st period	Mathematics	Mathematics	Mathematics	Mathematics	Mathematics
2nd period	Reading 2, 3, 6, 7 Vocabulary 4, 5	Reading 2, 3, 4, 5 Vocabulary 6, 7	Reading 2, 3, 6, 7 Vocabulary 4, 5	Reading 2, 3, 4, 5 Vocabulary 6, 7	German 4, 5, 6, 7, 8 Reading 2, 3
3rd period	English	English	English	English	English
4th period	Health 4, 5, 6, 7 Writing	Spelling Phonics	Health 4, 5, 6, 7 Phonics	Spelling Phonics	Health 4, 5, 6, 7 Writing

Table D.4. Sample School Schedule (Old Order Mennonite Teachers' Meetings)

	Monday	Tuesday	Wednesday	Thursday	Friday
1st period	Penmanship	Penmanship	Penmanship	Penmanship	Memory Verse
2nd period	Arithmetic	Arithmetic	Arithmetic	Arithmetic	Arithmetic
3rd period	English Reading/ vocabulary	English Reading/ vocabulary		English	Reading/ vocabulary
4th period	Spelling	Social studies	Social studies Health German	Health quiz Spelling, 2–5 Art	Spelling German

Table D.5. Hill and Valley School (Lancaster County)

	Monday	Tuesday	Wednesday	Thursday	Friday
1st period	Arithmetic	Arithmetic	Arithmetic	Arithmetic	Arithmetic
2nd period	English	English	German	English	German
3rd period	Health	Social studies	Reading	Social studies	Music
4th period	Spelling	Reading	Art	Reading	Spelling

Notes

Preface

1. As will be discussed in Chapter 1, the Old Order Amish do not have church buildings. Instead, "church" refers to both religious services and the worshipping community itself, a reality captured in the term *church-community*. For further discussion of terminology, see Chapter 1, note 4.

2. Hornberger cites Pelto and Pelto (1973).

Chapter 1. Private Schools and Old Order Life

1. See note 1 to the Preface and note 4 below.

2. These principles were laid out in the Schleitheim Articles, issued by a conference of the Swiss Brethren in February 1527. Because of their unwillingness to take up arms during wartime and their belief that violence in self-defense is also wrong, the Anabaptists have also been called "defenseless Christians." See Kraybill and Bowman (2001, 80–81).

3. In fact, Amman's quarrel was with the Mennonite group known as the Swiss Brethren and was, as Hostetler (1993, 33) points out, a bit of a "family squabble." Unlike many Dutch and Flemish Mennonite congregations, the Swiss Brethren had not, for the most part, accepted the Dordrecht Confession of 1632, which mandated *Meidung*, or social shunning (Article XVII) and footwashing (Article II). Amman insisted on both.

4. Technically, the majority of Old Order schools are not parochial schools since they are not owned and operated by the church. Instead, they are established, funded, and owned by the parents who operate the schools on behalf of the church-community. The distinction between "parochial" and "private" is not as sharp in Old Order communities as it is in non–Old Order society, for in Old Order communi-

ties parents act within church guidelines with the advice and support of church membership. In keeping with the Old Order Amish practice of referring to both the church (the religious service) and the church-community (those who worship together) with the Pennsylvania German word *Gmay*, Old Order writers often refer to the private Old Order schools as "church schools" or as parochial schools. I will refer to them as "private schools."

5. See Hostetler (1993, 91–92), who notes that "the Amish have developed a unique community structure in America." He defines a "settlement" as "Amish families living in a contiguous relationship" or "households in proximity to one another." Settlements can be small or large. They may consist of a single church-community or many. The church district is the basic governing body of a settlement, and is, as Hostetler points out, roughly equivalent to a "congregation": "The church district is a self-governing body with ceremonial and institutional functions reinforced by the preaching service." Each church district is independent from all others and makes its own decisions. There is no higher governing structure that unites Amish church districts, but a church district may be affiliated with another, meaning that they share similar *Ordnungs*, that ministers of one district preach in the other, and that marriage between members of the districts are sanctioned. Affiliated church districts are said to be "in fellowship." A church-community comprises those church districts that are in fellowship within a particular settlement.

6. It is difficult to compare Old Order Amish to Old Order Mennonite according to this high-low scale because the church-communities are organized differently.

7. There has long been an Anabaptist presence in upstate New York. For example, Croghan, in Lewis County, was settled by Amish from France in the early nineteenth century (see Luthy 1986, 287–91; Yousey 1987), and there are several different Mennonite churches in the Croghan-Lowville-Watertown area. In addition, in 1974 (a good year for Anabaptist settlement in the North Country), members from the Melitta Fellowship Church in Leola, Pennsylvania, founded a daughter community, the Philadelphia Christian Fellowship, in Jefferson County. (Lewis, Jefferson, and St. Lawrence counties are contiguous, each sharing a border with the other two.) In 2000 a new Old Order Amish community was founded in Lowville, New York, with settlers from Pennsylvania. This community has already established social ties with the Norfolk Old Order Amish community, and in 2001 Norfolk turned (unsuccessfully) to Lowville in its search for a new schoolteacher.

8. The prohibition against working in town means that farmers may not take their produce to local farmers' markets, and teams of carpenters may not work within village limits; carpentry teams may, however, work "in the country," and farmers may sell produce from their buggies outside of town. Farmers may sell in town, but only so long as they go door-to-door "like peddlers," although this appears to be changing.

9. Interviews with teachers, parents, students, and other members of the different Old Order communities that are the focus of this study undergird the author's observations and archival research of Old Order education. In addition, the author carried on an extensive correspondence with a number of those interviewed. Comments attributed to Old Order sources are taken from interviews and correspondence. A list of informants and a record of correspondence is included in Appendix A.

10. There are family ties between Swartzentrubers and other Old Order Amish groups. One Swartzentruber bishop, just returned from a visit to cousins in the large Old Order settlement in Kalona, Iowa, noted that his father had been the only one of that generation to join the Swartzentruber church. Consequently, none of the bishop's paternal cousins or their families is Swartzentruber Amish.

11. All quotations of scripture are from the King James Version.

12. Although the first Anabaptists did not dress or live differently from their neighbors in any obvious way, Enninger (1991, 21) suggests that it wasn't long before the speech of the Anabaptists was noticeably unlike that of their neighbors, largely due to the Anabaptist refusal to swear oaths.

13. Old Order Mennonites have considerable local input into conference decision making. Twice a year, before communion, individual congregations hold counsel meetings, during which individual members are expected to make known to their church ministry any concerns they might have. Following the counsel meetings, the ministry of the member churches gather for the conference meeting, at which spokesmen for the different churches present the results of the counsel meetings and, ideally, any differences are resolved.

14. While this book focuses on Old Order schools, it is important to note that not all Old Order children attend Old Order private schools. Particularly in the Holmes County, Ohio, and Centreville, Michigan, settlements, a number of children receive some or all of their education in public schools from public school teachers. This will be discussed further in Chapters 5 and 6.

15. Also working with the Old Order Amish and horse-and-buggy Mennonite groups have been the Weaverland Conference or "Horning Mennonites," car-driving conservative Mennonites often called "black bumper" Mennonites because of the group's insistence that automobiles owned by members be entirely black. While some of the exclusively Horning schools now offer 9 or 10 grades rather than 8, many Horning children attend the 8-grade Old Order Mennonite schools, and these schools often employ Horning teachers.

16. Joseph Stoll, one of the founders of the Pathway Publishers in Aylmer, Ontario, points out that in Ontario, where Old Order Mennonites outnumber the Old Order Amish, it is the Old Order Mennonites who have taken the lead in the private school movement, the reverse of the situation in Lancaster County.

17. Both John A. Hostetler and Donald A. Erickson testified before the Supreme Court on behalf of the Amish. Two resources of particular value in understanding *Wisconsin v. Yoder et al.* are Albert N. Keim's 1975 work, *Compulsory Education and the Amish: The Right Not to Be Modern,* and Shawn F. Peters, *The Yoder Case: Religious Freedom, Education, and Parental Rights* (2003).

Chapter 2. Old Order Schools and Old Order Identities

1. This postcard was bought in Berlin, Ohio (Holmes County), at a local gift shop, April 2002.

2. "Reasons for not sending our children to school beyond the elementary eighth grade," addition to the Minutes of Sept. 11, 1954. Record of Proceedings, Holmes County Board of Education.

3. Kraybill (2001) attributes this quote to Aaron E. Beiler.

4. As noted in the first chapter, for the Old Order Amish, acceptance of a particular innovation is a congregational decision, while for the Old Order Mennonites, it is a matter for the conference, with each congregation offering its input. For both the Amish and Mennonites, disagreement over the decision may result in a schism in the church.

5. For example, members of the Swartzentruber Amish church-communities have refused to attach the slow-moving vehicle triangle to the backs of their buggies and wagons, which has often brought them into conflict with state authorities. Members of other Old Order church-communities greet the Swartzentruber refusal to use the triangle with bewilderment and even derision.

6. Throughout this work, the names of Old Order schools have been changed to protect the privacy of teachers, students, and parents. See Appendix B for a list of schools and their locations.

7. According to the teacher at the Crossroads School, "the trouble started when they needed to rebuild.[. . .] Someone made the remark that the school house is too big or something."

8. This is the cost quoted by the dissenting parents; they contrast it to the $15,000 cost of the River View School.

9. The Old Order Amish, in contrast to the Old Order Mennonites, meet for worship in members' homes. The building of a separate structure for religious observances would, for the Swartzentruber Amish and many other Old Order groups, seem a very worldly step to take, so comparing the new school to a church building would be tantamount to saying that those who built it were acting in a worldly way.

10. The Reidenbach Mennonites, also called "Thirty-fivers," separated from the Groffdale Conference (Wenger Mennonites) because they objected to the Wenger Mennonite participation in the Civilian Public Service camps, which were insti-

tuted by the Selective Training and Service Act of 1940 to provide "for alternative service for conscientious objectors" who were assigned "work of national importance under civilian direction." (*www.afsc.org/news/quaker-action/fall2004/ cps-camps.htm*, accessed June 9, 2005; see Wenger and Sauder 1968, 363; Toews 1996, 150–51).

11. An unmarried woman who had taught school for several years and then left teaching when she turned 21 has been hired to "teach school" for these children. At first, there were no plans to build a separate schoolhouse. The teacher told me that she would have a room in the home as a designated "classroom" and that she would probably teach only "a half-day school" because with only four scholars she'll "get through the books" easily. In the end, the community did construct a separate building for the school, which they put only about ten yards from the house. The school windows look out on the family cornfield. The schoolhouse was built on skids so that it could be moved to a more central location "because some other families might move in." The teacher, her family, and neighbors all talk about how the teacher has "taken a school." Clearly, the parents and the community will do their best to ensure that the children will not be "home schooled," and the teacher and her pupils will follow the routine of the other schools. The lack of other children is still seen as a problem.

12. Ervin N. Hershberger was a member of the Beachy Amish church; yet, he was asked to contribute to the *Blackboard Bulletin* by its Old Order Amish editor, Joseph Stoll. Stoll points out that Hershberger "may not be typical," yet acknowledges that he and others were in agreement with Hershberger's sentiments "or I wouldn't have asked him to write for the *Bulletin*." The Beachy Amish churches, like the Horning Mennonites, use automobiles (painted black), have electricity, and have adopted English for use in religious services. When the Old Orders were first establishing schools in great numbers, members of Beachy congregations were sometimes involved. Early school directories published in the *Blackboard Bulletin* acknowledged Beachy participation in a number of private schools.

13. Although the author does not acknowledge this in her letter, part of this passage, from "As public school instruction" to the end of the passage, appears to be a quote from the Foreword of the *Pennsylvania Standards*, p. 1.

14. See Pederson 2002, esp. p. 347.

Chapter 3. The Swartzentruber Schools

1. I was asked by a board member for the new Ridgeview School, then under construction, to purchase an alphabet chart at a local teachers' supply store, but none of those they had for sale, all decorated with pictures of animals or objects, were suitable in the eyes of the board. In the end, the board member told me that the teacher would "look elsewhere or would make her own."

2. While corporal punishment is acceptable and expected, it appears to be rare, and teachers do not like to use it. For example, this same teacher noted that her cousin, also a teacher, had to "spank a couple of her scholars, we heard," and commented that "we [she and other teachers] want to ask her about it all on Sunday." This teacher also admitted that she didn't know what she'd do if she had to spank one of the older pupils, but then added, "It's mostly the little ones who need it. The older ones know how they should behave."

3. By "higher class churches" the bishop means those Old Order Amish church-communities that have, in his eyes, moved closer to the world in their use of technology and in their dress, transportation rules, and interaction with the non–Old Order society.

4. Interestingly, another brother in this family never finished school; as another sister, a former teacher, put it, "he never finished eighth grade because he got through the books early." That one brother was "easy to learn" was nothing to be proud of, just as the other brother being "hard to learn" was nothing to be ashamed of.

5. In church services only men are *Vorsingers*, but in school, boys and girls share equally in the task. Singing is a very important group activity, and school provides training not only in the songs themselves but in the way group singing is carried out.

6. Every Swartzentruber school has a shelf for books to which the students can turn after they've finished their work; schools vary widely, however, in what that shelf has to offer and how much. Most often there are cast-off readers from the public school and children's books donated by neighbors (often non–Old Order). One school had an incomplete set of encyclopedias. Often the books are falling apart, and students bring back only a part of the book to read at their desks. By the end of eighth grade when a student graduates, he or she will have had ample opportunity to read everything on the shelf more than once.

7. E-Z Graders are produced in Chagrin Falls, Ohio, and sold in Old Order school supply stores. Setting the grader to the number of problems, one has only to note the number wrong to have the percentage score.

8. "How to be an interesting person," in *Penmanship Pad, Grade 5* (Gordonville, PA: Gordonville Print Shop, n.d.), 26.

9. Since Pennsylvania German is not standardized and can vary considerably in vocabulary and pronunciation from community to community, German also isolates and protects children from the influence of other plain groups.

10. Generally, parents want their children to be six years old by the time school starts or not long after; a child turning six in December, for example, is usually considered too young to start and must wait until the following year.

11. Although in Swartzentruber communities it is rare for preschool-aged children to speak any English, there are, of course, some differences between families.

One teacher noted that sometimes fluency in English "depends on the family business. If they have a shop where a lot of English people come, they know more than if they're just farmers."

12. Part of me remains convinced that one eighth grader I observed was not, in fact, reading the difficult paragraph he'd gotten but was instead saying "lalala." That the teacher often pays little attention to the reading itself became clear when, during one fifth grade reading class, two children in a row read the same passage. The teacher was busy at this time explaining an arithmetic problem (in German) to a third grader. Only when the second child fell silent because he didn't know a word, did the teacher turn her attention to the readers.

13. Swartzentruber teachers, unlike teachers in other communities that also use these texts (see Chapter 4), do not tear out the answer section at the back of the book. Children routinely check the back after doing their assignment.

14. See H. C. Pearson and H. Suzzalo, *Essentials of Spelling* (1919), part 2.

15. More than once when visiting schools, I observed children practicing their spelling words on the board interrupt the teacher to ask her what word it was that they had just written.

16. Among the sentences accepted by one teacher for the spelling word "jealous" were "I am *jealous* for my tongue," "You made me very *jealous* for that candy," and "I am *jealous* for candy." The spelling words "struggle" and "drown" yielded "I saw a little boy *struggle* to keep out of water before he has to *drown*" and "Some people have to *struggle* to keep them from *drown*."

17. Of the seven Swartzentruber schools visited regularly for this study only two had a guest book. Only I had signed one of the books. The other recorded only six visits over a two-year span, most from out-of-town visitors to the community. None of the schools had a visitor's chart.

18. Neither parents nor teacher seems to have considered the incident a serious one. After agreeing that the teacher should have sent the girl home, the father pointed out that if she had, the other children wouldn't have had the buggy to get back themselves. Showing typical Swartzentruber conservatism in dealing with the medical establishment, the parents did not take the girl for medical treatment until the following day.

19. The board turned down her request.

20. In New York State the Swartzentruber Amish schools operate in isolation from any outside agency. Clive B. Chambers, superintendent at Heuvelton Central, a district that includes more Amish schools than any other in New York, wrote: "We go out once or twice a year and take a census and ask if there is anything they need. Sometimes they say lower school taxes. They occasionally ask for a bell or some slates, but that's all." Chambers went on to say, "We do not have any idea of what their curriculum is" (*Watertown Daily Times*, 21 September 1997, A1).

21. There are no duplicating machines in Swartzentruber schools; nevertheless, teachers do find "ditto masters" useful for homemade duplicating purposes. When photocopying is difficult or too expensive for the teacher and her family, she may prepare a "hectograph," a homemade duplicating material. See Appendix C for the recipe.

22. This was in 2003.

Chapter 4. Small Schools in Small Settlements

1. When the teacher married, she and her husband wished to complete the house, and a new one-room schoolhouse, with a cellar, was built for the 2003–2004 term.

2. There appear to be no differences in men's dress between the two communities.

3. When questioned about other Old Order Amish groups, the Swartzentruber Amish generally reply simply, "They're not like us."

4. These are settlements in fellowship with those under discussion.

5. The Grove School was built in 1991 and had 17 students in 2002.

6. Several schools in these settlements have clocks that need winding. The presence of battery-powered clocks in some schools in the same church-district indicates that battery-powered clocks are acceptable to the church, although perhaps unavailable to all the schools.

7. To "take a class" means bringing a grade to the front so that the teacher can present the lesson, grade workbooks, or hear oral reading.

8. This teacher noted in her letter that her father had helped her formulate this statement.

9. In the Brookside School in Ashland, for example, grades six through eight use *Learning to Spell*, and the other grades use the *Essentials of English Spelling*. In the Valley View School, also in Ashland, grade eight is now using *Learning to Spell*, while the rest use *Essentials*; this is a recent change.

10. *Learning Numbers With Spunky (the donkey)*, a first grade text, and *Counting Numbers With Spunky (the donkey)*, a second grade text. These were copyrighted by Schoolaid, an Old Order Mennonite press in East Earl, Pennsylvania, in 1995 and 1996, respectively.

11. The first graders were using Gordonville Print Shop reprints of the Laidlaw Brothers' 1951 *My First Health Book*.

12. According to others in the Somerset community, the "sis-in-law," who taught several years in the Somerset school, added the Pathway vocabulary texts (*Working with Words*) to the curriculum and changed the English texts from *Plain and Fitting English*, a Gordonville publication, to *Climbing to Good English*, which is published by Schoolaid.

13. Emphases in this paragraph are mine.

14. Of the different schools visited as part of this study, only two did not fit this pattern, and both were recognized in the community as not being well run. In one school, while the teacher met with a reading class at the front table, children waved books in the air to get her attention, and they responded slowly to the teacher's instructions. During the singing, one boy shouted the words, while two others talked to each other during the song. The reaction of a teacher who was also visiting suggested that none of this was acceptable behavior. Similarly, in another school in the same settlement, children walked around, talked loudly to each other, and even hummed while the teacher, holding class at the front of the room, did not seem to notice. Aware of problems in this latter school, the community has hired a helper, a married woman whose children are grown, to come in several days a week. Several community members commented that the helper kept the school orderly. It must be noted that both of these teachers were only 17 years old and in their first year of teaching. As another teacher in the same settlement noted, "What do we expect, taking a young girl with no experience."

15. The children took delight in this activity, which in the adult world is one that bridges the divide between the Amish and their non–Old Order neighbors. The older children demonstrated their awareness of the boundaries of their church community: "Nobody wants to be without a light," the auctioneer informed his audience. "Buy a candle in case the electricity goes out."

16. In a later letter, this teacher wrote, "If I have any problems with a child, I can talk to his/her parent about it!"

17. The Old Order Amish community in Clyde, New York, like the communities specifically mentioned in the text, is small and relatively isolated. It fellowships with the Norfolk community and is bound by family, social, and spiritual ties to the other communities discussed.

18. After teaching several years in the Norfolk community, this teacher also taught in the Clyde, New York, Old Order Amish community.

19. At the time of the interview, three weeks into the start of the term, the teacher had decided that she most certainly needed a helper.

20. These homogeneous church-communities vary in their interaction with the state. An Ashland teacher indicated, for example, that she regularly sent an enrollment report and attendance forms to the county superintendent, but a teacher from the Somerset settlement had never submitted either in several years of teaching.

Chapter 5. Mainstream Amish Schools

1. Donald Kraybill, quoted by R. Rhodes, "No Longer Living Off the Land," *Mennonite Weekly Review*, 21 October 2002, 1, 7.

2. Members of more progressive groups suggest that their less progressive counterparts have focused on the form rather than the meaning of biblical commandments and, taking refuge in unchanging, have lost sight of the scriptural basis and spiritual importance of many practices. Less progressive groups see the willingness of more progressive groups to adopt new technology or alter longstanding behaviors as evidence of "drift" or assimilation to the world that signals a failure to maintain the faith (and thus the practices) of their forebears.

3. Although the students attending these six schools are predominantly Amish, the schools are public, and non–Old Order children are enrolled as well. The East Holmes School District sets the curricula and chooses the texts, and students take the standard achievement tests and meet other district requirements. Each of these schools has an Old Order Amish Advisory Board. Interview, M. Zinck (East Holmes School Board), June 7, 2005.

4. Ibid.

5. Published in Apple Creek (Wayne County), Ohio, in 1958, these standards were "compiled and approved by bishops, committeemen and others in conference, Henry J. Hershberger, Chairman." Reprinted in Buchanan 1967, 233–39.

6. Byler (1969; 1980, 30; 37). Uria R. Byler, one of the first Old Order teachers in Ohio, was very active in the early growth of the Old Order Amish private schools. His manual for teachers, *School Bells Ringing*, solicited by Pathway editor Joseph Stoll, is based in part on questionnaires sent to a number of experienced teachers.

7. In providing aid to Old Colony Mennonites in Mexico, Holmes County area Old Order Amish are in company with Old Order Amish in other areas, most notably in Michigan and Indiana. The Holmes County area Old Order Amish are in fellowship with these other Amish church-communities. The October 2001 *Update* from Mexico Mennonite Aid notes: "Our Old Order Brethren will soon see some results of their investment" (1).

8. Again, there is variation. The teacher at the Crossroads School, a member of a Swartzentruber Amish church, notes, "[I] colored most of them [the charts] myself. My sister helped a little too."

9. According to the *Ohio Minimum Standards* (Hershberger n.d.), "very few can deny that if the child has received the instruction that will enable it to earn an honest living and lead a Christian life, then that child has been 'adequately' educated. The Amish schools of Ohio have been set up with that principle as their objective" (see Buchanan 1967, 233–39).

10. Achieving *Gelassenheit*, which is to trust in God so completely that one questions nothing, to curb one's individual desires, and to subordinate one's will to God's will as expressed in the Bible and the *Ordnung*, is the means of preparing oneself for eternal life (Cronk 1977; 1981; see also Hostetler 1993).

11. These lists, "compiled by the pupils of Buckeye School, Sugarcreek, Ohio," and "sent in by the teacher, Susie Yoder, November 1965," were reprinted in *The Challenge of the Child*, 209–10.

12. According to one special education teacher, "there are now 16 or 17 Special Ed classes throughout Wayne and Holmes Co." (personal communication).

13. Notes from the Special Needs Session, Aylmer, Ontario, Friday, August 13, 1999. Unpublished transcript.

14. The *Ohio Minimum Standards* define a school district as "the area within a radius, a reasonable walking distance of the school. Where the distance is greater, and other means of transportation is used, the problem of transportation rests with the parents" (cf. Buchanan 1967, 237).

15. Editorial, *Blackboard Bulletin*, September 1962; reprinted in *The Challenge of the Child*, 131–32.

16. The North District Teachers' meeting was held in Geauga County, northeast of Cleveland.

17. Not only have Holmes County area teachers gone to Old Colony communities in Mexico, but Old Colony Mennonites have also visited Holmes County area schools, attended Old Order Amish church services, and participated in Old Order Amish young folk gatherings.

Chapter 6. Progressive Amish Schools

1. Remarks presented by an Amish bishop at the fourth annual Indiana Amish parochial teachers' class held in Parke County, Indiana, on July 13, 2000.

2. Ibid.

3. Noted in *Indiana Regulations* (2002, 2).

4. The 1995 *Indiana Amish Directory of Elkhart, LaGrange, and Noble Counties* notes: "Then all pupils in the corporation from the seventh grade and higher had to attend Westview High School or an Amish private school. Pupils in the lower grades could attend Shipshewana, Topeka, Honeyville, or Clay Township schools. As a result, eight new Amish schools were built that summer. More have been built since."

5. *Michigan Amish Directory* 2002 (D. Miller 2002, 65); although the directory says that the current building was constructed "approximately around 1973," a retired teacher remembers attending school there in the 1930s. The school has been called "Pine Trees" only since 1995.

6. Huntington (2001, 27) suggests that Michigan classrooms are quite plain: "A bulletin board, posters displaying the name and grade of each child, some mottoes, and perhaps drawings done by the pupils or teacher are the only decorations." This was not the case in the Centreville schools.

7. Although the display noted that the verse was from the Psalms, no chapter or verse was indicated.

8. The Beachy Amish, like the Horning Mennonites, drive cars that must be painted black, and they no longer use German in their church services. The schism in the Centreville church-community occurred in the early 1990s; the Tobe Yoder Church is acknowledged to be stricter in its *Ordnung* than the main body from which it split.

9. The A Beka Book Web site, retrieved August 2, 2004, from www.abeka .com. According to the founders, Dr. and Mrs. Arlin Horton, "The hundreds of traditional Christian educational materials developed by *A Beka Book* have been developed and refined over a period of 50 years in the classrooms of Pensacola Christian Academy, an independent Baptist college in Pensacola, Florida.

10. Ibid.

11. Teachers at one school, noting that all the upper grade students had older people in the community as "pen friends," commented that "it gives them practice writing."

12. *School Echoes*, December 2001, 19.

13. Ibid.

14. As noted earlier, many Old Order schools are technically private schools— supported by the families of children who attend—rather than parochial schools— supported by the church. The *Indiana Regulations*, noting that teachers employed in parochial schools cannot be required to take out Teachers Unemployment Compensation, strongly recommends that "we have our Amish Private Schools really become Amish Parochial Schools, which are supported by all members of the church and not only by the parents involved in the school" (2002, 5). The schools in the Nappanee area are church schools, not neighborhood schools.

15. This does not always work. One board member noted, "We're not sale people here [at the local school]. We used to have bake sales at the flea market but haven't for the last two years. The ladies decided it was time for the men to do some work, and nothing happened."

16. The chairman of the Executive Committee noted that, in addition to non− Old Order teachers, Old Order Mennonites have been hired for Amish schools. He also pointed out that a Nappanee area Old Order Amish bishop was teaching at an Old Brethren school. In *The Amish Schools of Indiana: Faith in Education* (2004), Stephen B. Harroff also documents the presence of non−Old Order teachers in Amish private schools.

17. As quoted in "From the Staff," *Blackboard Bulletin*, December 1992, 14.

18. Ibid., 14−15.

19. Interview with W.B.; two male Amish teachers, one of whom had been a pupil of W.B.'s, expressed surprise that his salary was so low.

20. This is "O Gott Vater, Wir Loben Dich." It is the second song sung at Amish worship services. Written in 1590 by Lenhardt Clock, the "Loblied" also plays a role in ordination services. The *Ausbund*, the oldest Protestant hymnal in continuous use, contains songs written by Anabaptist martyrs in the early sixteenth century; the first known printing of the text was in 1564. See Mary M. Miller (2000, 109–10) and John A. Hostetler (1993, 227–33).

21. One retired teacher noted that "in a lot of places I taught the parents didn't start their children to school so young. If they become seven before [the start of the term] they'd start that fall; if not, they waited for the next year. That's so they don't get out of school so young, to prevent sending them to vocational school."

22. Letter from H. J. Miller addressed to "Dear Friend" and dated 1974; Heritage Historical Library, Aylmer, Ontario.

23. Letter from HJM, dated April 1995; Heritage Historical Library, Aylmer, Ontario.

Chapter 7. Old Order Mennonite Schools in Lancaster County

1. There are also Old Order Brethren in Lancaster County. According to Kraybill (2001, 15), these number roughly 300 adult baptized members. While they also have their own private schools, these are entirely in English and go through the twelfth grade. They will not be discussed in this work.

2. The Horning Mennonites are sometimes called "Black Bumper" Mennonites because the cars they drive must be entirely black.

3. See Hoover n.d.

4. *Blackboard Bulletin*, November 2000; Kraybill 2001, 178–79.

5. *Background of the Old Order Mennonite Parochial Schools of Pennsylvania* 1985, 13–14.

6. According to an Amish teacher now teaching in a Mennonite school, "There are no Mennonite teachers in Amish schools."

7. The Mid-Atlantic Mennonites and the Hope Mennonites have adopted the automobile. The Hope Mennonites, more progressive than the Horning Mennonites, have Sunday Schools; like the Horning Mennonites and the Mid-Atlantic group, they no longer use German in their church services.

8. The teacher reports a visit to the school by an elderly woman who stated that she had come to see the schoolhouse in which her grandfather had taught in 1850.

9. One Horning Mennonite involved in school issues commented that the Old Order Amish "like to have a Mennonite on the school board when they can because then the school can be wired for electricity."

10. Meetings for Beginning Teachers, Old Order Mennonite, Riverside School (8/02).

11. This teacher questioned further, "How's education going to help? Besides, how can you get educated if there's no respect?" A Mennonite teacher reading this quote noted, "We had Amish students and they were very polite [. . .] polite but not always respectful." As noted earlier, for the Amish, "respect" is often synonymous with "obedience."

12. Compiled by J. D. Brunk. First published in 1902 and reprinted in 1976 by the Mennonite Publishing House in Scottdale, Pennsylvania.

13. Shaped notes denote the note on the scale by a particular shape.

14. Teachers use flash cards that reinforce the children's recognition of the notes through color and mnemonic devices. For example, on one card △ or "do" is colored green, and the teacher tells the children that this note is "firm but restful"; □ or "la" is colored black, and the note, according to the teacher, is "mournful and sad."

15. An important part of growing up Old Order Amish or Old Order Mennonite is joining "the young folk" at age 16. Old Order young people remain with "the young folk" until they marry. As Hostetler and Huntington (1992, 30) note, the young folk peer group "is of supreme importance, for most of the Amish young person's socialization takes place within this group rather than within the church or the family." This is also true for the Old Order Mennonites.

16. While young women teach music in the schools, only men may teach music in the singing schools.

17. Weaverland Conference or Horning Mennonites no longer use German in their church services, so there is little motivation for the retention of the language, and many of the younger generation are no longer learning it at home (Johnson-Weiner 1998); similarly, children whose parents are members of the Mid-Atlantic Conference or the Lancaster Conference are unlikely to speak any German when they begin school.

18. This teacher noted further that "Mennonite schools are changing from Strayer-Upton to Rod and Staff arithmetic for example, but Amish schools are not. When you're in a mixed school, you go along with the school. We hold the line in our own schools. There was a problem in one school in which the director went ahead and bought *Pathway Readers* without consulting the parents. The Amish were upset and wanted to stick with what they had, which was *Dick and Jane*."

19. For example, in Book 2^2 of Upton's *Arithmetic Workbook*, reprinted in 2000 by Gordonville Print Shop, Nan buys a doll at the store for 4¢, while Mary buys a doll at the fair for 3¢. In *Counting Numbers with Spunky* 2^2, Sadie's Bake Shop sells bread for $1.59 a loaf, and doughnuts for $1.29, and in a later exercise, a baseball costs $4.39, while a whistle costs $1.29.

20. *Mathematics for Christian Living Series: Exploring Numbers*, Grade 3 (Crocket, KY: Rod and Staff Publishers, Inc., 1982), 81.

21. *Mathematics for Christian Living Series: Mastering Numbers,* Grade 7 (Crocket, KY: Rod and Staff Publishers, Inc., 1988), 59.

22. At least one Lancaster school is using the A Beka arithmetic series, although the teacher notes that it may be the only one. She likes the series but complained that A Beka "is revising too often and it's too expensive to keep up." Moreover, she added, "there's a more modern trend."

23. *Pennsylvania Standards* 1969, 32. The *Pennsylvania Standards* defines a "substitute" teacher as "the best available teacher for this school at this time."

24. There were 228 teachers at the first day of the 2003 meetings. Of this number, 9 had taught more than 16 years, 11 had taught between 10 and 15 years, 13 (including one male) had taught between 6 and 9 years, and 42 had taught two to three years. There were 50 beginning teachers, 14 from Lancaster County and 36 (including 2 males) from elsewhere in Pennsylvania and out-of-state (including New York, Ohio, and Wisconsin).

On the first day of the 2004 meetings, there were 227 teachers attending, 7 of them men. Of the total number, 10 (including one Amish woman) had taught for 16 or more years, 11 (including one Amish woman) had taught between 10 and 15 years, 11 had taught between 6 and 9 years, 14 (including 1 Amish woman) had taught 4 or 5 terms, and 46 (including 3 men and 9 Amish women) had taught 2 to 3 terms. Five of the men attending were from a Horning community.

25. The dividing line for these regional meetings is route 322 in Lancaster County.

26. The same article also notes that fewer than 5 percent of Old Order Mennonite teachers are male (December 1992, 14).

27. See Lapp 1991, 573–74, for a discussion of the history of "special schools" in Lancaster County.

28. "Topics of the Times: Their Own School," *New York Times,* 30 November 1938, 22.

Chapter 8. Publish or Perish

1. Alta Hoover, a founder of the Schoolaid Publishing Company, an Old Order Mennonite textbook publisher, confirms that "the schools could get used public school books cheaply." Interviews with Hoover were conducted over a period of several years beginning in the late 1990s. John Martin was interviewed in 2001 and 2003.

2. Interview, W. Hershberger (owner, Gordonville Print Shop), June 2001.

3. The Old Order Book Society has often influenced Old Order church-communities in other states, but it has not imposed (and cannot impose) its decisions on them.

4. Pearson and Suzzallo, *Essentials of English Spelling* (1919), iii.

5. Interview, W. Herschberger, June 2001.

6. Upon receiving a circle letter, each participant takes out the page he or she had written for the previous circle, writes something new, adds it to the letters from the other participants, and sends the whole packet on to the next person on the list. If there are ten participants, then there will be ten letters circulating. It is a form of communication in which all participants must play an active role and for which all must assume responsibility. It is, in fact, a version in writing of an Old Order community, with all members participating equally and actively.

7. *Blackboard Bulletin*, April 1958; rpt. in *Challenge of the Child*, 67–69.

8. Rpt. in Keim 1975, 18.

9. Joseph Stoll, a founder of and editor at Pathway Publishing, was interviewed in 2002 and 2003.

10. Announcement for the "New Newsletter for Teachers," 1957.

11. Letter from D. Luthy (Pathway editor) to D. W. Bowling, November 25, 1995. Heritage Historical Library, Aylmer, Ontario.

12. Letter from J. Stoll to A. S. Kinsinger, May 30, 1966. Heritage Historical Library, Aylmer, Ontario.

13. Letter from J. Stoll to I. Leid, May 16, 1966. Heritage Historical Library, Aylmer, Ontario.

14. Letter from D. Luthy to J. R. Squire (editor-in-chief, Ginn & Co.), February 4, 1969. Heritage Historical Library, Aylmer, Ontario.

15. Letter from D. B. Peachey to J. Stoll, January 31, 1968. Heritage Historical Library, Aylmer, Ontario.

16. In fact, the first Old Order Amish textbook written specifically for the Old Order schools was Noah Zook's *Seeking a Better Country*, published by the Gordonville Print Shop in 1963 (Yoder 1990, 145).

17. Letter from J. Stoll to Mr. and Mrs. J. Borntrager, May 16, 1966. Heritage Historical Library, Aylmer, Ontario.

18. Letter from D. Luthy to D. W. Bowling, Nov. 25, 1995. Heritage Historical Library, Aylmer, Ontario.

19. Ibid.

20. Letter from D. Luthy, read at a gathering of Old Order schoolteachers in LaGrange County, Indiana, 7/3/66. Heritage Historical Library, Aylmer, Ontario.

21. Interestingly, while they use *McGuffey's Readers* in grades one through five, the Swartzentruber Amish do use the *Pathway Readers* for the higher grades. Thus, they are using the Pathway texts that draw heavily on archaic non–Old Order sources, but rejecting the lower-grade readers that focus on Old Order life.

22. Letter to J. Stoll from Crist M. Hershberger, Burton, Ohio, 1966; Heritage Historical Library, Aylmer, Ontario.

NOTES TO PAGES 219–236

23. Personal communication, J. Stoll (November 2002).

24. "Schoolaid: Its purpose, origin, and organizational structure," n.d. In 1993, Martin Fox died and was replaced on the board by David Hoover.

25. Introduction, *Wir lesen Geschichten aus der heiligen Schrift*, Lancaster: Schoolaid, 1984.

26. This is not to say that the Old Order Mennonites are actively evangelizing. Rather, Old Order Mennonites do support such organizations as Christian Aid Ministries.

27. Although the letterhead on Study Time stationary gives the company name as two separate words, founder Delbert Farmwald consistently spells it as one, "Studytime." I use the two-word version here because that is what is used on published materials.

28. Personal correspondence, August 2, 2004.

29. Ibid.

30. Minutes of OOA Steering Committee (4th vol.), Sept. 9, 1987, 21st annual meeting (printed by Gordonville, Penna. Print Shop), p. 7.

31. Ibid.

Chapter 9. What's Education For?

1. More succinctly, Kachel (1989, 94) asserts that Old Order schools are "fact and application oriented, related specifically to the values of the Amish and to the information they will need throughout their lives as members of the Amish community."

2. Personal communication, A. Hoover (August 2002).

3. Ultimately, the education of Old Order children continues beyond the eighth grade as children go to work for Old Order or non–Old Order employers and enter *Rumspringa*, the "running around years." During *Rumspringa*, which begins at age 16 or 17, depending on the church-community, life for young people revolves around the peer group. In more conservative church-communities, *Rumspringa* may involve gathering for singings on church Sundays, excited whispering about who will be going home with whom, and courtship. In more progressive communities, young people join youth groups or gangs, dress "English," own automobiles, have parties and dances, and experiment with alcohol. Exploring their options in the company of other young people, Old Order youth have, to varying degrees, the opportunity to "enjoy the delights of the world" (Kraybill 2001, 147).

Kraybill suggests that *Rumspringa* likely only provides Old Order young people deciding whether to join church the illusion of choice and that "thinking they had a choice, adults are more likely to comply with the demands of the Ordnung later in life" (2001, 186). Approximately 90 percent of Old Order young people do, finally, join a church-community. Nevertheless, those that decide to leave the Old Order world generally fare well, often seeking higher education and entering a variety of occupations (cf. Kraybill 2001; Hostetler 1993, esp. ch. 14; for another perspective, cf. Garrett 1998; Garrett and Farrant 2001). It is important to note that, while leaving the church-community is always difficult emotionally and socially, those who leave after becoming baptized and joining church face excommunication (*Bann*) and social shunning (*Meidung*), while those who leave without joining church do not.

4. Peters observes that "although the piety of the Amish ostensibly had little bearing on the legal questions at the heart of [*Wisconsin v.*] *Yoder*, it clearly struck a chord with the straitlaced [Chief Justice Warren] Burger." Peters goes on to note that "the chief justice gushed that 'the Amish communities singularly parallel and reflect many of the virtues of Jefferson's ideal of the sturdy yeoman'" (2003, 152; Keim 1975, 164).

5. In the Centreville, Michigan, community, for example, Amish who take part in disaster relief refer to their efforts as "missionary work."

Bibliography

A Plea to Men of Authority. 1937. A petition signed by 40 representatives, November 17, 1937, and republished in various works, including Esh (1965, 3–4), and Lapp (1991, 140–41).

Anonymous. 1996. *The Beginning and Development of Parochial Special Schools: 1975–1996*. Gordonville, PA: Gordonville Print Shop.

Arons, S. 1972. Compulsory Education: The Plain People Resist. *Saturday Review* 55:52–57.

Articles of Agreement Regarding the Indiana Amish Parochial Schools and Department of Public Instruction. 1967. Indianapolis, IN: Department of Public Instruction.

Background of the Old Order Mennonite Parochial Schools of Pennsylvania 1969–1980. 1985. Gordonville, PA: Gordonville Print Shop.

Bandman, B. 2001. A Friendly Critique of a Child's Right to an Open Future. *Philosophy of Education Yearbook*. Retrieved June 22, 2005, from www.ed.uiuc.edu/EPS/PES-Yearbook/2001/Bandman%2001.pdf.

Barker, B. O. 1986. The Advantages of Small Schools. *ERIC Digest*. No. ED265988.

Barker, R., and P. Gump. 1964. *Big School, Small School*. Palo Alto, CA: Stanford University Press.

Beiler, A. E. 1961. *Record of Principles Pertaining to the Old Order Amish Church Sect School Committee as of September 2, 1937. Reaffirmed and Approved through Counsel of the Committee August 9, 1961*. Gap, PA.

Blackboard Bulletin. (A journal for Old Order teachers published by Pathway Publishing Company, Aylmer, Ont.)

Borkholder, O. E. 2001. *Nappanee Amish Directory including the Rochester, Kokomo, and Milroy Communities 2001*. Nappanee, IN: Owen E. Borkholder Family.

Borntrager, John M. 1989. The Challenge Before Us. In J. A. Hostetler, *Amish Roots*. Baltimore: Johns Hopkins University Press.

Bourdieu, P., and J.-C. Passeron. 1977. *Reproduction in Education, Society and Culture*. London: Sage.

Brown, R. G. 1991. *Schools of Thought: How the Politics of Literacy Shape Thinking in the Classroom*. San Francisco, CA: Jossey-Bass.

Buchanan, F. S. 1967. *The Old Paths: A Study of the Amish Response to Public Schooling in Ohio*. PhD diss., Ohio State University.

Byler, A. M. 2001. *Amish Directory. Fredericktown Settlement*. Gordonville, PA: Gordonville Print Shop.

Byler, U. R. 1963. *Our Better Country*. Gordonville, PA: Old Order Book Society.

———. 1969; 1980. *School Bells Ringing: A Manual for Amish Teachers and Parents*. Aylmer, Ont.: Pathway Publishing Corporation.

———. 1992. *As I Remember It*. Aylmer, Ont.: Pathway Publishing Corporation.

Chalkdust: Selections from Blackboard Bulletin (1978–1985). 1991. Aylmer, Ont.: Pathway Publishing Corporation.

The Challenge of the Child: Selections from "The Blackboard Bulletin" 1957–1966. 1967. Aylmer, Ont.: Pathway Publishing Corporation.

Cronk, S. 1977. *Gelassenheit: The Rites of the Redemptive Process in Old Order Amish and Old Order Mennonite Communities*. PhD diss., University of Chicago.

———. 1981. Gelassenheit: The Rites of the Redemptive Process in Old Order Amish and Old Order Mennonite Communities. *Mennonite Quarterly Review* 55:5–44.

Dauenhauer, N. M., and R. Dauenhauer. 1998. Technological, Emotional, and Ideological Issues in Reversing Language Shift: Examples from Southeast Alaska. In *Endangered Languages: Language Loss and Community Response*, ed. L. A. Grenoble and L. J. Whaley, 57–98. Cambridge: Cambridge University Press.

Delisio, E. R. 2003. Responsive Classroom Practices Teach the Whole Child. *Education World*. Retrieved September 11, 2003, from www.educationworld.com/a_issues/schools/schools016.html.

Delval, N. 1986. The Amish Educational System Seen through the Blackboard Bulletin: Maintenance of a Minority Identity. Unpublished manuscript, Heritage Historical Library, Aylmer, Ontario.

Dewalt, M. W., and B. Troxell. 1988. Case Study of an Old Order Mennonite One-Room School. Paper presented at the Annual Meeting of the American Educational Research Association, Washington, D.C., April 9.

Ediger, M. 1998. Teaching Science in the Old Order Amish School. *Journal of Instructional Psychology* 25 (1): 62–66.

Enninger, W. 1987. On the Organization of Sign-Processes in an Old Order Amish (OOA) Parochial School. *Research on Language and Social Interaction* 21: 143–70.

———. 1991. Linguistic Markers of Anabaptist Ethnicity Through Four Centuries. In *Language and Ethnicity: Focusschrift in Honor of Joshua A. Fishman*, ed. J. R. Dow, 23–60. Amsterdam: Benjamins.

———. 1999. Continuity and Innovation in the Bilingual Education Among the Amish. In *The Construction of Knowledge, Learner Autonomy and Related Issues in Foreign Language Learning: Essays in Honour of Dieter Wolff*, ed. B. Missler and U. Multhaup, 213–24. Sonderdruck: Stauffenburg Verlag.

Erickson, D. A. 1969. Freedom's Two Educational Imperatives: A Proposal. In *Public Controls for Nonpublic Schools*, ed. D. A. Erickson, 159–75. Chicago: University of Chicago Press.

Esh, J. F. 1965. *The Amish Moving to Maryland, 1940*. Gordonville, PA: A. S. Kinsinger.

Ferster, H. 1983. The Development of the Amish School System. *Pennsylvania Mennonite Heritage* 6: 7–14.

Fisher, S. E., and R. K. Stahl. 1997. *The Amish School*, rev. ed. Intercourse, PA: Good Books.

Fisher, W. L. 1996. *The Amish in Court*. New York: Vantage Press.

Fishman, J. A. 1966. *Language Loyalty in the United States: The Maintenance and Perpetuation of Non-English Mother-Tongues by American Ethnic and Religious Groups*. The Hague: Mouton.

———. 1976. *Bilingual Education: An International Sociological Perspective*. Rowley, MA: Newbury.

Fletcher, S. W. 1950. The Rural School, 1640–1840. Rpt. in C. Lapp, *Pennsylvania School History, 1690–1990*, 59–75. Gordonville, PA: Christ S. Lapp, 1991.

From the Staff. 1992. *Blackboard Bulletin*, December, 14–15.

Garrett, O. 1996. *The Guidebook to Amish Communities & Business Directory*. Kalona, IA: Hitching Post Enterprises, Inc.

Giles, H., and N. Coupland. 1991. *Language: Contexts and Consequences*. Pacific Grove, CA: Brooks/Cole.

Gilmore, P., and A. A. Glatthorn, eds. 1982. *Children In and Out of School: Ethnography and Education*. Washington, DC: Center for Applied Linguistics.

Giroux, H. 1983. Ideology and Agency in the Process of Schooling. *Journal of Education* 65 (1): 12–34.

———. Introduction. In *Restructuring for Integrative Education: Multiple Perspectives, Multiple Contexts*, ed. T. E. Jennings, vii–x. Westport, CT: Bergin and Garvey.

Giroux, H., and P. McLaren, eds. 1994. *Between Borders: Pedagogy and the Politics of Cultural Studies.* New York: Routledge.

Goals and Guidelines for Amish Parochial Schools. n.d. Geauga County, Ohio.

Goodenough, W. 1961. Education and Identity. In *Anthropology and Education,* ed. F. C. Gruber, 84–102. Philadelphia: University of Pennsylvania Press.

Grenoble, L. A., and L. J. Whaley, eds. 1998. *Endangered Languages. Language Loss and Community Response.* Cambridge: Cambridge University Press.

Gross, H. H., R. E. Gabler, and A. McIntire. 1962. *Exploring Regions Near and Far.* Chicago: Follett.

Guthrie, J. 1979. Organizational Scale and School Success. *Educational Evaluation and Policy Analysis* 1 (1): 17–27.

Gutmann, A. 1999. *Democratic Education,* rev. ed. Princeton, NJ: Princeton University Press.

Harroff, S. B. 1998. Value-Oriented Teaching in a Contemporary Indiana Amish Parochial School: Preparations for Adult Life through Faith, Responsible Behavior, and Community Interaction. *International Journal of Educational Reform* 7 (3): 243–54.

———. 2004. *The Amish Schools of Indiana: Faith in Education.* West Lafayette, IN: Purdue University Press.

Heath, S. B. 1983. *Ways with Words: Language, Life, and Work in Communities and Classrooms.* New York: Cambridge University Press.

Hershberger, E. N. 1958. Why Do We Have Our Own Schools? Rpt. in *The Challenge of the Child: Selections from "The Blackboard Bulletin" 1957–1966,* 67–69. Aylmer, Ont.: Pathway Publishing Corporation.

Hershberger, H. J. n.d. *Minimum Standards for the Amish Parochial or Private Elementary Schools of the State of Ohio as a Form of Regulations. Compiled and Approved by Bishops, Committeemen and Others in Conference (Ohio Minimum Standards).* Apple Creek, Ohio. Rpt. Gordonville Print Shop, 2003.

Hoover, A. B. n.d. *A Return to Parochial Schools.* Unpublished manuscript.

Hornberger, N. 1988. *Bilingual Education and Language Maintenance.* Providence, RI: Foris.

Horst, I. R. 2000. *A Separate People: An Insider's View of Old Order Mennonite Customs and Traditions.* Waterloo, Ont.: Herald Press.

Hostetler, J. A. 1956. The Amish and the Public School. *Christian Living,* September, 4–6, 41–43.

———. 1962. *The Amish in American Culture,* ed. D. M. Kent and W. A. Hunter. Harrisburg, PA: Commonwealth of Pennsylvania, Historical and Museum Commission. Pamphlet.

———. 1963. The Amish Use of Symbols and Their Function in Bounding the Community. *Journal of the Royal Anthropological Institute* 94, pt. 1, 11–12.

——. 1969. *Educational Achievement and Lifestyles in a Traditional Society, the Old Order Amish.* Philadelphia: Temple University for the U. S. Department of Health, Education, and Welfare. Project 6-1921, Contract OE 1-6-061912-1621.

——, ed. 1969. *Conference on Child Socialization.* Washington, DC: U.S. Department of Health, Education, and Welfare.

——. 1970. Old Order Amish Child Rearing and Schooling Practices: A Summary Report. *Mennonite Quarterly Review,* April, 181–91.

——. 1975. The Cultural Context of the Wisconsin Case. In *Compulsory Education and the Amish: The Right Not to Be Modern,* ed. A. N. Keim, 99–113. Boston: Beacon Press.

——. 1989. *Amish Roots.* Baltimore, MD: Johns Hopkins University Press.

——. 1993. *Amish Society,* 4th ed. Baltimore, MD: Johns Hopkins University Press.

Hostetler, J. A., and G. E. Huntington. 1976. The Amish Elementary School Teacher and Students. In *Schooling in the Cultural Context,* ed. J. I. Roberts and S. K. Akinsanya, 194–205. New York: David McKay.

——. 1992. *Amish Children. Education in the Family, School, and Community,* 2nd ed. New York: Harcourt Brace Jovanovich College Publishers.

Hostetler, J. A., and C. Redekop. 1962. Education and Assimilation in Three Ethnic Groups. *Alberta Journal of Educational Research* 8 (4): 189–203.

Howe, K. R. 1997. *Understanding Equal Educational Opportunity: Social Justice, Democracy, and Schooling.* New York: Teachers College Press.

Howley, C. 1989. What Is the Effect of Small-Scale Schooling on Student Achievement? *ERIC Digest,* ERIC Clearinghouse on Rural Education and Small Schools, Report No. EDO-RC-89-6.

Huntington, G. E. 1993. The Contemporary Relevance of the Amish Family, Education, and Health. Paper presented at the Conference on Three Hundred Years of Persistence and Change; Amish Society 1693–1993. Young Center, Elizabethtown College, Elizabethtown, Pennsylvania.

——. 1994. Persistence and Change in Amish Education. In *The Amish Struggle With Modernity,* ed. D. B. Kraybill and M. A. Olshan, 77–96. Hanover: University Press of New England.

——. *Amish in Michigan.* East Lansing: Michigan State University Press.

Jackson, N. N. 1969. Perverse Amish. MA thesis, Washington University. (Heritage Historical Library, Aylmer, Ont.).

Jakobsh, F. 1993. German in Old Order Mennonite Schools. *Journal of Mennonite Studies* 11: 162–73.

Johnson-Weiner, K. M. 1993. Community Expectations and Second Language Acquisition: English as a Second Language in a Swartzentruber Amish School. *Yearbook of German-American Studies* 28: 107–17.

———. 1997. Reinforcing a Separate Amish Identity: English Instruction and the Preservation of Culture in Old Order Amish Schools. In *Languages and Lives: Essays in Honor of Werner Enninger*, ed. J. R. Dow and M. Wolff, 67–78. New York: Peter Lang.

———. 1998. Community Identity and Language Change in North American Anabaptist Communities. *Journal of Sociolinguistics* 2/3: 375–94.

———. 2001a. Katie. In *Living North Country: Essays on Life and Landscapes in Northern New York*, ed. N. Singer and N. Burdick, 207–20. Utica, NY: North Country Books, Inc.

———. 2001b. The Role of Women in Old Order Amish, Beachy Amish, and Fellowship Churches. *Mennonite Quarterly Review* 75 (2): 231–56.

Kachel, D. 1989. What Can We Learn from Amish Education? *Education Digest* 55 (3): 61–63.

Kaplan, R., and R. Baldauf Jr. 1997. *Language Planning from Practice to Theory*. Clevedon: Multilingual Matters, Ltd.

Kauffman, G. 2002. *Heartland Amish Business Directory 2002–2003*. Goshen, IN: Diamond Design.

Kauffman, J. E. 1959. Why We Have Our Own Private Schools. Rpt. In *The Challenge of the Child: Selections from "The Blackboard Bulletin" 1957–1966*, 69–71. Aylmer, Ont.: Pathway Publishing Corporation.

Keesing, R. M. 1992. *Custom and Confrontation: The Kwaio Struggle for Cultural Autonomy*. Chicago: University of Chicago Press.

Keim, A. N. 1975. *Compulsory Education and the Amish: The Right Not to Be Modern*. Boston: Beacon Press.

Kinsinger, A. S. 1997. *A Little History of Our Parochial Schools and Steering Committee from 1956–1994*. Compiled by S. A. Kinsinger. Gordonville, PA: Gordonville Print Shop.

Kinsinger, S. A. 1988. *Family and History of Lydia Beachy's Descendants 1889–1989*. Gordonville, PA: Gordonville Print Shop.

Klimuska, E. n.d. (c.1989). *Amish One-Room Schools: Lessons for the Plain Life*. Pictures by M. Heisey. Lancaster, PA: Lancaster Newspapers, Inc.

———. 1995. County's 174 Plain-Sect Schools Open. *Lancaster New Era*, 28 August, C-16.

———. 1997. Amish Pupils Getting Back to the Six R's. *Lancaster New Era*, 26 August, B-1.

———. 1998. *Lancaster County*. Stillwater, MN: Voyageur Press, Inc.

Koehl, R. 1977. The Comparative Study of Education: Prescription and Practice. *Comparative Education Review*, June/October, 177–94.

Kollmorgen, W. M. 1942. Culture of a Contemporary Community: The Old Order

Amish of Lancaster County, Pennsylvania. *Rural Life Studies*, no. 4. Washington, DC: U.S. Department of Agriculture.

Koret Task Force on K-12 Education. 2003. Findings and Recommendations. In *Our Schools and Our Future . . . Are We Still at Risk?* ed. P. E. Peterson, 3–22. Stanford, CA: Hoover Institution Press.

Kraybill, D. B. 1993. *The Amish and the State.* Baltimore, MD: Johns Hopkins Press.

———. 1994. Plotting Social Change Across Four Affiliations. In *The Amish Struggle with Modernity*, ed. D. B. Kraybill and M. A. Olshan, 53–74. Hanover, NH: University Press of New England.

———. *The Riddle of Amish Culture*, 2nd ed. Baltimore, MD: Johns Hopkins University Press.

Kraybill, D. B., and C. F. Bowman. 2001. *On the Backroad to Heaven.* Baltimore, MD: Johns Hopkins University Press.

Kraybill, D. B., and M. Olshan. 1994. *The Amish Struggle with Modernity.* Hanover, NH: University Press of New England.

Kraybill, D. B., and S. M. Nolt. 1995. *Amish Enterprise: From Plows to Profits.* Baltimore, MD: Johns Hopkins University Press.

Kreps, G. M., J. F. Donnermeyer, and M. W. Kreps. 1997. *A Quiet Moment in Time: A Contemporary View of Amish Society.* Sugarcreek, OH: Author.

Kulick, D. 1992. *Language Shift and Cultural Reproduction: Socialization, Self, and Syncretism in a Papua New Guinean Village.* New York: Cambridge University Press.

Lapp, C. 1991. *Pennsylvania School History 1690–1990.* Gordonville, PA: Christ S. Lapp.

Lee, V. E., and J. B. Smith. 1995. Effects of High School Restructuring and Size on Early Gains in Achievement and Engagement. *Sociology of Education* 68 (4): 241–70.

Loyd, Linda. 1975. Amish Building One-Room Schools as Bastions against Worldly Ways. *Philadelphia Inquirer*, 8 December, 1-B, 3-B.

Luthy, D. 1986. *The Amish in America: Settlements That Failed, 1840–1960.* Aylmer, Ont.: Pathway Publishers.

———. 1993. A Turnpike Traveler in 1854 Views an Amish School. *Family Life*, March, 17–19.

———. 1998. The Origin and Growth of the Swartzentruber Amish. *Family Life*, August/September, 19–22.

McIntire, A., and W. Hill. 1962. *Working Together*, 2nd ed. Chicago: Follett.

Meier, D. 1995. *The Power of Their Ideas: Lessons for America from a Small School in Harlem.* Boston, MA: Beacon Press.

Mennonite Confession of Faith. 1966. Crockett, KY: Rod and Staff Publishers, Inc.

Meyers, T. 1993. Education and Schooling. In *The Amish and the State*, ed. D. B. Kraybill, 87–106. Baltimore, MD: Johns Hopkins University Press.

Miller, D. 2002. *Michigan Amish Directory 2002*. Millersburg, OH: Abana Books.

Miller, J. E. 1995. *Indiana Amish Directory: Elkhart, LaGrange, and Noble Counties, 1995*. Middlebury, IN: J. E. Miller.

Miller, L. 1992. *Our People: The Amish and Mennonites of Ohio*. Scottdale, PA: Herald Press.

Miller, M. 2000. *Our Heritage, Hope, and Faith*. Shipshewana, IN: Mary E. Miller.

Miller, W. 1969. A Study of Amish Academic Achievement. PhD diss., University of Michigan.

Mulhausler, P. 1994. Language Teaching=Linguistic Imperialism? *Australian Review of Applied Linguistics* 17 (2): 121–30.

———. 1995. *Linguistic Ecology: Language Change and Linguistic Imperialism in the Pacific Region*. London: Routledge.

Newcomb, T. L. 1986. A Study of Amish and Conservative Mennonite Schooling in Ohio (1982–1985). In *Internal and External Perspectives on Amish and Mennonite Life 2*, ed. W. Enninger, J. Raith, and K.-H. Wandt, 54–72. Essen, Germany: Unipress.

Northeast Foundation for Children. 2004. *Responsive Classroom: Principles and Practices*. Retrieved October 8, 2004, from www.responsiveclassroom.org/about/principles.html.

Ochs, E., and B. B. Schieffelin. 2001. Language Acquisition and Socialization: Three Developmental Stories and Their Implications. In *Linguistic Anthropology: A Reader*, ed. A. Duranti, 263–301. Malden, MA: Blackwell.

Ohio Legislative Service Commission. 1969. *Sectarian Amish Education*. Columbus, OH: Res. Rpt. No. 44.

Olshan, M. A. 1994. Amish Cottage Industries as Trojan Horse. In *The Amish Struggle with Modernity*, ed. D. B. Kraybill and M. A. Olshan, 133–46. Hanover, NH: University Press of New England.

Pederson, J. M. 2002. "She May Be Amish Now, but She Won't Be Amish Long": Anabaptist Women and Antimodernism. In *Strangers at Home: Amish and Mennonite Women in History*, ed. K. D. Schmidt, D. Zimmerman Umble, and S. D. Reschly, 339–63. Baltimore, MD: Johns Hopkins University Press.

Pelto, P. J., and G. H. Pelto. 1973. Ethnography: The Fieldwork Enterprise. In *Handbook of Social and Cultural Anthropology*, ed. J. J. Honigmann. Chicago: Rand McNally.

Peters, S. F. 2003. *The Yoder Case: Religious Freedom, Education, and Parental Rights*. Lawrence: University Press of Kansas.

Pittman, R. B., and P. Haughwout. 1987. Influence of High School Size on Dropout Rate. *Educational Evaluation and Policy Analysis* 9 (4): 337–43.

Postman, N. 1995. *The End of Education: Redefining the Value of School*. New York: Alfred A. Knopf.

Raywid, M. A. 1999. Current Literature on Small Schools. *ERIC Digest*. No. ED425049.

Redekop, C. 1989. *Mennonite Society*. Baltimore, MD: Johns Hopkins University Press.

Regulations and Guidelines for Amish Parochial Schools of Indiana [*Indiana Regulations*]. 2002. Middlebury, Indiana.

Reich, R. 2002. *Bridging Liberalism and Multiculturalism in American Education*. Chicago: University of Chicago Press.

Rhodes, R. 2002. No Longer Living Off the Land. *Mennonite Weekly Review*, 21 October, 1, 7.

Riddle, W. 1910. *Cherished Memories of Old Lancaster—Town and Shire*. Lancaster, PA: Intelligencer Printing House.

Rochester, J. M. 2002. *Class Warfare: Besieged Schools, Bewildered Parents, Betrayed Kids, and the Attack on Excellence*. San Francisco, CA: Encounter Books.

Roellke, C. 1996. Curriculum Adequacy and Quality in High Schools Enrolling Fewer than 400 Students. *ERIC Digest*. Report No. EDO-RC-96-7.

Rogers, S. C. 1978. Women's Place: A Critical Review of Anthropological Theory. *Comparative Studies in Society and History* 20 (1): 123–62.

Sahlins, M. 1981. *Historical Metaphors and Mythical Realities: Structure in the Early History of the Sandwich Islands Kingdom*. Ann Arbor: University of Michigan Press.

———. 1985. *Islands of History*. Chicago: University of Chicago Press.

Savells, J. 1990. Social Change among the Amish in Eight Communities. *Pennsylvania Mennonite Heritage* 3: 12–16.

Schoolaid: Its Purpose, Origin, and Organizational Structure. n.d. Pamphlet.

Schoolteachers' Signposts. 1985. East Earl, PA: Schoolaid.

Scott, J. C. 1990. *Domination and the Arts of Resistance*. New Haven, CT: Yale University Press.

Shirk, E. M. 1939. *Report of Committee of Plain People Making Pleas for Leniency from Depressive School Laws*. Ephrata, PA.

Simons, M. 1983. *The Complete Works of Menno Simons*. Aylmer, Ont.: Pathway Publishers.

Snauwaert, D. T. 2001. *Wisconsin v. Yoder* and the Relationship between Individual and Group Rights. *Philosophy of Education Yearbook*. Retrieved June 22, 2005, from www.ed.uiuc.edu/EPS/PES-Yearbookj/2001/snauweart%2001.pdf.

Standards of the Old Order Amish and Old Order Mennonite Parochial and Vocational Schools of Penna. [Pennsylvania Standards]. 1969 (rev. 1973 and 1988). Rpt. 2003. Gordonville, PA: Gordonville Print Shop.

Stockard, J., and M. Mayberry. 1992. *Effective Educational Environments.* Newbury Park, CA: Corwin. ERIC Document No. ED350674.

Stoll, J. 1969. German and English. *The Blackboard Bulletin* (May), 207–9.

———. 1975. Who Shall Educate Our Children? In *Compulsory Education and the Amish: The Right Not to Be Modern,* ed. A. N. Keim, 16–42. Boston: Beacon Press.

Testa, R. 1992. *After the Fire: The Destruction of the Lancaster County Amish.* Hanover, NH: University Press of New England.

Tips for Teachers: A Handbook for Amish Teachers. 1970; rev. ed. 1991. Aylmer, Ont.: Pathway Publishers.

Toews, P. 1996. *Mennonites in American Society, 1930–1970.* Scottdale, PA: Herald Press.

Walbert, D. 2002. *Garden Spot: Lancaster County, the Old Order Amish, and the Selling of Rural America.* New York: Oxford University Press.

Wenger, E. D., and G. G. Sauder. 1968. *The Weaverland Mennonites.* North Holland, PA: Lewis B. Groff.

Wengerd, M., ed. 2000. *Ohio Amish Directory. Holmes, Tuscarawas, and Wayne Counties, 2000 Millennium Edition.* Walnut Creek, OH: Carlisle Press.

Wittmer, J. 1970. Homogeneity of Personality Characteristics: A Comparison between Old Order Amish and Non-Amish. *American Anthropologist* 72:1063–68.

Yoder, E. S. 1990. *I Saw It in The Budget.* Hartville, OH: Diakonia Ministries.

Yoder, P. 1993. The Amish View of the State. In *The Amish and the State,* ed. D. B. Kraybill, 23–40. Baltimore, MD: Johns Hopkins University Press.

Yousey, A. 1987. *Strangers and Pilgrims: History of the Lewis County Mennonites.* Croghan, NY: Author.

Index

CENTER BOOKS IN ANABAPTIST STUDIES

Carl F. Bowman, *Brethren Society: The Cultural Transformation
of a "Peculiar People"*

Perry Bush, *Two Kingdoms, Two Loyalties: Mennonite Pacifism
in Modern America*

John A. Hostetler, ed., *Amish Roots: A Treasury of History, Wisdom, and Lore*

Julia Kasdorf, *The Body and the Book: Writing from a Mennonite Life*

Donald B. Kraybill, *The Riddle of Amish Culture,* revised edition

Donald B. Kraybill, ed., *The Amish and the State,* 2nd edition

Donald B. Kraybill and Carl Desportes Bowman, *On the Backroad to Heaven:
Old Order Hutterites, Mennonites, Amish, and Brethren*

Donald B. Kraybill and Steven M. Nolt, *Amish Enterprise:
From Plows to Profits,* 2nd edition

Werner O. Packull, *Hutterite Beginnings: Communitarian Experiments
during the Reformation*

Benjamin W. Redekop and Calvin W. Redekop, eds. *Power, Authority,
and the Anabaptist Tradition*

Calvin Redekop, Stephen C. Ainlay, and Robert Siemens,
Mennonite Entrepreneurs

Calvin Redekop, ed., *Creation and the Environment: An Anabaptist Perspective
on a Sustainable World*

Steven D. Reschly, *The Amish on the Iowa Prairie, 1840 to 1910*

Kimberly D. Schmidt, Diane Zimmerman Umble, and Steven D. Reschly,
Strangers at Home: Amish and Mennonite Women in History

Diane Zimmerman Umble, *Holding the Line: The Telephone in
Old Order Mennonite and Amish Life*

David Weaver-Zercher, *The Amish in the American Imagination*